PRACTISING INTERDISCIPLINARITY

Edited by Peter Weingart and Nico Stehr

Academic disciplines provide a framework for the transfer of knowledge from one generation to the next. Not only do they shape our education and understanding, they structure our professional lives. Interdisciplinarity, the reconfiguration of academic disciplines and the boundaries between them, has lately become a field of major interest to scholars and policy-makers. This collection brings together the latest research and analysis from this emerging field.

The editors take as their central thesis the idea that the existing matrix of disciplines is dissolving, leading to fundamental changes in the traditional order of knowledge. Contributors to the volume include specialists from Canada, Australia, Europe, and the United States who focus on the actual practice of interdisciplinarity: the ways in which it is researched, organized, and taught in institutes and universities around the world. The role of funding bodies is also considered, revealing the relationship and the delineation of disciplines and their resource bases. Together, the essays offer first-hand insights into the operations and successes of some of the world's foremost interdisciplinary research centres. In acquainting us with the current state of interdisciplinary research the volume also considers the social and economic contexts that make such research possible.

Peter Weingart is a professor at the Institute for Science and Technology Studies, University of Bielefeld, Germany.

Nico Stehr is Senior Research Associate in the Sustainable Research Development Institute of the University of British Columbia and DAAD Professor at the Universität Duisburg, Germany. He is a Fellow of the Royal Society of Canada and editor of the *Canadian Journal of Sociology*.

Edited by PETER WEINGART and NICO STEHR

Practising Interdisciplinarity

UNIVERSITY OF TORONTO PRESS
Toronto Buffalo London

© University of Toronto Press Incorporated 2000
Toronto Buffalo London
Printed in Canada

ISBN 0-8020-4328-3 (cloth)
ISBN 0-8020-8139-8 (paper)

Printed on acid-free paper

Canadian Cataloguing in Publication Data

Main entry under title:

Practising interdisciplinarity

Includes bibliographical references.
ISBN 0-8020-4328-3 (bound)   ISBN 0-8020-8139-8 (pbk.)

1. Interdisciplinary research.   I. Weingart, Peter.   II. Stehr, Nico.

Q180.55.I48P72 1999   001.4   C99-932559-0

The University of Toronto Press acknowledges the financial assistance to its
publishing program of the Canada Council for the Arts and the Ontario Arts
Council.

University of Toronto Press acknowledges the financial support for its publishing activities of the Government of Canada through the Book Publishing
Industry Development Program (BPIDP).

Canadä

Contents

PREFACE   vii
INTRODUCTION   xi

**Part I. The Popularity, Functions, and Paradoxes of
Interdisciplinarity: The Discourse   1**

1 A Conceptual Vocabulary of Interdisciplinary Science   3
   JULIE THOMPSON KLEIN
2 Interdisciplinarity: The Paradoxical Discourse   25
   PETER WEINGART

Part II. The Changing Topography of Science   43

3 What Are Disciplines? And How Is Interdisciplinarity
   Different?   46
   STEPHEN TURNER
4 The Interdisciplinary Nature of Science: Theoretical Framework
   and Bibliometric-Empirical Approach   66
   ANTHONY F.J. VAN RAAN
5 Mapping the New Cultures and Organization of Research
   in Australia   79
   TIM TURPIN AND SAM GARRETT-JONES

Part III. Nurturing Environments of Interdisciplinarity   111

 6 Beyond One's Own Perspective: The Psychology of Cognitive
    Interdisciplinarity   115
    RAINER BROMME
 7 Practising Interdisciplinary Studies   134
    RHODRI WINDSOR LISCOMBE
 8 Cognitive Science as an Interdisciplinary Endeavour   154
    MARC DE MEY
 9 Inducing Interdisciplinarity: Irresistible Infliction? The Example
    of a Research Group at the Center for Interdisciplinary Research
    (ZiF), Bielefeld, Germany   173
    SABINE MAASEN
10 Interdisciplinary Research at the Caltech Beckman Institute   194
    ERIC R. SCERRI
11 Major Discoveries and Biomedical Research Organizations:
    Perspectives on Interdisciplinarity, Nurturing Leadership,
    and Integrated Structure and Cultures   215
    ROGERS HOLLINGSWORTH AND ELLEN JANE HOLLINGSWORTH

Part IV. The Perspective of the Funders   245

12 Interdisciplinary Research Initiatives at the U.S. National
    Science Foundation   248
    EDWARD J. HACKETT
13 Beyond the Ivory Tower: Some Observations on External Funding
    of Interdisciplinary Research in Universities   260
    WILHELM KRULL

Concluding Comments   270

REFERENCES   273
CONTRIBUTORS   291

Preface

Both in academia and in science policy a renewed interest has emerged in interdisciplinarity, its opportunities, and its institutional obstacles. This interest derives its urgency from the perception of an uninhibited trend towards ever more specialization in science driven by the search for novelty and efforts to achieve visibility. Specialization of research and its solidifying organizational structures are seen as impediments to innovation.

This was the motive to bring together scholars who had pertinent experience either in institutions devoted explicitly to interdisciplinary research or in funding agencies supporting such research in various programs, or who had done research on such institutions.

In January 1995 Peter Weingart organized a first conference at the Center for Interdisciplinary Research (ZiF) in Bielefeld, Germany, entitled 'Centers for Interdisciplinary Research – A Model for Institutional Innovation in Science in Europe.' Participants came from research institutes with a strong interdisciplinary commitment and higher education institutions with some experience in implementing centres of excellence and/or interdisciplinary postgraduate programs. The purpose of this conference was to explore needs and opportunities of institutional innovation within and outside the university system. Participants were Maurice Aymard, Director, Maison des Sciences de l'Homme, Paris; Graeme Clarke, Australian National University, Canberra; Jutta Fedrowitz, Centrum fuer Hochschulentwicklung, Guetersloh, Germany; John R. Grace, University of British Columbia, Vancouver; Rogers Hollingsworth, University of Wisconsin, Madison; Wilhelm Krull, General Secretary, Volkswagen Foundation, Hanover, Germany, previously Max Planck Society, Munich; Sabine Maasen, Research Coordinator,

Max Planck Institute for Psychological Research, Munich, previously ZiF, Bielefeld, Germany; Marc De Mey, University of Ghent; Johan Mouton, Director, Center for Interdisciplinary Research, University of Stellenbosch, South Africa; Torsten Nybom, Council for Higher Education, Stockholm; Tim Turpin, Centre for Research Policy, Wollongong, Australia; Volker Ullrich, University of Konstanz, Germany; Bjoern Wittrock, Director, Swedish Collegium for Advanced Study in the Social Sciences, Uppsala, Sweden; Peter Weingart, Director, Institute of Science and Technology Studies, University of Bielefeld, previously Director, ZiF, Bielefeld.

At the conference in Bielefeld it was decided to reconvene for a second conference that would pursue the discussions of the Bielefeld meeting and bring contributions to a final form, widen the spectrum to North American/Canadian participants, and include theoretical reflections as well as additional institutional experiences of interdisciplinarity. John R. Grace of the University of British Columbia, a participant at Bielefeld, offered the newly founded Peter Wall Institute for Advanced Studies, Vancouver, for the conference. By the time the second meeting was planned and funding was obtained he had left his post as dean and Nico Stehr, then Fellow at the Peter Wall Institute and at Green College, took on the organization of the conference at Vancouver. The conference, entitled, like this book, 'Practising Interdisciplinarity,' took place in March 1997 and reflected the broader scope but also the focus on actual practice.

Not all participants at the first conference could attend the second. In their place others were recruited to bring new ideas: Rainer Bromme, University of Muenster, Germany; Sam Garrett-Jones, University of Wollongong, Australia, who took Tim Turpin's place; Julie Thompson Klein, Wayne State University, Detroit; Stephen Turner, University of South Florida, Tampa; and Rhodri Windsor Liscombe, University of British Columbia, Vancouver. Others who could not attend but volunteered to submit papers included Edward J. Hackett, Arizona State University, Tempe, and Wilhelm Krull, Volkswagen Foundation, Hanover, Germany. We want to thank all participants of the two conferences for their contributions, whether they were in the form of discussion or a paper. That this gratitude includes everyone is all the more justified since some papers were, indeed, reworked, and others were stimulated by the discussions of the first meeting and edited once more on the basis of input from the second.

The conferences could not have taken place without the generous support from various sources. The first meeting was hosted by the Center for Interdisciplinary Research (ZiF) of the University of Bielefeld, Germany's first centre for advanced study and unique insofar as it is devoted to interdisciplinary research, either carried out by groups residing at the centre for a full academic year or in conferences. Support for that meeting also came from the Istituto Italiano per gli Studi Filosofici in Naples, an interdisciplinary study centre devoted to the humanities that collaborates with ZiF in organizing conferences.

The second meeting was hosted by Green College, University of British Columbia. This was quite appropriate since Green College is an innovative and sucessful graduate college that nurtures interdisciplinarity. The second meeting was sponsored by the Royal Society of Canada and co-funded by the Social Sciences and Humanities Research Council, Ottawa, Canada, as well as the Stifterverband für die Deutsche Wissenschaft, Essen, Germany. We are also grateful for the financial support received for the Vancouver conference from Dr Daniel Birch, Vice-President Academic, and Dr Bernard Bressler, Vice-President Research, of the University of British Columbia.

When all papers were submitted, Lilo Jegerlehner of the ZiF prepared the manuscript for print. We thank her and all these institutions for their respective support, and hope that the resulting volume meets their expectations.

PETER WEINGART
NICO STEHR
BIELEFELD, APRIL 1999

Introduction

Scientific disciplines are, in a sense, the eyes through which modern society sees and forms its images about the world, frames its experience, and learns, thus shaping its own future or reconstituting the past. *Disciplines* are the intellectual structures in which the transfer of knowledge from one generation to the next is cast; that is, they shape the entire system of education. Likewise, disciplines have a great impact on the structure of occupations – the world of practice – and they do so increasingly as societies move from primary (agricultural) and secondary (industrial) to tertiary (knowledge-based) economic orders. Finally, disciplines are not only intellectual but also social structures, organizations made up of human beings with vested interests based on time investments, acquired reputations, and established social networks that shape and bias their views on the relative importance of their knowledge. As social organizations, disciplines participate in and contribute to conflicts over political, economic, legal, and ethical decisions, over the distribution of resources and life chances. In all these functions, scientific disciplines constitute the modern *social order of knowledge*, and the order of knowledge is in this sense a political order as well. It therefore seems self-evident that it is critical to understand the inner workings of this order, the changes that it undergoes as well as their impact on the society at large.

Something quite fundamental is happening to the established order of knowledge as it has emerged with the modern universities in the nineteenth century: the organizational matrix of disciplines is beginning to dissolve.

Observers note a growing pluralism both in the locations of knowledge production and in the patterns of initiation, production, and use of knowledge as well as its disciplinary combinations. These observers suggest that one may have to add a postdisciplinary stage to the predisciplinary stage of the seventeenth and eighteenth centuries and the disciplinary stage of the nineteenth and twentieth centuries.

This development is uneven; it does not affect all disciplines in the same way. The natural sciences seem to be more affected than the humanities. Where production of knowledge is fast and the half-time of knowledge short (i.e., its becoming is superseded), the disciplinary boundaries seem to be more fluid than in areas where a less hurried pace prevails. Besides, disciplines are prevalent organizational principles in universities, where the goal of knowledge production is to *understand*; they do not seem to command great respect where the goal is to generate practical knowledge in order to *solve problems*. In fact, there they are even frowned upon as obstacles to innovation or as providing a skewed perspective.

The scope and impact of this development are still contested, the reasons for it are only partially known and understood, and the ultimate consequences are far from clear. But as it will affect the fabric of all of society, it is undoubtedly a highly relevant issue of social, economic, and political concern. We do not know yet what is going to take the place of the traditional disciplines. But it is already apparent from a cursory contact with the issue of disciplinarity/interdisciplinarity that it is a moving target. Only three decades ago the student movement of the late sixties called for radical university reforms, one central element of which was the elimination of the traditional academic disciplines in favour of holistic notions of training that were closer to the practical problems of life. *Interdisciplinarity* became a programmatic, value-laden term that stood for reform, innovation, progress. However, when the open conflicts subsided and the mundane academic routine had returned to the universities, the call for interdisciplinarity became much less urgent. 'Project study' programs were labelled 'soft' and quietly discontinued; interdisciplinary institutes and research groups struggled to survive and in many cases failed. What had seemed progressive only a few years before appeared outdated, if not quaint.

Yet, under the surface of declining public attention, university politics, and academic propaganda, changes began, driven not so much by student enthusiasm or well-meaning educators but by other, converging forces both inside and outside of science. Prominent among them is, of course, the persistent development of research itself. The outstanding case of research-induced interdisciplinarity during the first quarter of the twentieth century was the merger of physics and chemistry. But it took Walter Nernst fifteen years of being nominated for the Nobel Prize until he finally earned it in 1920 (for chemistry); chief among the reasons for the long deliberations of the committee was the fact that the physics and chemistry classes of the Swedish Academy could not make up their minds where Nernst belonged with his Third Law of Thermodynamics. Further dramatic changes set in during the First World War, when science was instrumentalized for military ends on a grand scale. The National Laboratory and the organization of Big Science were institutional innovations also in the sense that they merged different disciplines in the attempt to target research more efficiently and to profit from synergetic effects. However, the war effort was short-lived, and the scientists returned to their academic settings, where the disjunction of research from applications was the prevalent mode of work. Yet, another famous interdisciplinary revolution occurring in the 1950s had its beginnings in the 1930s and also involved the physicists. Max Delbrück, Leo Szilard, and others became interested in biology and in the problem of cell reproduction in particular. This initiated what twenty years later culminated in Watson and Crick's discovery of the DNA model and the revolutionary developments in biology.

More recently an enthusiasm among scientists has emerged for what they perceive to be an unprecedented – yet not completed – coupling and amalgamation of disciplines: under the label of 'cognitive sciences,' neurobiology, psychology, parts of computer science (artificial intelligence), and, across the great divide to the humanities, philosophy of mind have found common ground and research interests. Likewise, under the 'dynamic paradigm,' the development of 'chaos theory' has demonstrated its utility in a wide array of disciplines, ranging from physics and mathematics to economics and psychology, thus revealing the isomorphism of the problem of explaining change. Finally, in a similar vein, the expansion or transfer of the evolutionary paradigm from biology into the social sciences, notably economics and sociology, and its combination with game theory and population statistics hold the promise to bridge paradigmatically the chasm between micro and macro perspectives.

All these cases exhibit a similar pattern: disciplinary interests, boundaries, and constraints are dissolving; disciplines are merging in areas where their overlap forms a new field either providing stimulus for other new developments or responding to challenges from outside. Systems research, materials science, environmental science, and so on reflect both sources of this development. This suggests that it becomes increasingly futile to ponder the pros and cons, the epistemological virtue or impossibility of interdisciplinarity, or to spend much time on defining disciplines, fields, specialties, and the like. More elucidating insights are to be gained from taking a more distanced view from above.

Disciplines are diffuse types of social organizations for the production of particular knowledge; they differ in size, in their goal orientation, and in their structure. Their boundaries are very difficult to draw, as is easily exemplified by trying to categorize the vast number of scholarly journals under disciplinary headings. A comparative look at 'disciplines' used to consider organizational frameworks that oriented ('disciplined') inwardly the process of knowledge production and drew the boundary between relevant and irrelevant, problematic and unproblematic, admissible and inadmissible communication. In the course of time disciplines have assumed the function of an interface between knowledge production on the one hand and its patrons as well as its clients on the other. This relationship has become closer. Science has been drawn out from its relative social isolation, its élite status, and moved closer to the mundane concerns of society. Knowledge production as well as academic training has been coupled more directly than before to political, economic, and social problems. That entails that the already fairly fluid organizational structures of disciplines have acquired additional functions, mediating between knowledge production and knowledge markets. They are, thus, required to adapt more quickly and to change, a process that has been interpreted as their losing their original role as guardians of intellectual pursuit.

As long as disciplines seemed to constitute strongly established institutional structures interdisciplinarity was but the counter-image. Now, as disciplines are more diffuse, their boundaries become more malleable, and the number of new fields and specialties is growing by the day, interdisciplinarity has become a fairly common experience. But this does not mean that it has become unproblematic. Interdisciplinary organization of research carries the image of a progressive endeavour, but at the same time is claimed to be the present reality and certainly the future order of knowledge. In the face of an estimated 9000 distinguishable fields of knowledge the promise of a reductionist *unified science* is no longer credible as an institutional clamp holding together the very diverse activities that are pursued in the academy. Thus, the project of interdisciplinarity has assumed a more pragmatic and realistic stance.

The focus is on its innovative functions and on the psychological, ideological, and organizational obstacles that stand in its way.

These are some of the considerations that have led to this book. Its title signals that the focus is on the actual *practice* of interdisciplinarity, the ways in which interdisciplinary research is organized in specialized institutes of advanced study (Maasen), in and between university departments (Hollingsworth and Hollingsworth, De Mey), in interdisciplinary research institutions (Scerri), and in teaching programs (Windsor Liscombe). Here, the interest is in teasing out the psychological dispositions (Bromme), the specific organizational mechanisms – its 'nurturing environment' – (Hollingsworth and Hollingsworth), and the interplay between these and the intellectual problems of the respective disciplines that make *interdisciplinary research* work and account for its fruitfulness.

This interest makes up the major part of the book. But what is happening in the institutions of knowledge production should also be seen from a more distanced viewpoint. Thus, in order to put the detailed accounts of interdisciplinary practice in the greater temporal and social perspective, the analysis of the 'nurturing environments' is preceded by views on the changing topography of the landscape of knowledge production. These views reveal the close relationship between (as well as the historical contingency of) the delineation of disciplines and their resource bases (Turner), and show the topicality and scope of cognitive as well as institutional changes that have occurred among the disciplines (van Raan, Turpin and Garrett-Jones). And since the type of knowledge production at issue here – academic research – is dependent on resources from outside, interdisciplinarity is in some measure dependent on but also has an impact on funding agencies and patrons. Thus, two views, one from a government funding agency (Hackett), and the other from a large private foundation (Krull), are included.

As mentioned, the concept of interdisciplinarity has moved through a development that may be characterized as ranging from 'programmatic' to actual 'practice.' This development is reflected in the social discourse about interdisciplinarity, in the metaphorical resources used (Klein, Weingart). The discourse is a reflection of the perspectives, interests, conflicts, and changing views of the actors participating in it, and shapes them in turn. To look at the discourse on interdisciplinarity, therefore, provides an insight into the interpretive framework in which interdisciplinary knowledge production is situated, socially sanctioned, and unfolding. The view on the discourse is yet another perspective on the fundamental changes of the social order of knowledge.

The scope of the issue of interdisciplinarity as it is represented here, as well as the differential weights given to its different trajectories, provide, the editors hope, access to understanding these changes and their relevance, albeit more as stimuli for further inquiry than as a complete set of answers.

PART I

THE POPULARITY, FUNCTIONS, AND PARADOXES OF INTERDISCIPLINARITY: THE DISCOURSE

After years of being eclipsed, *interdisciplinarity* has re-emerged as a pervasive term to gain great popularity both in science and in policy contexts. In both contexts interdisciplinarity has become a label almost synonymous with creativity and progress, signalling reform and modernization in science and scientific institutions. The desired and the real developments of interdisciplinary research are almost unanimously taken to be superior to the traditional disciplinary pursuit of knowledge production. Yet, such popular use of a term rarely reflects actual developments. In many instances there is little or no concrete concept or experience with the *actual* practice of interdisciplinarity. Such discrepancy alone is reason enough to be inquisitive and to raise questions about the purposes the widespread use of the term serves. How is it possible that interdisciplinarity has such positive connotations if at the same time it is often contradicted by the reality of intellectual and social organization of the scientific community? To which realities does to the term refer that are deemed desirable?

Distinguishable discourses constituted by and focusing on certain concepts are a fruitful target of inquiry for social research. The dynamics of these discourses can shed light on social change in that they provide the perspectives available at a given time, but also set the limits to thought and action. They reflect and shape social reality at the same time. Thus, before looking at the actual practice of interdisciplinary research (and teaching), the organizational environments, and the intellectual substances, it is instructive to look at the *discourse* of interdisciplinarity itself.

Julie Thompson Klein explores in her paper the many dimensions of the term 'interdisciplinarity,' the different meanings it assumes in connection with different fields and their combinations, as well as illustrative examples of interdisciplinarities. Peter Weingart's paper addresses the issue of the apparent paradox of the discourse on interdisciplinarity: a growing specialization in scientific practice contrasts with an ever more urgent call for interdisciplinarity. A closer look at the metaphors being attached to disciplinarity and interdisciplinarity not only reveals their complementarity but also hints at the function of the discourse itself. One may speculate that the renewed popularity of interdisciplinarity indicates a fundamental shift in the image and self-concept of science as a unified though heterogeneous institutional arrangement. From the early nineteenth century onwards, when the differentiation and specialization of science became apparent, the *unity of science* had become a promise of some future synthesis, be it by way of synthesizing principles such as evolution or energy conservation, as Du Bois Reymond suggested, or by reduction through the methodology of logical empiricism, as was the hope of Otto Neurath and the Unity of Science Movement in the 1930s. Today's discourse on interdisciplinarity seems to have given up this promise in exchange for the recognition of heterogeneity and the promise of cognitive and organizational innovation through evolution by variation, diversity, and combination.

1

A Conceptual Vocabulary of Interdisciplinary Science

JULIE THOMPSON KLEIN

It is a most unfortunate consequence of human limitations and the inflexible organizations of our institutions of higher learning that investigators tend to be forced into laboratories with such labels as 'biochemistry' or 'genetics.' The gene does not recognize the distinction – we should at least minimize it.

G.W. Beadle, 'The Genetic Control of Biochemical Reactions,'
The Harvey Lectures, 1944–5

The reality I want to report on is much more complicated and, consequently, the concept of interdisciplinarity more ambiguous.

Marc De Mey, 'Cognitive Science as an Interdisciplinary Endeavour,' Practising
Interdisciplinarity Conference, Vancouver, 1997

For most of the twentieth century, the question of knowledge has been framed by disciplinarity. In recent decades a different view has emerged. Research is becoming increasingly interdisciplinary. New social and cognitive forms have altered the academic landscape, new practices have emerged, and disciplinary relations have realigned. Talk of *re*negotiation, *re*organization, and *re*configuration abounds. As a result, even the most basic terms – 'discipline' and 'interdisciplinary' – are no longer adequate. A new conceptual vocabulary is needed.

Defining Interdisciplinary Science

Understanding is complicated by the current 'jungle of phenomena' (Huber 1992: 195). Ask three scientists what interdisciplinarity means, and they will likely give three answers. A geologist might reply plate tectonics, a life scientist molecular biology, and a physicist materials science. On the Internet, a multitude of websites support interdisciplinary interests as wide-ranging as global networks, information science, pharmacy, psychiatry, chaos theory, the environment, robotics, system dynamics, and electrical engineering. In the first half of this century, interdisciplinarity was not a major force in science. By mid-century, cross-fertilizations across the sub-branches of physics, grand simplifying concepts, the emergence of systems theory, and new fields such as biochemistry, radioastronomy, and plate tectonics marked increased activity. The most prominent event was the Second World War. Formation of institutes and laboratories to solve military problems legitimated interdisciplinary problem-focused research (IDR) and accustomed academic administrators to large-scale collaborative projects on campus. The Manhattan Project and operations research reinforced an instrumental discourse focused on technical problems akin to Peter Weingart's notion of pragmatic or opportunistic interdisciplinarity (1995: 6). After the war, many projects were dismantled, though influential laboratories continued to operate. Over the ensuing decades new laboratories and institutes were established in nuclear science, radiobiology, biophysics, marine physics, and atomic research (Etzkowitz 1983: 214–5).

Government support was a strong legitimating factor in the new social contract between government and academy. In the late 1950s, the U.S. Department of Defense (DoD) funded the first materials research laboratories and, by the early 1960s, the Interdisciplinary Research Laboratories. In the 1970s, international economic competition created added pressure for a new technology initiative. At least two areas of cutting-edge technology – computers and biotechnology – were closely tied to academic science (*New Alliances* 1986: 7). In response, the National Science Foundation (NSF) launched new initiatives. In the late 1970s, NSF provided seed money through the University–Industry Cooperative Research Centers. In 1985, NSF established an Engineering Research Centers program, followed by a Science and Technology Centers program. The long–term role of centres is unclear, but they have altered organizational structures and cultural practices of research (Turpin and Hill 1995). When centres existed primarily on a private basis and in applied research, they were not regarded as serious threats to academe. In recent decades, they have proliferated, due to accretion of problem- and mission-oriented research (Halliday 1992: 23).

New organizational structures have also emerged, including offices of technology transfer, industrial liaison programs, joint mergers and ventures, research networks, consortia, contract research, and entrepreneurial firms. They are not always interdisciplinary. Yet, research is typically problem-focused and often collaborative. Innovations in product design utilize new ideas and methods born at the interfaces of disciplines. The areas attracting the greatest attention today are advanced engineering materials and methods, computer sciences and complex systems software, molecular biology, and biomedical specialties (Sproull and Hall 1987: 3). Heightened links with product innovation and new discoveries support Weingart's contention (this volume) that interdisciplinarity is a discourse of innovation. The term 'innovation' connotes everything from new ideas to product design, though it tends to be equated with improvements in sociotechnical systems of manufacture and increased performance of products, services, and costs (Kline 1995: 180).

Instrumentality is not the only discourse of interdisciplinary science. Epistemological interests span traditional questions about knowledge, sociological studies of practices, and post-modern critique. Instrumental discourse driven by a policy agenda or social problems demands accommodation of problem solving but leaves existing disciplines and institutions intact. Interdisciplinarity forged in critique demands their reconstitution, akin to notions of 'critical interdisciplinarity' (Klein 1996) and interpenetration of existing discourses (Fuller 1993). It also promotes second-order reflection, akin to Weingart's notion of reflexive interdisciplinarity. Strategic and critical discourses are not always separate, though. Both critique and instrumentalism shape the environmental field.

Several movements have promoted unified knowledge, most notably the Unity of Science campaign in the 1930s and 1940s. The search for grand simplifying concepts – the second law, the mass-energy equivalence, and quantum mechanics – also promoted general theory. So has general systems. Transdisciplinary ambitions persist, but a different level of activity has gained attention more recently. The first prominent notice appeared in 1972, when the Organization for Economic Cooperation and Development identified development of science as the first need for interdisciplinarity. This need is manifested in an apparent contradiction: increasing specialization limits the focus of research, though it also leads to intersections of disciplines (OECD 1972: 44).

In a landmark study, Darden and Maull (1977) examined how theories bridge two fields. They depicted science as a network of relations, not a hierarchical succession of reductions. The term 'field' designates a central problem, domain of related items, general explanatory factors and goals, techniques and methods, and related concepts, laws, and theories. 'Interfield theory' designates relations between entities or phenomena in different fields and their explanatory role. In science, integrations are typically local. Exemplars include the bridging of genetics and cytology through the chromosome theory of Mendelian heredity, relating genetics and biochemistry through the operon theory, and connecting biochemistry and physical chemistry through the theory of allosteric regulation.

Nearly a decade later, a conference on life sciences focused on problems that lend themselves to interdisciplinary investigation. The case studies were biochemistry, the evolutionary synthesis, and cognitive science. Editor William Bechtel (1986: 46–7) identified five patterns of disciplinary relations:

- developing conceptual links using a perspective in one discipline to modify a perspective in another discipline
- recognizing a new level of organization with its own processes in order to solve unsolved problems in existing fields
- using research techniques developed in one discipline to elaborate a theoretical model in another
- modifying and extending a theoretical framework from one domain to apply in another
- developing a new theoretical framework that may reconceptualize research in separate domains as it attempts to integrate them

Several lines of inquiry characterize recent studies. The literature on management continues to grow. Increased attention is also being paid to local practices in specific domains, such as Marc De Mey's study of cognitive science, and in organizational structures, such as studies of centres by De Mey, Sam Garrett-Jones, Rogers Hollingsworth, Sabine Massen, Eric Scerri, and Stephen Turner, all in this volume. Paralleling the expanding field of knowledge studies, multiple methods are employed, including genealogy, ethnography, interviews and surveys, bibliometrics, discourse analysis, archival research, organizational analysis, social theory, and critique. Disciplinary histories are also being updated.

Physics is a striking case. In 1972 the National Research Council (NRC) in the United States declared there was 'no definable boundary' between physics and other disciplines (*Physics in Perspective* 1971: 67). In 1986, the Council highlighted new disciplines arising from interfaces of physics and other sciences, plus applications in technology, medicine, and national defense (National Research Council 1986). Almost all significant growth has occurred at 'interdisciplinary borderlands' between established fields. The five prominent areas of fundamental research are biological physics, materials science, the physics–chemistry interface, geophysics, and mathematical physics and computational physics. The six outstanding areas of technical applications are micro-electronics, optical technology, new instrumentation, the fields of energy and environment, national security, and medical applications.

New developments have blurred boundaries by relocating scientific and technological work away from discrete sites to problems and puzzles characterized by unpredictability, complexity, and a quickening pace. In many areas of advanced technology, the intellectual boundary between engineering and physics is vanishing, creating a continuum that speeds innovation and technology transfer. The postgraduate demands of many scientists and engineers are pulling them inexorably into the continuum. At major synchrotron facilities the cultures of physicists and chemists are merging, and, in macromolecular research, boundaries among chemistry, physics, and biology are blurring.

The NRC defines new patterns of interaction as 'true interdisciplinary science.' Traditionally, techniques and discoveries were transferred from physics to other disciplines. Today, both physicists and chemists are building on and enriching areas to create new subfields. Even the NRC acknowledges the limits of this picture. Synergistic interactions between physicists and chemists far from the traditional interface have usually occurred in spite of department structures. Institutions are not always ready to adapt to complexity, promote borrowing, or accommodate effective problem solving (Carole Palmer, personal communication, 16 October 1996).

An apparent paradox emerges. New programs, centres, and activities proliferate. However, interdisciplinarity is impeded. There is no paradox, Weingart (this volume) rightly contends, only terminological confusion. Interdisciplinarity and specialization are parallel, mutually reinforcing strategies. The relationship between disciplinarity and interdisciplinarity is not a paradox but a productive tension characterized by complexity and hybridity.

Complexity and Hybridity

An old saying comes to mind – interdisciplinarity exists in the 'white space' of organizational charts. Many activities, such as De Mey's 'wandering professor,' are not tracked. While lamenting the lack of systematic data, Weingart (this volume) repeated a telling estimate. One expert speculated that only about 20 per cent of projects in targeted research programs of the German government encouraged interdisciplinarity. However, the rate was apparently higher in a standard funding program that is supposedly disciplinary. Interdisciplinary activity does not always fit the preconceptions administrators have (Bechtel 1986: 4, 29).

Activities are located across an expanse of sites and relations. An enormous amount of interdisciplinary traffic occurs in less visible forms such as common interests and problems; shared use of facilities, instrumentation, and databases; and borrowed tools, methods, results, concepts, and theories. The least visible activities are often in disciplines, in interdisciplinary traditions, new practices, and research on strategic and intellectual problems. Instruments also play a key role. When it comes to big machines such as spectroscopies, Turner remarked (this volume), chemistry begins to look like physics.

One signal, specialty migration, is familiar. Migration implies boundedness, but specialties possess no inherent boundaries. They are defined by relative concentrations of interests. The underlying metaphor of migration, Hoch (1987) cautioned, may be ill-conceived. Most migration occurs because research areas are in constant reformulation. Boundaries shift and overlap because ideas and techniques do not exist in fixed places. Researchers carry them through multiple groups (Becher 1990: 344; Chubin 1976: 464, note 35). Interdisciplinarity, Turner observed, starts by creating novel divisions of labour for novel ends. Consequently, 'frontier' is a popular metaphor of interdisciplinarity, connoting expansion into uncharted domains and 'the cutting edge.' Understandably, interdisciplinarity is associated with pathbreaking ideas, discoveries, and lines of investigation. Yet, the frontier metaphor creates a rigid realism. The space of interdisciplinary work is not just *out* there – interdisciplinary activity these days may be *in* the heart of disciplinary practice. In some areas knowledge production is no longer occurring strictly within disciplinary boundaries, especially in the Human Genome Project, biotechnology, molecular biology, risk assessment, and technology assessment (Gibbons et al. 1994: 138, 147).

These developments suggest that territorial metaphors may be obsolete. Spatial metaphors – turf, territory, boundary, and domain – highlight formation and maintenance. Boundary formation occurs as categories and classifications stake claims. Organic metaphors – boundary crossing, interdependence, and interrelation – highlight connection. Organic models compare intellectual movements to processes in ecology and the evolution of plant and animal species. 'Ecology,' Winter (1996) recalls, derives from a Greek word, *oikeos*, meaning household or settlement. The verbs associated with *oikeos* suggest inhabiting, settling, governing, controlling, managing, and other activities in a complex interweaving of fields of social action. Knowledge, simply put, cannot be depicted in a single metaphor. Spatial dynamics of place and organic dynamics of production occur simultaneously. Spatial and organic models may even be combined to form a third type, highlighting interactions between social groups and environments. Organism and environment, Winter emphasizes, imply one another mutually. Both are territorial, competitive, and expansionist. The underlying idea is to make and reinforce jurisdictional claims, analogous to territorial claims humans and animals make in ecological niches. Organism and environment also exploit resources to produce new life forms and settlements.

The simultaneity of spatiality and organicism – of location and generation – is apparent in the hybrid character of interdisciplinary activity. Hybridization is a biological metaphor connoting formation of new animals, plants, or individuals and groups. A hybrid emerges from interaction or cross-breeding of heterogeneous elements. In organizational theory, the metaphor marks tasks at boundaries and in spaces between systems and subsystems (Gibbons et al. 1994: 37). Communities that facilitate interdisciplinary research exhibit properties that Gerson (1983) attributed to intersections in science. An intersection is a system of negotiating contexts. Most intersections involve techniques, specialized skills, and instruments. Intersections, though, also occur in interpretive phases, from borrowing vocabulary and ideas to theoretical explanations, such as new groundings of 'valance' and 'gene' in other disciplines.

Intersections are accommodated in a variety of hybrid communities, from centres and programs to projects, networks, invisible colleges, and matrix structures. Matrix structures are alternative forms superimposed on organizations dominated by disciplines or functions. Matrices have long facilitated innovations in the realms of pharmacy, engineering, and social and technological problem solving (Pearson, Payne, and Gunz 1979: 114; Klein 1990: 121–39). In science policy circles, 'hybrid community' has a technical meaning, designating a group of researchers, politicians, bureaucrats, and others who formulate a research program. New organizations such as the Work Research Institute in Norway are hybrid, problem-solving communities. They encompass organizational frameworks of policy making and social research as well as the new hybrid discourse coalitions in which problems are defined, investigated, and handled (Mathiesen 1990: 411–13; Hagendijk 1990: 58–9). These organizations are interinstitutional as well as interdisciplinary.

Two additional concepts – trading zone and enclave – shed light on intersections. Galison (1992) proposed the concept of 'trading zones' to explain heterogeneous interactions of scientific cultures. Interactions range from a stabilized 'pidgin zone,' a linguistic term for an interim form of communication, to a 'creole zone,' a main subculture or native language of a group that develops a new hybrid role and professional identity. Trading zone is also an economic metaphor connoting exchange of goods, trade agreements, and embargoes (Fuller 1992, 45–6). Lowy (1992), Fuller (1993), the authors in a special issue of the journal *Social Epistemology* (1995), and Klein (1996) have extended the notion of trading zones to explain disciplinary interactions.

Turpin and Hill call the organizational structures emerging from research centres 'enclaves of collaborating research practitioners' (1995: 10). These structures create new boundaries of alliance, identities, and professional roles. They operate partially as counter-cultures and partially as components of new cultures. Some individuals participate fully, others in a transitory fashion. Historically, such enclaves mark the growing diversification of strata formation and crossing of political, sectoral, and occupational formations (Eisenstadt 1992: 57). Enclaves are loci of changing roles and cultural orientations. The enclaves where interdisciplinary interests are segmented often exhibit a 'semi-liminal' character.

Hybridization connotes both form and process. Dogan and Pahre (1990) view hybridization as a characteristic of knowledge production today. As innovative scholars move from the core to margins of their disciplines, specialties are recombined continuously, with two results:

1 formally institutionalized subfields of one or another formal discipline or permanent committees or programs that regularize exchanges
2 informal hybridized topics, such as development, that may never become institutionalized fields

The higher up the ladder of innovations, the greater the chances boundaries will disappear, Dogan asserts (1995: 103). Hybrids, moreover, beget other hybrids, especially in natural sciences where higher degrees of fragmentation and hybridization occur. Their formation is not continuous. Yet, specialty interaction is a prominent feature of knowledge production today. The second type of hybrid is difficult to map, because relations cannot be easily defined in spatial terms. The current interface between physics and chemistry has been crossed so often in both directions, the authors of an NRC report remarked, that 'its exact location is obscure; its passage is signaled more by gradual changes in language and approach than by any sharp demarcation in content.' Interactions and cross-fertilizations that characterize the interface have been sources of continual advances in concept and application across the science of molecules and atoms, surfaces and interfaces, and fluids and solids (National Research Council 1986: 53).

Two prominent activities – borrowing and problem solving – further illuminate the hybridity and complexity of interdisciplinary activity.

BORROWING

A great deal of crossfertilization occurs in the daily flow of influence signified by the metaphor of borrowing. The simple borrowing of tools, data, results, and methods does not tend to transform boundaries. Yet, concepts from one level may permeate to other levels in a process called 'pivoting' (Kedrov 1974) and 'whirlpool effects' (Intrilligator 1985). Methods of mathematics, statistics, and systemology are used in mechanics, physics, chemistry. Methods used in the latter disciplines are used, in turn, in astronomy, geosciences, and biosciences (Dahlberg 1994: 68). Borrowing is an important signal. When, over time, genetic techniques became primary tools and knowledge of mechanics of gene action and regulation provided primary insights for many basic problems, borrowing became more frequent as a mode of unification in biology (Burian 1993: 312).

Borrowing is difficult to map. Sometimes a borrowing is assimilated so completely it is no longer considered foreign, or it transforms practice without being considered 'interdisciplinary.' Many physical techniques have become so fully integrated into biological research that their origin may be forgotten; for instance, electron microscopy, X-ray crystallography, and spectroscopies. Current pressure on scientists to do interdisciplinary work derives in part from borrowing techniques and instruments to address problems raised in another discipline (Bechtel

1986: 282–3). One of Scerri's interviewees remarked, 'The philosophy of our lab is to try to steal as many technologies as we can from other disciplines and apply them to our problem' (this volume).

Palmer's study of one institute lends insight. The institute houses research programs in physical sciences, engineering, computational science, life sciences, and behavioural sciences. Research exhibits a dual action. Centrifugal forces help move people, things, and ideas outward into other domains. Centripetal forces hold elements together in established frameworks. Diversity of membership opens up networks, skills, and ideas otherwise not accessible to individuals. Concrete things are a pivotal feature of boundary crossing:

> Data (numbers) and data sources (rabbits) are shared between labs and sometimes brought together for comparative analysis. Databanks of raw data are amassed and then added to by allied researchers. Molecules built by one research group are analyzed by another, with both sides bringing insights to the final results. It is common for apparatus to be borrowed and applied in new ways and to different types of data. New computational technologies are often combined with established disciplinary science to 'push the frontier end of studies' in the area. (Palmer 1996)

Concepts and theories are also influential sources of interaction. Hübenthal (1991) identifies 'concept interdisciplinarity' as a specific type, citing system theory, cybernetics, information theory, synergetics, game theory, semiotics, and structuralism. Star and Griesmer (1988) proposed the term 'boundary concept' to explain heterogeneous interactions between different professional groups. Concrete and conceptual objects are robust enough to maintain unity across fields but plastic enough to be manipulated. Weakly structured in common use, they are strongly structured at individual sites. As negotiable entities, they simultaneously delimit and connect. In cognitive terms, they facilitate hybrid intellectual work. In social terms, they facilitate inter-group alliance. In this volume, Maasen, commenting on the transfer of concepts in research groups, recalled Bono's (1995) observation that concepts act as sites and media of exchange. Boundary concepts exhibit both generality and particularity. The theory of the genetic code and protein synthesis exhibits features of universality and broad scope, plus particularization to specific organisms (Schaffner 1993: 320).

Chaos is a timely example. Traditionally, Hayles (1990) explains, turbulence was viewed from the perspective of fluid flows. Today it has become a general phenomenon. When concepts circulate within a cultural field, they stimulate cross-fertilization. Yet, they bear traces of local disciplinary economies. Literary theorists value chaos because they are concerned with exposing ideological underpinnings of traditional ideas of order. Chaos theorists value chaos as the engine that drives a system towards a more complex kind of order. Hayles theorizes interdisciplinarity as an 'ecology of ideas' that neither demands unity nor overrides differences. Commonalities and differences create dual emphasis on cultural fields and disciplinary sites. The discourse of chaos is both fragmented and unified: 'Any description presupposes a frame of reference that limits, even as it creates, what is said.' What is known is a function of what is noticed and considered important. Both spatial and organic dynamics operate. Activities 'locate' in intersections but continue to circulate across spheres (1990: 135, 144).

PROBLEM SOLVING

Palmer highlights an added feature of scientific work – researchers tend to work *on* problems not *in* disciplines. Problems are focal points where disciplinary social worlds intersect. The figurative common ground of problem areas such as oscillating reactions, photosynthesis, and membranes is fluid. It changes as science progresses through discoveries and interactions between fields (Palmer 1996: 57, 119). All problems, moreover, are not the same. Reynolds identified three kinds of problems (Sigma Xi 1988: 21):

- *Problems of the first kind:* intellectual problems in a traditional discipline;
- *Problems of the second kind:* multidisciplinary problems that are basically intellectual not policy-action in nature but cannot be successfully undertaken within boundaries of one discipline;
- *Problems of the third kind:* distinctly multidisciplinary problems generated increasingly by society and distinguished by relatively short-time courses calling in some cases for a policy-action result and in other cases for a technological quick fix.

With problems of the first kind, disciplinary boundary work is strongest. Problems of the second kind heighten boundary crossing. Boundary concepts such as 'text,' 'discourse,' 'interpretation,' and 'culture' have been catalysts for interaction across humanities and social sciences. 'Role,' 'status,' and 'area' have cross-fertilized social sciences.

The multi- and interdisciplinary nature of research problems is often highlighted in centres: when, for instance, a polar research centre addresses problems of ice core research, polar ecology, Antarctic tectonics, and glaciology (OSU 1991: 18). The urgency of problems of the third kind has heightened the discourse of instrumentality.

In describing this change, Gibbons et al. (1994) proposed the concept of Mode 2 knowledge production. Mode 1, the traditional form, is primarily academic, homogeneous, and hierarchical. It is dominated by disciplinary boundary work and comprised of ideas, methods, values, and norms of Newtonian science. Mode 2 is non-hierarchical. It is distinguished by heterogeneously organized forms, transdisciplinarity, and closer interaction among scientific, technological, and industrial modes of knowledge production. Mode 2 has garnered wide attention in science policy circles. Weingart (this volume) judges the claim overstated and empirical evidence weak. Nonetheless, Mode 2 provides a name for traits closely associated with innovation and boundary crossing. Human resources have become more mobile, and organization of research is more open and flexible. The weakening of disciplinary boundaries has been accompanied by collapse or erosion of monopoly power. As organizational boundaries of control blur, 'competence' is redefined and criteria of quality broaden.

Multidisciplinary competencies, as Garrett-Jones and Tim Turpin forecast in this volume, are becoming more than a secondary 'add-on' to disciplinary identities. In the future, portfolios of identities and competencies must be managed. As resources, knowledge, and skills are continuously reconfigured, Gibbons et al. add, both theoretical and practical knowledge are generated in new configurations of intellectual and technological work. Since exploitation of knowledge requires participation in its generation, discovery and application are more closely integrated. In a dynamic and socially distributed system with feedback loops, markets set new problems more or less continuously. In human genome discourse, Rheinberger (1995) predicts, boundaries of basic research and medical applications will be inverted. The opportunistic ideology of medical application and goals-directed research will produce keys for attacking 'fundamental' problems in other areas, such as developmental biology, protein folding and function, and the brain (Gibbons et al. 1994: 178).

Metaphors of knowledge shift in turn. Gibbons et al. liken organizations that carry projects at the forefront of science, technology, and high-value enterprises to a spider web. Connections are spun continuously, with growing density and connectivity. Problems in genetics, electronics, mathematics, and physics possess an intrinsic intellectual interest nourished by the research and practical interests of other users. Older terms – 'applied science,' 'technological or industrial research,' 'technology transfer,' 'strategic research,' 'mission-oriented research,' 'research and development' – are no longer adequate. In the linear model, science led to technology and technology satisfied market needs. In many advanced sectors of science and technology today, however, knowledge is being generated *in* the context of application. New social contracts between industry and academe make 'interchange' a more appropriate word than 'transfer.' A greater number of scientists, moreover, are working on problems outside traditional specialties and entering into new social arrangements.

Research, Garrett-Jones and Turpin add, is not unidirectional. Clark coined the term 'restless research' to describe research that moves out in many directions from traditional university settings (1995, 195). Definitions of a 'good' scientist and science become more pluralistic. Problem solvers, problem identifiers, and strategic brokers are working with knowledge resources held in government laboratories, consultancies, and other businesses (Gibbons et al. 1994: 23, 32, 37, 65, 76, 145). Skilled 'boundary riders' must 'beat the boundaries' in order to relocate science into productive and localized forms (Turpin and Hill 1995: 16). Managers in higher education, in turn, are beginning to operate in a parallel mode.

The current push of high technology and international competition has made 'collaboration,' 'competitiveness,' 'problem solving,' 'systems,' 'complexity,' and 'interdisciplinary' new descriptors of knowledge. Instrumental discourse has not rendered IDR central to the academy. Yet, problem complexity, economic competition, costs of instrumentation and facilities, the desire to transfer knowledge rapidly to application, and the interchange of applied and basic research have heightened the legitimacy of hybrid organization and modes of knowledge production. As new 'technostructures' intersect with traditional university departments, new commercial strategies are accompanied by changes in organizational values, structure, culture, and intertextuality of scientific discourses with elements of public political discourse and popular discourse (Stehr and Ericson 1992: 196). Grappling with the need to address complex problems, governments are making decisions that increase the likelihood of the deinstitutionalization of science as greater control passes to non-scientists. Elzinga (1985) coined the term 'epistemic drift' to account for the shift from strictly internalist criteria and reputational control to externally driven criteria that are more open to external regulation in the policy arena. The likelihood of interdisciplinary work involving at least one party who does not work at a university also increases (Fuller 1995: 204).

When interdisciplinarity is cast as a principal means of achieving targeted objectives, the problem of interdisciplinarity is drawn closer to the general problem of knowledge policy (Fuller 1995: 33). Outcomes may be determined more by a power battle between disciplinary groupings and hybrid communities than by scientific validity, social need, or the legitimacy of integration and collaboration (Hoch 1990, 45). Discourses of epistemology and second-order reflection are also shortchanged, as motivation and social consequences are minimized or even ignored.

The Disciplinary Question

Another popular metaphor – knowledge 'explosion' – signifies a development that further strains conventional notions and standard models. By 1987, there were 8530 definable knowledge fields (Crane and Small 1992, p. 197). By 1990, roughly 8000 research topics in science were being sustained by related networks (Clark 1995: 193). A significant number of specialties today are 'hybrid creatures' (Clark 1995: 245; Winter 1996: 24). Intensification of interests in new areas has produced new domains that fall between older disciplines, such as sociobiology and biochemistry, and at extremes of prior capability, such as particle physics and cosmology. Extensification of interests has produced new areas that draw together disciplines to model more complex phenomena, such as concrete economic and public health problems (Fuller 1988: 285). Disciplines also routinely experience the push of prolific fields and the pull of strong new concepts and paradigms (Jantsch 1980: 306).

Invoking the metaphors of mapping and geography, Becher (1990) highlights the variety of current forms and practices. The earth is comprised of many topographical patterns; cross-national connections; economic, functional, and occupational similarities; and broad social and cultural features. Their counterparts in knowledge territories include *basic characteristics* (e.g., quantitative and qualitative, pure or applied), *shared theories or ideologies* (e.g., catastrophe theory, Marxism), *common techniques* (e.g., electron microscopy, computer modelling), and *sociocul-*

tural characteristics (e.g., incidence of collaborative work, nature of competition).

These forms and practices are not the result of a simple increase in the number of activities – they also represent a change in kind. Specialization works against systematic integration by leading to greater fragmentation, but it also gives rise to a characteristic style of connection or mutual interdependence that provides some sense of unity (Winter 1996: 6). Becher (1990) uses the analogy of a biological culture viewed under a microscope. At close range, a discipline is a constantly changing 'kaleidoscope of smaller components,' varied in form but still related through a general process of specialization. Individual cells are in a 'state of constant flux' – subdividing, recombining, and changing shape and disposition. One of the salient features of subdisciplinary groupings is their relative lack of stability compared with parent disciplines. Some sub-units even exhibit an 'anarchic tendency' to appear more closely allied with counterparts in heartlands of other disciplines. These groupings create 'counter-cultures' that may conflict with and even undermine the parent disciplinary culture.

The current extent of boundary crossing at this level suggests that specialty interactions may be more reliable indicators of interdisciplinary activity than the emergence of new hybrid disciplines, even perhaps of knowledge production in general (Lepenies 1978: 302; Dogan and Pahre: 64). Academic subject labels are also strained. Traditional labels may suffice for teaching but are less accurate for research or faculty identity (Pinch 1990: 299). Palmer found that 'physics,' 'chemistry,' 'psychology,' and 'biology' were not meaningful knowledge domains for researchers working in an interdisciplinary institute (1996: 207). To call someone a biologist doesn't tell much about what she/he or her/his professional peers do (Bechtel 1986: 279). One biochemist reported that her approach has become more integrative as her field has grown more multidisciplinary on an international scale (Palmer 1996: 56). In one university, moreover, the subject area of 'biology' is spread across thirteen discipline-based departments and seventeen interdisciplinary programs (Clark 1995: 142).

Disciplinary loyalties, Turner (this volume) rightly notes, undermine interdisciplinary work. Yet, the pull of disciplinary careers is not so strong as it used to be. Changes in the organization of scientific research have weakened the monolithic character of departments. Disciplines have become decentralized into smaller units that exert day-today social control over what is studied and how. These units neither certainly nor inevitably lie within conventionally defined boundaries. Alternative sites – programs, centres, institutes, and laboratories – have further weakened disciplinary control over subject definition, conceptual approaches, cognitive structures, goals, and norms (Whitley 1984: 12, 18–20).

The view of disciplinarity that emerges does not deny the value of specialization, the inevitability of differentiation, the inertial strength of institutionalized formations, or the regulative mechanisms that discipline interdisciplinary work (Stocking and Leary 1986: 57; Calhoun 1992: 184). It does, though, dispute oversimplifications. Standard models stress stability, predictability, autonomy, maturity, progress, unity, and consensus (Salter and Hearn 1996). Discipline, however, is not a neat category (Becher 1990: 335). Disciplines vary in the ways they structure themselves, establish identities, maintain boundaries, regulate and reward practitioners, manage consensus and dissent, and communicate (Squires 1992: 203). Heterogeneous practices, hybrid activities, and interdisciplinary fields have rendered disciplines fissured sites. Comprised of multiple strata and influenced by other disciplines, a discipline is a 'shifting and fragile homeostatic system' that evolves and adapts to changing environments (Heckhausen 1972: 83; Easton 1991: 13).

This view of disciplinarity also challenges the popular notion that a successful interdisciplinary practice becomes 'just another discipline.' 'Border interdisciplinarity,' 'interdisciplinarity of neighbouring disciplines,' 'borderland interdisciplinarity,' 'zone of interdependence,' and 'zone of proximal development' are names for high-level integration. The reconstructive capacity of interdisciplinary research alters the architectonics of knowledge by strengthening connections outside the discipline 'proper.' Connections weaken divisions of labour, expose gaps, stimulate cross-fertilization, and fix new fields of focus. They also imply new divisions of labour, redistribution of resources, realignment of institutional structures, and redefinitions of epistemological and ontological premises (Landau, Proshansky, and Ittelson 1961).

All hybrid disciplines are not the same, however. Interrelations may be postulated between entities examined in one discipline and entities in another. The conceptualization of genes as part of chromosomes linked genetics to molecular biology. Or, two disciplines may become conceptually connected while retaining different but overlapping foci, principles, or theories. Physics and chemistry were linked through the bridge laws of thermodynamics. Or, one discipline may be absorbed into another, as astronomy was absorbed into physics. Or, two disciplines may join into a more general discipline through translatability of their fundamental principles, as geometric and arithmetic sciences became unified into mathematical science (Paxson 1996).

Likewise, outcomes differ. Cognitive science is an interdisciplinary field. At this point, however, it does not constitute a new discipline that stands alongside artificial intelligence, cognitive psychology, theoretical linguistics, cognitive anthropology, and philosophy. Practitioners share resources through interdisciplinary programs, societies, conferences, and journals while remaining identified with their 'home' disciplines. A psychologist working in the field is likely to hold an appointment in psychology and belong to the American Psychological Association and subscribe to its journals. Bechtel calls such affiliations 'cross-disciplinary research clusters.' In contrast, molecular biology became a new 'way of life' in biological research. Its 'technical fallout' exceeds and subverts boundaries of existing biological disciplines (Rheinberger 1995: 175). In cognitive science the central problem – what processes underlie cognition? – was already a topic of inquiry in the disciplines being bridged. In cell biology, the task of explaining cell function in terms of cell structures was not a central task in contributing disciplines (Bechtel 1986: 295).

Hybrid disciplines are not handled uniformly, either. Biochemistry, for example, is structured as an independent department, joined with a department of biochemistry and biophysics, merged into a department of physiology and chemistry, and organized by an interdisciplinary committee composed of members of departments of biology and chemistry (Bechtel 1986: 16). The biological metaphor of a niche implies formation of a new species, variation, or mutation. Survival is indeed tied to the ability to create new niches. Not all interdisciplinary work, though, results in a new niche. The speciation model, De Mey remarked (this volume), is only a loose metaphor. It does not necessarily extend to all levels of aggregation in science. The biological counterpart is an ecosystem, not a single species. Yet, restricted speciations, such as De Mey's example of spatial cognition, arise.

Most scientists working across disciplinary boundaries are not attempting to achieve ontological simplification and unification (Bechtel 1986: 42–3). The redrawing of boundaries through 'ontological gerrymandering' is more typical (Woolgar and Pawluch 1984: 216; Fuller 1988: 197). Only partial spheres tend to be integrated, and convergence often means tolerance, not a change of world-view (Hübenthal 1994: 61;

Falersweany 1995: 167). In a critique of general theories, Van der Steen (1993) charges that selected case studies have been overemphasized and limits to integration minimized. 'Peripheral integration' is more common. The modern synthetic theory of evolution, for instance, does not cover all disciplines that may pertain. Their generality resides in terminology, not substantive unity. When concepts of taxis and kineses in animal orientation carry a conceptual overload, the result is 'pseudo-integration,' not unity. The concepts cannot account for a great diversity of phenomena. Encompassing theories of evolution have a loose structure. As integrative force moves outward from the core of evolutionary biology, it becomes more peripheral. When used for a heterogeneous category of processes, selection and allied concepts become diluted notions that express a limited array of analogies.

Conceding overstatements, Burian (1993) insists the evidence is representative of many cases. Coherence and integration are typically achieved in middle-range norms that play a guiding role in long-term treatment of biological problems. To recall Darden and Maull (1977), theories in biology are typically interlevel. Innovations do not tend to span whole disciplines or even major parts, but rather a few subfields (Dogan and Pahre 1990: 13). Less formal higher-order norms operate at a meta level or as rules of thumb. Middle-range theories are not wide-ranging, but they are not mere summaries of data either. They are midway between extremes. Schaffner cites two examples. Neurosciences and biological theories are interlevel prototypes that embody causal sequences; they are related through strong analogies. Interlevel models are levels of aggregation; they contain component parts that are often specific in intermingled organ, cellular, and biochemical terms (Schaffner 1993: 321).

The norm of unification has value. It improves the content of biological knowledge and offers greater coherence of description and explanation. The specificity of cases, though, means that different terminologies do not map easily onto each other and may yield contradictions. Nonetheless, they overlap in regard to entities, process, or mechanisms. Significant change in disciplinary relations may take the form of a progressive blurring and amalgamating of distinctions between mechanisms and generalizations.

In sum, local sites and interlevel integration are prominent features of interdisciplinary science. 'The task of interdisciplinary research,' Hübenthal cautions, 'is not to be solved with a global interdisciplinary theory that cannot supply concrete directives for subject-overlapping research on a specific topic. It must be pursued within individual sciences in daily usage' (1994: 55, 57). The level at which bridging or integrating is attempted affects the kinds of problems that arise (Bechtel 1986: 7). Generalizations must be supplemented with details of specific connections and more finely structured elements. The applicability of integrationist ideals, the value of pursuing them, and their consequences depend on a variety of local historical circumstances, including the power of available techniques, the character of conceptual contacts between pertinent disciplines, and current opportunities. In short, generality and particularity coexist.

Landscaping Knowledge

Over the course of this century, metaphors of knowledge have shifted from the static logic of a foundation and a structure to the dynamic properties of a network, a web, a system, and a field. Perceptions of academic reality, though, are still shaped by older forms and images. Simplified views of the complex university only add to the problem of operational realties that outrun old expectations, especially older definitions that depict one part or function of the university as its 'essence' or 'essential mission' (Clark 1995: 154). Repeating the same metaphors, Goldman (1995) cautions, impedes understanding of new knowledge and relationships. Even the metaphor of levels, so pervasive in science, presumes a hierarchy and a foundational logic at odds with images of free-floating constructions and non-linear, non-vertical perspectives that are multidimensional and multidirectional. A wider range of physical and topological or architectural metaphors describes relations of elements that make up innovations and their contexts – dimensions, joints, manifolds, points of connection, boundedness, overlaps, interconnections, interpenetrations, breaks, cracks, and handles (Clark 1995: 222–3).

Bechtel defines interdisciplinarity as an 'ongoing process for discovery,' not an attempt to systematize what is known (1986: 43–4). The real benefit, Salter and Hearn (1996) contend, is not necessarily in subject matter or new journals and publications. Interdisciplinarity is a set of dynamic forces for rejuvenation and regeneration, pressures for change, and the capacity for responsiveness. It is the necessary 'churn' in the system. Interdisciplinarity entails knowledge negotiation and new meanings, not one more stage in 'normal' science. There is a danger, though, in perceiving interdisciplinarity and innovation at the single moment of inception, as isolated events. They continue throughout the circulation, diffusion, elaboration, revision, modification, and appropriation of new ideas, and their incorporation into intellectual and social life. Social practices and their material bases generate openings for ideas that lead to development of newer practices that help, in turn, to institutionalize new ideas (Goldman 1995: 212).

Interdisciplinary cognition, Paulson (1991) proposed, lies in the attempt to construct meaning out of what initially seems to be noise. The idea of self-organization from noise emanates from information theory. When there is noise in an electronic channel during transmission, the information received is diminished by the ambiguity of the message. The message received is neither pure nor simple. Importing terms and concepts from other disciplines creates a kind of noise in the knowledge system. Perceived as unwanted noise in one context, variety and interference become information in a new or reorganized context. New meaning is constructed out of what first appears to be noise as the exchange of codes and information across boundaries is occurring, whether the activity is borrowing, solving technical problems, developing hybrid interests, or disrupting and restructuring traditional practices.

The metaphor of noise acknowledges the roles of disequilibrium and complexity. The subtle subversion of meanings introduced by the improper creates a space for mobile, shifting meanings, the exchange of meaning among different discourses, and new positions and practices (deCerteau 1984; cited in Bono 1995: 132). The starting point of interdisciplinarity, Roland Barthes declared, is an 'unease in classification.' From there a 'certain mutation' may be detected. It must not be overestimated, however: 'It is more in the nature of an epistemological slide than a break' (Barthes 1977: 155). Noise, Paulson explains, is a signal: 'What appears to be a perturbation in a given system, turns out to be the intersection of a new system with the first.' What is extra-systemic at one level may be an index of another level, another system with a new kind of coding (1991: 44, 49). Interdisciplinarity implies idiosyncrasy, but novel work can create a new common wisdom (Bazerman 1995: 195).

The analogy to postmodernism is striking. Heightened boundary crossing in knowledge is paralleled by widespread crossing of national, political, and cultural boundaries. A central feature of this process is reversal of the differentiating, classificatory dynamic of modernity and increasing hybridization of cultural categories, identities, and previous certainties. New forms of interdependence and cooperation call attention to a worldwide changing cultural configuration that places all cul-

tural categories and boundaries at risk (Bernstein 1991; Muller and Taylor 1995: 258). Contests of legitimacy over jurisdiction, systems of demarcation, and regulative and sanctioning mechanisms continue. Yet,
boundaries are characterized by ongoing tensions of permanency and
passage. Intersecting pressures created by new corporate research models have not simply blurred organizational boundaries – they represent
a new phase in the relation between knowledge and society. Turpin
and Hill (1995) acknowledge the link between post-modernism and the
apparent paradox of a global sea change coexisting with heightened
local conditions of knowledge production and personal relations. In
this instance, relational and articulational dimensions, border-crossing,
seepage, and hybridity take on heightened roles. If framed only in terms
of instrumental discourse, however, the critical function of epistemological discourse is absent.

The implications for knowledge studies are striking. Once framed by
questions of epistemology, knowledge studies today are defined by
intersections of individuals from an eclectic assortment of fields such as
philosophy, sociology, education, English, cultural studies, political science, economics, and anthropology (Pahre 1995: 242). Some approaches,
Harvey Goldman explains, denote a deep structure of intellectual or
linguistic enterprise, such as episteme, discursive formation, mental
equipment, paradigm, disciplinary matrix, generative grammar, and language games. Other approaches illuminate the structure of practices,
institutions, and relations, such as field, complex of power/knowledge,
regime of truth, invisible college, exemplar, network, system, and grid.
Others yet point to a broad social and collective mental foundation of
mentalité, habitus, cultural unconscious, hegemony, and culture. These
and other tools are being brought to bear on a fuller conception of
interests, histories, structures, and relations that account for production
of knowledge that goes beyond reproduction of the conventional
(Goldman 1995: 213, 221).

The next step in interdisciplinary science is already under way. Burian
forsees the next decade of work in biology addressing difficult questions regarding the matching of tools, organisms, institutions, and conceptual frameworks required to solve major problems (Burian 1993:
311). The task for philosophers of science is to specify conditions that
promote integration and to formulate criteria to evaluate integrations
(Ven der Steen 1993: 222–3). There is no universal interdisciplinary language. Even powerful cross-fertilizing languages, such as mathematics
and general systems, have limits. Interdisciplinary work requires the

creation of what Hollingsworth and Hollingsworth (this volume) call 'horizontal communication' within an 'interdisciplinary/integrated culture.' A working language emerges through the negotiation of meanings. The dynamics of negotiation are captured in Hollingsworth and Hollingsworth's notion of triangulating depth, diversity, and tensions, and in Rainer Bromme's triangulation of diversity, difference, and tension (this volume). The resulting 'common ground' is not an artificial unity that eschews differences. The boundary between disciplinarity and interdisciplinary 'flows,' Bromme's image, depends on difference.

Greater interest in the exigencies that move people to traverse disciplinary domains and practices does not mean that calls for a general practice of interdisciplinarity will cease. The two are not necessarily contradictory. A general crisis could be expressed in what appears to be many local crises (Bazerman 1995: 193). Declarations by scientists about the desirability of interdisciplinary research, Weingart cautions in this volume, can no more be taken at face value than normative appeals will change scientists' attitudes. Neither can knee-jerk dismissals. One of Scerri's interviewees proclaimed there is no 'real interdis-ciplinarity.' It is a bogus argument. Proponents overstate the extent, opponents understate it.

2

Interdisciplinarity: The Paradoxical Discourse

PETER WEINGART

The Apparent Contradiction

As far back as 1969, at the height of the student revolt and reform euphoria in higher education, Norman Birnbaum observed: 'For years an official critique of the division of the world of learning into disciplines has accompanied the growth of ever more rigid compartments of the mind. The very men who as scholars, teachers, and administrators perpetuate the academic division of labor argue persuasively that it is nonsense.' He then went on to comment on the student critique of the scope and direction of scholarship, which he thought 'mirrored, in distorted fashion, the crisis of the disciplines ...' (Birnbaum 1986 [1969]: 53).

At the end of the 1960s and into the 1970s, a time of planning euphoria, of technology gaps and forecasting, 'interdisciplinarity' and derivatives such as 'pluridisciplinarity' or 'transdisciplinarity' were traded as panaceas of higher education reform. Few if any tracts attained the sophistication of the OECD/CERI's volume, *Interdisciplinarity* (1972, edited by a committee composed of Leo Apostel, Guy Berger, Asa Briggs, and Guy Michaud), in which Erich Jantsch published his seminal study of interdisciplinarity in research and education. A decade and a half later, the OECD took another look, *Interdisciplinarity Revisited*, in which it observed that its first effort had had little impact. The verdict was that the concept of interdisciplinarity had lost its momentum; the departments and faculties as the main organizational structures of the university had not only survived but apparently had been strengthened (Levin and Lind 1985: 9).

Another decade later Gibbons et al. (1994) diagnose the emergence of a new mode of knowledge production that they term 'Mode 2.' Knowledge production in this mode is no longer limited to universities but is taking place in many types of institutions. Its main feature is 'transdisciplinarity': Problem contexts or contexts of application, rather than disciplines, are the crucial frames of reference for both continuation and validation of research. Disciplines are losing their function of orientation and control. Knowledge production in Mode 2 is organized in highly flexible and transient forms of organization. These are the institutional counterparts of the temporary and opportunistic clusterings and configurations of knowledge driven by the exigencies of the contexts of application rather than by aspirations to the discovery of natural laws and ultimate theories (Gibbons et al. 1994: 3–44).

These are but three examples of an apparent contradiction from a discourse that has evolved over a span of at least thirty years. One could find hundreds more, all revealing the same contradictory pattern: interdisciplinarity (or transdisciplinarity and similar derivatives) is proclaimed, demanded, hailed, and written into funding programs, but at the same time specialization in science goes on unhampered, reflected in the continuous complaint about it. How is it possible that, in the face of all available evidence to the contrary and very little reason for hope, the discourse on interdisciplinarity can persist?

Robert Merton's (1973 [1963]) analysis of another contradiction endemic to scientists' behaviour comes to mind: the contradiction between their zealous race for priority and their (mostly autobiographical) renunciation of self-interest in fame and glory. His conclusion in the study of the ambivalence of scientists: The stronger the denial of interest in priority, the greater that interest actually is. In similar fashion one may approach this contradiction: What is the underlying rationale for the positive valuation of interdisciplinarity in the face of its constant violation?

The thesis is that, on the *social-psychological level*, the values of universalism and organized scepticism suggest openness to all relevant knowledge, whether supportive or contradictory, as crucial to innovativeness (i.e., the highest value in scientific activity). This translates into 'interdisciplinarity' as a programmatic value tantamount to innovation. It is another example of Merton's theory on the ambivalence of scientists because the actual activity of knowledge production contradicts this squarely. The prevailing strategy is to look for niches in uncharted territory, to avoid contradicting knowledge by insisting on disciplinary competence and its boundaries, to denounce knowledge that does not fall into this realm as 'undisciplined.' Thus, in the process of research, new and ever finer structures are constantly created as a result of this behaviour. This is (exceptions notwithstanding) the very essence of the innovation process, but it takes place primarily within disciplines, and it is judged by disciplinary criteria of validation.

The same reasons account for the fact that interdisciplinarity is also prominent in the rhetoric of organizational innovation in science. Here the programmatic pronouncements of 'interdisciplinarity' and its identification with innovation contrast with very vague mechanisms, if any, of implementation. In other words, a very similar pattern can be observed in the science policy arena to that in the scientific community. Since science policy makers cannot be assumed to have the same psychological dispositions or interests as scientists, their reasons must be different.

Yet, the answer to why the discourse continues in spite of the fact that the reality to which it refers is so much different must be different again. I will attempt to give it at the end.

I will first look at the discursive juxtaposition of 'disciplinary' organization of knowledge production and interdisciplinarity, largely relying on examples collected by authors writing on interdisciplinarity. (I cannot represent the discourse but can give only illustrations. By focusing on writings that praise interdisciplinarity that side is privileged, while the opposite position appears mostly in response to it. This does not seem to be a misrepresentation, though, because innovation by *disciplinary* research is the 'normal' case and not an issue of debate.) Second, I present some examples of proclaimed organization of interdisciplinarity in order to identify operationalizations of that goal. In the final section I will argue that the positive estimation of interdisciplinarity that is coextensive with that of innovation cannot have direct organizational correlates but at best indirect ones. Thus, the apparent contradiction is solved by pointing to the implicit function of the call for interdisciplinarity as well as the reason for the apparently paradoxical continuation of the discourse.

Elements of the Discourse on Interdisciplinarity

Julie Klein refers to the 'inevitable paradox when talking about interdisciplinarity': Since we are predisposed to classify and categorize, we are predisposed to think in terms of disciplines (Klein Thompson 1990:

77). This predisposition, she claims, has created some metaphoric structures in the discourse. On the basis of her collection the most obvious structural concept delineating disciplines is geographical or geopolitical. Knowledge is pictured as territorial; we speak of research areas or fields, partitioned into disciplines that are separated from one another by 'boundaries' (Weingart 1995; Klein Thompson 1996).

Viewed from the side of writings on interdisciplinarity, disciplines are characterized pejoratively in terms of rule, defence, and attack: 'private property' with 'no trespassing notices,' 'empire,' 'territory,' 'balkanized region of research principalities,' 'feudalized fiefdoms,' 'bastions of medieval autonomy,' 'academic nationalism,' 'jealously protected' (all examples and references in Klein Thompson [1983] 1986: 91).

Now notice the contrast when the focus shifts to interdisciplinarity: ventures to the 'borderlands,' to the 'frontiers' of knowledge, 'breaching' boundaries, crossing 'no man's land' between the disciplines, 'cross cultural exploration,' driven by 'cutting-edge questions' are taken to be threats to the status quo. Interdisciplinary research is seen as 'alien intrusion' that if successful can establish 'enclaves,' and so on (Klein Thompson [1983] 1986: 91; 1990: 77).

There are other categories that characterize the discourse on interdisciplinarity: the organic metaphor, images of diffusion and extension, of centripetal and centrifugal forces (cf. Klein Thompson 1990: 82–84). But they are used to describe the structure of disciplines in relation to one another, their differences, their relation to 'nature,' and their dynamics. Although systematic analysis of these metaphors would probably reveal interesting features of the discourse, too, I will leave them aside.

So far, in presenting the images of disciplinarity and interdisciplinarity I have sided with the explorers. What about those who stay home? What are their reasons for remaining behind? In other words, there is a reverse side of valuations of disciplinarity and interdisciplinarity that throws a quite different light on the two positions. Interestingly enough it is much more difficult to find examples of positive connotations to discipline in science, and likewise collections of metaphors. 'Discipline' is entered in *Webster's New World Dictionary* as (1) 'a branch of knowledge or learning; (2) training that develops self-control, character, or orderliness and efficiency ... (4) acceptance of or submission to authority and control.' The positive valuation of discipline in science is tied to self-control as a crucial character trait needed for good work. There will be little doubt that orderliness and efficiency have their positive functions. A typical reaction to interdisciplinarity is to insist on disciplinary competence as a prerequisite (cf. Mittelstrass 1987: 154). From this perspective interdisciplinarity is a slightly suspicious endeavour, too soft for real tough minds. Discipline signals methodological rigour, drilling deep, exactness. Klein also notes: 'When tied to the detection of error and the value of an epistemic community for testing new work, "discipline" has an undeniably positive value' (Klein Thompson [1983] 1986: 86).

Both interdisciplinarity and disciplinarity are, thus, given positive valuations for different functions: innovation on the one hand and rigour and control for error on the other. Both are plausible valuations with respect to the operation of the research process in spite of their apparent contradiction, and both are crucially important. They are complementary rather than contradictory. No new discovery is made without a frame of mind that allows one to distinguish between new and old, and relevant and irrelevant, and to record and remember.

The crucial feature of the discourse that interests us here is the polarized structure: Disciplines carry the connotation of and are valued (!) as being static, rigid, conservative, and averse to innovation. Interdisciplinarity carries the connotation of and is valued as being dynamic, flexible, liberal, and innovative. But then there is the reverse view: disciplines are hard, they stand for tough-mindedness, (necessary) order, and control, all features deemed to be prerequisites of progress and innovation. From this vantage point interdiscipinarity is suspicious of vagueness and lack of rigidity. Without pursuing it further it is obvious that the same polarity underlies the valuation of specialization (negative) and integration (positive). Examples of the complaint about the specialization of knowledge production in view of 'the whole' of the 'world' or 'truth' are countless. The disenchantment with the 'diffraction of truth' ('*Zersplitterung der Wahrheit,*' C.F. v. Weizsäcker) relates to the disappointment of the deep-seated religious anticipation that the quest for knowledge would result in revelation. The religious motives have disappeared from knowledge production. Only an abstract connotation of an inadequate fit between a fractured organization of knowledge and its needed integration or restructuring in order to 'match' and come to grips with the 'real problems' remains (Mittelstrass quotes environment, energy, and technology assessment as examples. Mittelstrass 1987: 155). Implicit in this is, again, the notion that the disciplines do not keep up with rapid developments in modern societies. The map of knowledge, in a sense, is always outdated.

This points to another aspect of the same discourse: Behind the positive valuation of interdisciplinarity lies an implicit and crude theory about innovativeness in science. Heisenberg pointed out that narrow and conscientious specialism can no longer play a leading role. Instead, scientists in physics, chemistry, and biology are forced to look across the boundaries into the neighbouring disciplines in order to make real progress. Schelsky, sociologist and architect of a centre of interdisciplinary research, claimed that the greatest chance of success in science lies in the cooperation of several, even distant, disciplines. Norbert Wiener considered those areas most fruitful for the flourishing of science that are neglected in the no man's land between the disciplines. Heisenberg generalized this implicit theory about scientific progress to the thesis that the most fruitful developments in the history of human thought arose where two different kinds of thinking have met (all citations in Hübenthal 1991: 3–5). And Mittelstrass stressed that interdisciplinarity has to begin in one's own head, asking questions no one has asked before, to learn what the discipline itself does not know (Mittelstrass 1987: 157).

The discourse on interdisciplinarity is, in effect, a discourse on innovation in knowledge production. Since science is ruled by the primacy of 'novelty' it is a non sequitur that all knowledge that has already been codified and given a social organization is looked upon as past achievement, as superseded, and as constraining the search for new knowledge. The hope is in the future, but the future is unknown, without structure. This hope is perennial, part and parcel of the research endeavour that endures in spite of the continuous sedimentation of knowledge into disciplinary structures.

This may explain to some extent the positive emphasis placed on interdisciplinarity in the face of ongoing differentiation and specialization. In fact, it reveals the seemingly paradoxical mechanism that the more differentiation of knowledge production the more intense will be the call for interdisciplinarity. The communal experience is one of an ever-expanding structured landscape of knowledge of which, from the perspective of every individual, only a constantly shrinking part is known to anyone. This fundamental frustration finds its consolation only, to return to our original metaphor, in visions of a yet uncharted, unclaimed, pristine territory where one can still roam freely without fear of transgressions, border controls, and conflicts over claim stakes and water rights.

But this still does not explain why interdisciplinarity and disciplinarity are seen as contradictory, and why not only on the level of public discourse but also on the level of individual motivation in terms of proclamations and actions the two orientations are kept independent from one another. Is it accidental that there is a substantial body of literature on interdisciplinarity but that the large majority of titles are normative and speculative (cf. the enormous bibliography by Klein Thompson 1990; Schurz, 1995: 1080)? Or is it accidental that scientists when asked seldom consider themselves a 'typical' representative of their own discipline but perceive their colleagues as being so (Schurz 1995: 1082)?

One explanation of the seemingly paradoxical discourse and the underlying behaviour of scientists may be seen in the same pattern that R.K. Merton has analysed as the ambivalence of scientists. He diagnosed an apparent contradiction between the values of originality and modesty as the psychological basis of the contradictory attitudes towards priority disputes (Merton 1973: 383). The same pattern is reproduced with respect to attitudes towards disciplinarity and interdisciplinarity: Public pronouncements of scientists will regularly reflect an openness towards interdisciplinary research, since it is concurrent with the value of originality. And they will, conversely, contain denials of 'discipline-mindedness' except in connection with efforts to secure innovations. On the other hand, identification with the discipline and adherence to its rules, standards, and orthodoxies are declared characteristics of the 'other.' And, true to the mechanism of projection, one can hypothesize that the more pronounced the declarations of 'openness,' the stronger the disciplinary rigidity, i.e., pursuit of specialized research interests, niche seeking, boundary demarcating, etc. Attitudes vis-à-vis interdisciplinarity are one expression of the 'Essential Tension' in science, the conflict between change and tradition (Kuhn 1977). Kuhn's characterization of 'normal' science and scientific revolutions taken as part of the discourse on innovation in science also reflects the polarity and the ambivalent valuations to some extent. Thus, on the level of the normative and descriptive discourse that pertains to the behaviour of scientists, the apparent contradiction between demands for interdisciplinarity and the reality of specialization may be resolved.

If the preceding analysis is correct the entire debate on interdisciplinarity would have to be seen in a different light. Declarations by scientists about the desirability of interdisciplinary research cannot be taken at face value, nor can it be expected that normative appeals will change scientists' attitudes. At their basis is an amalgam of social-psychological motives and expectations. One could also regard this as opportunism in the search for novelty checked by standards of control and competence. The whole issue of interdisciplinarity must then be shifted to the organizational level, and the question becomes one of how the behaviour in question can be influenced in such a way that interdisciplinary research is enhanced.

Organizational Representations of Interdisciplinarity

Before suggesting an answer I briefly want to look at another part of the discourse on interdisciplinarity, namely at proclamations of interdisciplinarity as a type of research organization. On this level, too, the question is how these proclamations relate to the organizational reality. How is interdisciplinarity introduced as an organizational feature? How do institutions that claim to be interdisciplinary organize this research? Because of familiarity I will look at examples of German funding agencies and research institutions only.

The Deutsche Forschungsgemeinschaft, or DFG (German National Science Foundation) entertains a number of funding programs that are designed to accumulate, combine, and coordinate research proposals from individual scientists under an umbrella theme. The two principal programs are the Schwerpunktverfahren (SPPs, or focal point funding) and the Sonderforschungsbereiche (SFBs, or priority research areas). In the case of the former one of the declared goals and criterion of selection is the 'creation of fruitful, new mutual relationships between hitherto separately working disciplines ...' In the case of the SFBs the DFG simply states that they are 'characterized by cooperation beyond the boundaries of disciplines, institutes, departments and faculties' (DFG 1996: 202). No further rules and regulations are spelled out that would operationalize the interdisciplinarity implicit in these goals. Anybody who has experience working under one of the funding schemes knows that, apart from a few exceptions, at least no *systematic* effort is made to establish and monitor the degree of interdisciplinarity. To my knowledge, no systematic data exist about the success of these programs with respect to interdisciplinary research. At a conference an inside expert reported that according to his informal estimate only up to 20 per cent of the projects in the SPPs and SFBs were interdisciplinary, while that rate was considerably higher in the standard funding program that is supposedly disciplinary and has no programmatic orientation whatsoever.

The Bundesministerium für Bildung und Forschung, or BMBF (Science Ministry) has two funding programs that are similarly of relevance to our theme: the so-called Innovationskollegs, which are again groups of researchers that work under one theme, coordinated by a university professor, and the Interdisciplinary Centers for Clinical Research in University Hospitals. The first program is designed to help the universities in former East Germany to reform, and to secure their future through 'competitiveness, internationality and inter-university research cooperation as well as interdisciplinarity' (BMBF 1996).

As is typical for funding programs there is no detailed prescriptive catalogue of criteria defining either interdisciplinarity or the procedures for how to achieve it. The project descriptions, which are always self-accounts of the research group coordinators, use a variety of definitions, many of which are implicit. In some cases they refer to specialties within one discipline (biology), in others to fields of very diverse breadth (molecular biology, genetic engineering, neuromorphology, neurophysiology, neurochemistry, neuropharmacology), in still others to organizational entities (three faculties and ten different disciplines). In all cases the research projects are highly specialized, and although there is apparently no consensus about what 'discipline' and 'interdisciplinarity' mean, the latter term is used liberally.

One reading is that interdisciplinarity serves the opportunism of proposal writing; the other that, indeed, a reality is being described, the main feature of which is a problem-specific and problem-driven combination of stocks of knowledge. Here again opportunism rules, opportunism of the moment that is oriented to innovation, not to conservation and control, let alone to unification.

In the second program the Science Ministry supports Interdisciplinary Centers for Clinical Research in University Hospitals. The main goal is to establish 'efficient structures for clinical research on a transdisciplinary level' and to enable universities to develop a specific research profile. The expectation is that the program allows them to design 'innovative and efficient management structures for clinical research.' It is hoped that the 'scientific concept of the centers transgressing departments, subjects and possibly faculties' will lead to a truly interdisciplinary cooperation. One means to achieve that is an organizational structure that reflects intellectual themes and projects rather than existing structures of departments, clinics, and institutes. The universities are free to devise the interface between clinics and non-clinical institutes, but their proposals should make clear 'in what ways the exchange between clinic and science is supposed to work' (BMBF 1996).

Here, again, 'interdisciplinarity' remains a purely formal label that is mostly an organizational principle: to organize research across existing boundaries of institutes and departments. How superficial with respect to the contents of research these declarations are, but at the same time how politically useful, is demonstrated by a remark of the science minister in 1997. Interviewed about the future role of the troubled big science laboratories he said: 'I don't like the term *big science* ["Grossforschung"]. They [the centers] should be called "Centers for Interdisciplinary Research"' (Interview with Minister Jürgen Rüttgers, *Die Zeit* 8, 14 February 1997). In due course they were relabelled accordingly.

As far as the real centres for interdisciplinary research are concerned I will elaborate on just three particular Institutes for Advanced Study explicitly devoted to interdisciplinary research.

CAESAR, the new Center for Advanced European Studies and Research, is supposed to concentrate on research at the interfaces between physics, chemistry, biology, and information sciences. The idea is that interdisciplinary topics will be chosen that fall into this broadly described area and that are not already worked on in existing institutions. In fact, the search for research topics focuses on existing fields, on research frontiers. The implicit mechanism of innovation is to identify highly specialized areas of research that are a combination of different disciplines. However, the descriptive level of the research areas is much more specific than that of the disciplines to which parts of them can be attributed. In other words, very little is being said about a particular mechanism that creates – organizationally – interdisciplinarity, but the issue is the selection of research themes that are innovative and are assumed to be interdisciplinary.

Another project well under way is the Hanse-Kolleg. Also shaped after other centres for advanced study, it is supposed to 'improve cooperation between subject fields by means of intensive discussion of overarching aspects' (Bremische Bürgerschaft 1995: 2). The authors of the founding charter have reflected on the ways the Institutes for Advanced Study operate and how in relation to them the Hanse-Kolleg is to achieve its goals. As they see it, all of the Institutes rely primarily on the 'productivity of a spontaneous scientific exchange of first rank scientists of different disciplines, theoretical orientation and nationality.' The Kolleg should set annually two to three 'relatively open and preferably interdisciplinary themes that link up with qualitatively important research foci already existing at the universities.' They envisage the Hanse-Kolleg as steering a middle course between the more liberal, Humboldtian idea of convening a number of outstanding scientists, no matter of which disciplinary denomination and methodological orientation, to pursue their inspirations, and the University of Bielefeld's Center for Interdisciplinary Research (ZiF) with its supposedly more planning oriented concept (Blanke and Preuss 1994: 12).

This leads to the most prominent example of an institution that is directed explicitly and exclusively to interdisciplinary research: the Center for Interdisciplinary Research (Zentrum für interdisziplinäre Forschung, or ZiF) at the University of Bielefeld. Here the original rationale for setting up the institute was connected with the concept of a university and the diagnosis of its pitfalls (Schelsky 1971). But this diagnosis also focused on what was perceived to be an obstacle to the innovativeness of the university as the central institution of knowledge production and diffusion. The ZiF, too, was commissioned to 'initiate and promote interdisciplinary research.' The only organizational specification for this mission was (and still is) that research groups be set up for the duration of one academic year working on a particular topic.

After thirty years of operation, obviously, a work routine has been developed in which the very formal mandate has been put into practice. Also, a certain amount of reflection on this practice, though by no means systematic and continuous, has taken place (cf. Kocka 1987; Maasen, this volume). The surprising (?) point is that nowhere in the statutes nor in any procedural rules is there any codified definition of 'interdisciplinarity,' nor a list of criteria on which the selection of the research groups could be based. Each board of directors, whose members are rotated, decides on the basis of its intuitions and past practice as it evolves. Since so far the boards have abstained almost entirely from pursuing an active research policy role, that is, scanning the research landscape for interesting, problematic, promising, or untoiled areas where interdisciplinary projects could be established, they rely on whatever themes are suggested to them by scholars from outside. In a sense, the institute serves as a shell, an organizational environment that is attractive to scholars who want to carry out a particular research whose interdisciplinarity they determine for themselves. (Ironically, both the CAESAR and the Hanse-Kolleg blueprints provide for a theme-setting function for their directors while claiming more liberality and flexibility than the ZiF.)

Several conclusions can be drawn from these examples of inter-disciplinarity as an organizational principle. Not surprisingly one finds the same positive association of interdisciplinarity with innovativeness. But whenever the organizational mechanism is specified for how to achieve interdisciplinarity, two common concepts become apparent. First, on a formal level of description, the innovative function of interdisciplinarity is achieved by combining disciplinary aspects, bridg-ing gaps, crossing boundaries, and synthesizing differences. Evolution-arily minded observers may think of a variation/selection mechanism. Second, the choice of interdisciplinary problems inevitably leads to highly specialized research topics. One could describe this organizational dis-course as having two layers: on the descriptive level, interdisciplinarity is tantamount to innovation and means the synthesis or combination of different fields; on the operational level, interdisciplinarity means dif-ferentiation, the definition of specialized topics between fields.

The fact that synthesis and differentiation exist side by side in the organization of innovative research may seem paradoxical, but in fact it is not. In conclusion I will argue that it cannot be otherwise.

The Unity of Interdisciplinarity and Specialization

Among the various accounts of new modes of knowledge production or 'post-normal science' one finds a common topos: claims of inter- or transdisciplinary forms of research are supported by moral enthusiasm. It is indicative that the authors of the transdisciplinarity, post-normal, post-modern, and Mode 2 schemes are oscillating between empirical and normative statements; for example, Funtowicz and Ravetz speak of their 'model for scientific knowledge,' and the 'philosophical core of our programme' (Funtowicz and Ravetz 1993: 121). The supposedly new forms of science are hailed because they seem more democratic and participatory than the rigid organization of elitist, narrow-minded disciplines (cf. Funtowicz and Ravetz 1993: esp. 110). In this respect the post-normal and new modes of science resound the same theme that triggered the debate on interdisciplinarity at the end of the 1960s in connection with the issue of higher education reform (Jantsch 1972), and whose deeper roots are in the never-ending dispute over the merits of practical reason versus the universal claims to truth of the math-ematical sciences, over excellence versus relevance (Toulmin 1990: esp. ch. 5). The normative impetus supports the structural argument that also repeats the old tune: 'new,' post-modern, transdisciplinary, or interdisciplinary forms of science are said to emerge from taking account of a context of application. This entails a participatory role of non-scientists who are involved in producing and even validating the knowledge as users or stakeholders (Funtowicz and Ravetz: 1993; Gibbons et al. 1994: 3–16). Both conditions define the 'systems' under consideration as 'more complex,' which, in turn, calls for more encompassing organizational or guiding principles of producing knowledge. Another way of saying this is that the self-referential mode of knowledge production is inadequate to represent the real world, that the structure of disciplines is too simple to deal with its complexity, and that in order to correct this 'misfit' it is to be supplemented if not replaced by interdisciplinary organizations of knowledge production.

Behind these pronouncements of inter- and transdisciplinarity is a specific model of knowledge that, despite all declared modernity, is tied to an old-fashioned realist epistemology. The model presupposes the distinction between an 'outer world' on the one hand and human knowledge production that slowly accumulates a growing stock of knowledge on the other. The seemingly modern turn is introduced, first, by postulating the misfit between the structures of knowledge and the structure of 'real world problems,' and, second, by demoting the wardens of disciplinary structures in favour of reinstating everyday practitioners to oversee knowledge production.

This model itself is the dominant one in scientific practice and its descriptions, and the model is shared on both sides, that is, by proponents and critics alike. Both overlook an empirical fact as well as a systematic argument, and consequently do not draw the necessary epistemological conclusion. The empirical fact is that the 'real problems' are constituted by existing knowledge and its gatekeepers. Several mechanisms interact. The chief mechanism can be called 'scientification.' Areas of hitherto unreflected social practice become subject matters of systematic scientific analysis, often in conjunction with professionalization: political science, sexology, criminology, public health, and environmental engineering are pertinent examples. A derivative mechanism, on a lower level of generality, is that governments establish funding programs that involve the combination and rearrangement of the disciplinary landscape in order to achieve a tighter problem orientation and perhaps also a more convincing public image of their science policy. The most pertinent recent example is climate research. The establishment of such overarching 'interdisciplines' is primarily driven by political goals and needs of legitimation. In most if not all cases these programs are initiated by the scientific community in the first place, or at least they are the result of negotiations between scientists and policy makers. Under conditions of scarce resources and pressures of legitimation scientists will invent problem definitions and labels that appeal to the public and its representatives. The scientists relabel their research projects in order to 'fit in.' The analysis of the early phases of environmental research clearly revealed this (Küppers, Lundgreen, and Weingart 1978). Enhanced media sensitivity and policy orientation, above all in the natural sciences, has intensified this pattern. The prediction may be ventured that in the future the landscape of scientific knowledge will be characterized to a greater extent than before by the fashions of the political agenda, a development that is already apparent in the different kinds of representation of science in self-descriptions of disciplines and in funding programs (Weingart, Sehringer, and Winterhager 1990). Very little is known about the repercussions of these developments on science proper: in what time spans and to what degree does science become *captured* by the institutionalization of labels that are supposed to reorient research to *real* problems? But the social scientist observing these processes must be warned not to take the rhetoric of competing exaggerations at face value.

The systematic argument disregarded by proponents of the realist model of knowledge production concerns the role of 'structure.' The delineation of subject matters around which disciplines are organized is obviously variable over time. And, by consequence, so is the overall structure of the landscape of knowledge. Different historical circumstances may be responsible for the content of these structures, but structure there will be and has to be. Structures of knowledge production like any others reflect the fundamental distinctions, ordering categories, and social representations that are necessary to maintain the activity, to give it direction for the future by providing the memory of past achievements. Without such a structure that is by definition different from the unstructured world around us there could be no such thing as knowledge.

Even if various specialties of the biological, chemical, and physical sciences are combined to form a new research field called 'environmental science' that responds 'more adequately' to the exigencies of environmental problems, this new interdisciplinary delineation will also have its particular blind spots. It will be a misfit with respect to problems other than the destruction of the environment. To put it simply, every structure is selective. The difference between a disciplinary structure and a supposedly interdisciplinary one is not a mystical proximity or a better fit to 'reality' of the latter but lies in the reasons and circumstances by which these structures are constituted.

From both the empirical fact and the systematic argument follows a different model of knowledge production than the one underlying normative demands for interdisciplinarity. Instead of assuming a disciplinary structure that has to be adapted to the structure of the real world by approximation, it has to be recognized that the structure of knowledge, and the delineation of disciplines and their subject matters constitute perceptions of the world. The structures are by no means fixed and irreplacable, but they are social constructs, products of long and complex social interactions, subject to social processes that involve vested interests, argumentation, modes of conviction, and differential perceptions and communications. 'Misfit' and approximation are issues within social processes and not between them and another world.

What follows from this both for the structure of the discourse on interdisciplinarity and for its continuation? Interdisciplinarity may best be described as a result of opportunism in knowledge production. This opportunism occurs on two sides: Scientists seize opportunities to acquire knowledge and resources as a means to produce new knowledge; users of knowledge (policy makers, industrialists, etc.) seize opportunities to acquire knowledge by providing resources either for any knowledge betting on indirect benefits or for the solution of particular problems. In the first case (academic science, funding of basic research) interdisciplinary research as recombination of existing specialties may be the result. In the second case (applied, strategic research) interdisciplinary research as direction to non-scientific goals may emerge. However, the crucial point is that the latter is always referred back to the existing mode of knowledge production, its social organization, and its criteria of validation. No matter if the manipulation of scientists' behaviour is directed to 'external' problems or left alone to the procreation of 'internal' problems, whether the research fields are interdisciplinary or not, the expected outcome is 'true,' that is, reliable knowledge. To dispute this is to violate a fundamental fact of modern societies, namely their functional differentiation and the epistemological independence (from politics, religion, economics) of the social subsystem of science.

From this follows a certain rationale for interdisciplinarity as an *organizational principle* to be considered equivalent to innovation. Innovation, the discovery of new knowledge, according to Popper's fundamental and simple insight, cannot be planned or predicted. What can be done is to influence the conditions of creativity, or more reliably, to manipulate the parameters that orient scientists' opportunist behaviour. In this understanding to organize 'interdisciplinarity' is another way of saying that one wishes to organize scientific innovativeness by giving free reign to opportunism in knowledge production. I have argued in another context that the principle of interdisciplinary centres of advanced study is to shield at least temporarily the resident scientists from the exigencies of disciplinary competition (Weingart 1987: 164). Hollingsworth has shown in his extensive research on the conditions favouring major discoveries in biomedical science that most important among them are diversity (variety of disciplines and specialties), depth (size of community in each area and diversity of talents), and integration (frequency and intensity of interaction). As he argues, these are contradicting forces insofar as greater diversity and depth favours differentiation and loss of integration (Hollingsworth 1996: 22; cf. Hollingsworth and Hollingsworth, this volume, similarly De Mey, this volume). Clearly, there is no golden rule on how to balance these three parameters. Rather, to allow for innovativeness in knowledge production, organizational structures have to be kept flexible and diversified. But it is in the (social) nature of the process that they tend to become structured, rigid, and routinized.

In terms of its *contents* with reference to the existing structure of disciplines and subfields, the process of knowledge production is inevitably a process of specialization and further differentiation. Every new recombination of bits of knowledge from previously different fields, if it is novel, is bound to be more specialized and to create new boundaries. Eventually, social organization – training, communication, and certification – follow suit.

We now can unravel the apparent paradox of an ongoing and perhaps even intensified discourse on interdisciplinarity in the face of ever more specialization and fragmentation. In other words, interdisciplinarity and specialization are parallel. They are mutually reinforcing strategies, and, thus, complementary descriptions of the process of knowledge production. This points to an admittedly speculative answer to the initial question of why the discourse on interdisciplinarity can and does go on in spite of ongoing specialization. Originally interdisciplinarity was associated with the notion that the unity of science would be achieved at some distant moment in time by way of reducing all fragmented disciplinary knowledge to the fundamental laws of physics.

This belief has vanished, for different reasons. The idea of interdisciplinarity as the mode of innovation and progress has taken the place of the promise of the unity of science, and the discourse continues because only this prospect makes it possible to identify all the very diverse and heterogeneous activities going on in the disciplines as being part of the same social activity, namely science. Interdisciplinarity is not the promise of ultimate unity, but of innovation and surprise by way of recombining of different parts of knowledge, no matter which.

PART II

THE CHANGING TOPOGRAPHY OF SCIENCE

At the present time, there is substantial discussion about the changes in the institutional framework of knowledge production, in the organizational structure, and consequently in the *topography of science*. The focus of these proclaimed changes is based on the observation that disciplines constitute the core social organizations and intellectual structures of science.

Disciplines, thus this observation, are no longer the crucial frames of orientation for research nor for the definition of subject matters, methods, and interpretations. Instead, research is characterized by *transdisciplinarity*: Problem solutions emerge in contexts of application, and transdisciplinary knowledge has its own theoretical structures and research methods.

The empirical evidence for these observations, however plausible they may seem, remains impressionistic and sketchy. Actually, there is hardly any systematic empirical knowledge about the real changes in the disciplinary landscape that could either substantiate, qualify, or contradict these assertions and claims about growing interdisciplinarity. None the less, the significance of the message provided by these analyses is that the socioeconomic and sociopolitical environments of science change, and the structure of disciplines is affected by these changes. But the role the disciplines play in the new production of knowledge and its effect on society at large is ignored in this picture. From a sociological perspective it is fruitful to view the disciplines as the interface organizations that execute the transfer between knowledge production and the implementation and application of knowledge.

From such a perspective it becomes evident that the purported trend towards interdisciplinarity and transdisciplinarity is likely the result of several interacting forces: the operation of disciplines as reputational organizations organizing the motivation of scientists, the network of constantly developing fields of knowledge with changing research opportunities across the boundaries to other disciplines, and the differential utility of types of knowledge that lead to opportunities for expertise and jobs in academic and non-academic labour markets on which disciplines appear as actors.

Precisely these issues, although certainly not exhaustive with respect to the analysis of the dynamics of knowledge production, are addressed in the three following papers and provide the overarching theme to their seemingly heterogeneous topics.

Turner provides a perspective on the interaction between disciplines and their socio-economic contexts, focusing on an often overlooked aspect of disciplinarity: the link of disciplines to job markets and to 'internal' student markets. Markets are created by disciplines, but markets also affect disciplines since disciplines are subject to changes in the economic environment. This link, which is one of resource acquisition and dependency from the perspective of the disciplines, explains a lot of the dynamics between broader socioeconomic and political trends on the one hand and training as well as knowledge production on the other.

Van Raan provides the baseline for the following studies by starting out with a theoretical framework accounting for the interdisciplinary nature of science. This framework states roughly that the dynamics between socio-economic problems, scientifically interesting problems, and interdisciplinarity are driven by motivations, regulated by reputational systems in science, dominated by just a few disciplines, and continuously reinforced by instrumentation. This framework leads to research sites where empirical work can be done. Van Raan then presents three bibliometric methods for analysing interdisciplinarity and gives concrete examples. The most advanced methods of citation or co-word mappings are best suited to reveal changes in the *disciplinary topography* of science. As van Raan shows, this kind of observation method raises questions about the 'operationalization of science.'

Turpin and Garrett-Jones take a thorough look at the Australian research system, which has undergone drastic changes over the last decade. Australia may be a special case, but some of the developments could indicate the future direction of knowledge production. The impact of commercial imperatives on the science system and its paradoxical results are central to the analysis. During the latter half of the 1980s and 1990s the Australian system of higher education was reformed quite drastically to be more responsive to public expectations and market forces. In reaction to this, a plethora of interdisciplinary research centres has emerged in the Australian science system that reveal entirely new organizational forms of knowledge production and capture. The liberation from the hegemony of the disciplines is exchanged for the vagaries of the market and the commercialization of academic pursuits. This trend may well and already does change both the mechanisms and symbols of evaluation within science as well as the valuation of disciplines by society, thus creating new structures of hierarchies among the disciplines. This is, indeed, a major shift in the *topography of institutions of knowledge production*, which may eventually also lead to a change in the *topography of knowledge*. Thus, the Australian case described in this thorough study in a sense exemplifies the analyses by Turner and van Raan.

3

What Are Disciplines? And How Is Interdisciplinarity Different?

STEPHEN TURNER

In what follows I would like to try to extract a relatively small number of more or less universal themes about disciplinarity and inter-disciplinarity that follow from the differing 'market' and bureaucratic circumstances of disciplinarity and interdisciplinarity. The apparent difference is this: Academic departments representing disciplines (though of course there are uses of the department form by interdisciplinary units) are different in that departments in different universities in the same discipline are essentially interchangeable with one another. The problems, prospects, strategies, and so forth open to a particular department of philosophy, for example, is likely to more or less closely resemble those available to another department and the business of the department: Hiring, tenuring, promoting, teaching, advising, granting degrees, placing students, and so forth are, in a great many important respects, the same. Departments corresponding to disciplines have a long history in universities, and they represent, with some quite interesting national differences, a more or less standard worldwide organizational form; consequently, the disciplines they represent make for a quite different kind of collectivity, with more or less standardized collective interests that more or less correspond to the common intellectual interests and instructional tasks of a group of academics.

Interdisciplinary centres (which in my university system are categorized for budget purposes as 'centres and institutes') are considerably more diverse in form, both organizationally and intellectually. In the sciences especially they may involve hundreds of researchers with a dependence on a common technology, such as research vessels or space probes. Or they may be very small, essentially voluntary endeavours that cost very little and have very little meaningful organizational structure, but are nevertheless sensitive to the currents generated by the organizational structures around them. These differences may be thought of as strategies for realizing divisions of intellectual labour and creating certain kinds of collectivities, and in what I have to say here I wish to indicate why there is an enduring difference between intellectual work organized in a disciplinary way and work that is not, and what some of these differences are. My point is, so to speak, a theoretical one, and theory of some sort is needed to go beyond the appearances. The difference is not the same as the difference between departments and centres. Interdisciplinary work may be organized into departments and in many respects resembles disciplinary work. So the differences are to be found at another level.

Why Are There Disciplines at All?

To clarify the differences it would perhaps be useful to begin with a definition of disciplines, as well as some reasons why this definition is perhaps as serious and deep a definition as one can get.

Disciplines are kinds of collectivities that include a large proportion of persons holding degrees with the same differentiating specialization name, which are organized in part into degree-granting units that in part give degree-granting positions and powers to persons holding these degrees; persons holding degrees of this particular specialized kind are employed in positions that give degree-granting powers to them, such that there is an actual exchange of students between different degree-granting institutions offering degrees in what is understood to be the same specialization.

There are two elements to the definition. The first is nominal: the discipline must be called a discipline, and the name is shared and used. The second is not: there must be actual facts of employment involving persons trained in the name of the discipline and there must be the beginnings of a market. The definition sounds a bit like a philosopher's trick, because it is apparently but not quite circular. I have given you no criteria to recognize 'nominal identity as a discipline,' for example, though for any purpose I can see, self-identification with the notion of 'discipline' is sufficient. But I will suggest that this definition has some very practical 'economic' implications that fit very closely indeed with the history of disciplines.

Disciplinarity identity is just that, a name or an understood identity that is realized in degree-granting bodies, such as departments, using this distinguishing mark both to identify its degree holders and at least occasionally by employing holders of degrees from other institutions with the same identity. From a historical point of view, it must be said that this status was a long time coming for many disciplines in the liberal arts in the United States generally, and especially for the social sciences.[1] The actual forming of disciplinary collectivities in the social sciences in the United States occurred in a very rapid way at the end of the nineteenth and beginning of the twentieth century, with very similar kinds of national organizations attempting to carve up the landscape of existing literature and claim it for their own, or in some important cases to disclaim it.

This history shows that establishing a national organization was easy. But in several disciplines the organization of national and even very successful international organizations did not lead to the creation of a discipline. Regularizing an internal market was the more difficult step, and it took a great deal of time, time measured in decades. Sociology, for example, did not have a standard name for its degrees until 1940 or so, when Columbia, one of the two dominant departments up to that time, changed from 'Social Science.' Even then some notable exceptions remained at Harvard, Yale, and Johns Hopkins. It was common for appointments in departments of sociology at major universities to be made up of persons who had no actual training in the field, at the rank of professor, as late as the 1920s, and the practice continued to an astonishing extent even into the 1960s.[2]

This bit of history is relevant to our understanding of disciplinarity in the following way: It is tempting to think of disciplines as something like nations, existing in some sense apart from their embodiments in states, and sometimes being realized in the form of a state and sometimes not – a perspective that any historian of Germany or Poland would be glad to explain. But in a sense this is something of a mystification. Some forms of the division of intellectual labour turn into disciplines as I have defined the term, and some do not. Sociology, for example, was in large part made up of either scraps of existing failed near-disciplines, such as the kind of social statistical study that had emerged in the middle part of the nineteenth century (Hacking 1987; Turner 1991), and it provides an interesting test of the model, for one of the scraps was a major near-discipline, Social Statistics.

Statistics – understood not as it is now, as a discipline concerned with the mathematics of inference, but as an overarching science of statistical data – had a nice run in the nineteenth century. It successfully generated several conferences and international congresses and a genuine international body by the middle of the nineteenth century. But it never fully became academic in the same form, in part because of its association with official statistical bureaucracies, and in part as a result of the fact that much of the training was in actuality on-the-job training for national statistical offices. However, in at least one case, Engels's Prussian statistical office, this on-the-job training was relatively formal and approximated, not to say exceeded, in the way in which an academic research department would have been organized if there had been such a thing (Hacking 1987). Statistics also managed to become a section of the British Association for the Advancement of Science, though again without becoming anything like an academic discipline proper.

Was mid-nineteenth-century statistics a discipline? Interdisciplinary? Transdisciplinary? A failed attempt to realize the form of a discipline? Why did it succeed when it was dismembered into its mathematical and subject area components, such as public health statistics, social statistics, the mathematical theory of statistics, and so forth? Is this history simply an anomaly? In fact it is not. It bears comparison with such later disciplinary/interdisciplinary efforts as cybernetics, and in explaining each case what is striking is the role not of disciplinary essences but of accidents of fit with pre-existing bureaucratic structures and with temporary conditions of the existence of resource bases.

The story in the case of the sciences generally is in some respects quite similar: divisions of labour came and went until a genuine internal market was created, at which point the fields took a different path. One case in the sciences will suffice, and as it happens it is one that fits with the Humboldtian ideal, which matured in the nineteenth century into the idea of the survey. Geology was the most heavily subsidized of American sciences in the nineteenth century, with both federal and state bureaus of geology that did geological surveying, among other things. Geologists had their own collective bodies, and indeed geology was the base around which the American Association for the Advancement of Science developed. By the end of the century geology was the most successful American science, and the first scientific discipline in which American science reached world standards, though genetics was quickly to follow, after the turn of the century.

'Geologists' sometimes had academic appointments in Geology departments, but the geologists employed in surveys were seldom trained in geology, and even experts in very recondite areas, such as conchology, were likely to have either on-the-job training or a general scientific

background, typically as a 'civil engineer' – a term used in the ante-
bellum United States to describe what amounted to a general scientific
education – or as a physician, rather than an academic degree in geology. Specialization in particular aspects of the division of labour of
geological surveying long preceded the organization of geology as something even approximating the kind of 'discipline' that matches the minimal definition I have given here. When an academic market for geologists developed towards the end of the century, everything changed. To
a large extent the demands of this market came to shape the contents
and meaning of the disciplinary identity 'geology.'

Because, as I have defined it, becoming a discipline means having at
least a minimal 'internal' market for students, it is perhaps not surprising that disciplinary development is hastened by the adjacent development of another closed internal market. Disciplinarization, this suggests, is a kind of protectionist device that responds to the alteration of
markets by the actions of others. Since the process took place very
quickly, one may assume that these external factors, rather than internal factors, such as the reaching of some particular stage of intellectual
development or coherence, was crucial. I need hardly add here that the
idea of fields that expand in a territorial way promoted by Pierre
Bourdieu (1991) is improved in this analysis by providing something
that Bourdieu declines to provide: a motive for the actions that make
up the process. Placing students and preserving the value of one's teaching efforts as a means of improving students' opportunities is a substantial motive.

The same process, of course, happened to the social sciences and
humanities. The entire pattern of development of the social sciences
consisted of the eventual dominance of academics in what originally
were bodies that owed their existence to reformist ideas as much as to
scholarly ideas. This occurred first in economics. In political science and
sociology, only in the thirties did professional lawyers and directors of
social agencies and governmental agencies cease to pay their dues: the
organizations shrank, and then changed character.

So what about statistics? Why didn't it go through the same series of
developments? It had the oldest and strongest professional society in
American social science. It had, it seems, many other advantages of
coherence and demand as well. Why did it not emerge as a discipline
until much later, and in such a diminished form? One could give a
quite involved story here. There were some accidents of temporality:
statistics peaked before the process of university disciplinarization be-

gan in earnest. But in the end there is no good general explanation. There were enthusiastic backers of the idea of university training in statistics, good professors who held key positions, and a large number of government jobs ready for the properly trained. What was missing is perhaps best captured in the old lawyer joke, which goes like this: The town of such and such was too small to support its one lawyer; fortunately, a second lawyer moved into town, and there was plenty of work for both of them. Statistical training in the United States was concentrated at Columbia, and primarily housed within its faculty of political science, which was itself interdisciplinary. The only academic positions that statisticians could get were either at Columbia or in departments of other kinds – a process facilitated by the fact that the Columbia social science graduate curriculum of the time required students to be prepared in several areas, and consequently able to identify themselves not only as statisticians but as economists, historians, political scientists, or social scientists (i.e., sociologists) as well. Because these were the disciplines in which graduates could become employed and then produce students, they were the disciplines in which an internal market developed. Had it been the case that other universities had programs in statistics at the time, or lacked departments with titles corresponding to those of the Columbia departments, the outcome would have been different.

Disciplines, this suggests, are cartels that organize markets for the production and employment of students by excluding those job-seekers who are not products of the cartel. They arise under various conditions, but the main condition is that there is a market to cartelize. But disciplines are peculiar cartels: Since they are the consumers of what they produce, they are unconcerned with prices. And they have no incentive to limit internal competition, for departments benefit from competition as consumers more or less as much as they do as producers.

The Consequences of Disciplinary Markets

Let me summarize what I have said so far by saying that disciplinarity is a matter of two things: identity and exchange. Neither calling oneself a member of a discipline nor exchanging students is enough. Fully fledged disciplines are systems of multigenerational, multilateral exchange – that is to say, markets. Everything else about the notion of disciplinarity, including notions about canons and common intellectual cores – that is to say about the nature of knowledge contents – is, I think, open to challenge. The distinctions between forms of knowledge that figure heavily in discussions of the problems of interdisciplinarity and transdisciplinarity (Gibbons et al. 1994) are for the most part, as I shall suggest, the product of the historical accidents that created disciplines in the first place. But a great deal result from the sheer existence of these internal, partly protected markets.

The existence of internal markets and consequently internal market competition for a specified market creates certain similarities in products through competition. Both uniformity and competitive differentiation at the margins by degree-producing programs, usually departments but sometimes not, result from the dynamic of competition. Competition is thus an extremely powerful influence on the way people are trained and consequently on common standards. The rigours of internal markets contribute to a kind of standardization of training in which the demands of the market become demands placed on students. The students, willingly or not, internalize these demands, at least in the minimal sense of having gone through the experience of studying for a particular exam or performing a particular kind of procedure or research act. The fact that a lot of people are trained in fundamentally the same way makes it possible for them to effectively make judgements about the quality of the work done by other people and for regimes of training to themselves be evaluated for their rigour.

To put a name to this, call it communicative competence: what disciplinary training serves to do is to create a community or audience of persons who can understand what is said. However one would like to think of this competence – as tacit knowledge, skills, and so forth – it is closely connected to the forms of disciplinarity and disciplinary training, and also to the business of certification of skills and training that is an enormously large part of the daily activity of science, and of the 'knowledge' activity of the university generally. Max Delbrück is rightly considered the paradigm case of a twentieth-century scientist who crossed disciplinary boundaries to produce a new field with major results. But Delbrück had plenty of obstacles. His biographers describe his arrival at the California Institute of Technology (Caltech), and of his being placed in a room with a sheaf of genetics reprints: 'He couldn't understand them, for by that time the Drosophila terminology had become [as he later put it in an interview] "so specialized and esoteric that it would have taken ... weeks" for a newcomer to master it' (Fischer and Lipson 1988: 111). But being able to read the literature in one's research speciality is essentially what a disciplinary degree program certifies a person able to do.

Can this kind of competence be acquired in another way, or dispensed with entirely? In this case, Delbrück was fortunate. Calvin Bridges, the author of the papers, became a personal mentor, and though Delbrück never became very excited about Drosophila genetics, he learned a great deal from Bridges. Caltech provided unusual circumstances in which this sort of discipline crossing was encouraged, and he found other people to learn from. The Rockfeller Foundation made a massive commitment of funds to the general problem of the physical basis of biological phenomenon. And Delbrück was fortunate to find (and also very actively sought out) people who were doing work that fit into this larger program and could employ his own skills as a physicist. Yet the people he encountered did not always share this strategy or attitude. Emory Ellis, for example, who introduced him to the phage, which made Delbrück's career, was known as a biochemist who started, in Delbrück's words, 'from zero knowledge concerned with anything about microbiology' (Fischer and Lipson 1988: 113). But Ellis had developed techniques that allowed quantifiable data on virus particles to be generated quickly and simply – a kind of bubble chamber of molecular biology – and this gave Delbrück something to which to apply his skills as a quantum physicist.

Patterns of collaboration and exchange could doubtless be identified, and in this book, especially in the chapters by Hollingsworth and Hollingsworth and Scerri, they are. But in each case the collaborator brings skills that have been acquired in something like 'disciplinary' settings. Classical biochemistry, quantum physics, and so forth are discipline-like fields, specialities with a more or less standard list of things that a member has to be able to do in order to be certified as competent. Although obviously one might acquire the skills without the certification, and acquire a variety of skills that are potentially mutually relevant without being certified or being formally trained, it is evident that, in practice, training is important, and that the most powerful constraints on quality of training are to be found in the markets for disciplines.

But is there anything more to the value of disciplinarity than the sheer fact of market discipline? Are their cognitive reasons for disciplinarity? It is a commonplace that it is difficult to have interdisciplinary programs on the undergraduate level because students do not bring to them the kind of disciplinary training that one gets in a standardized program. There is a strong base in practical experience for these beliefs. In many cases interdisciplinary work actually is an attempt to break free from these standards, which are in some respects arbitrary. Is it really necessary, for example, for someone to master Anglo-Saxon linguistic history in order to teach literature? Is it appropriate to demand of everyone who teaches ancient history a high level of competence in the classical languages? In both of these cases there has been a great deal of discussion of the extent to which these are essential or essentially arbitrary. It may seem odd to claim that ancient history can be done very nicely without strong qualifications in the relevant languages. But in fact a good deal of work in the area is done by people without these qualifications. As these disciplines find it useful to expand their audiences by teaching undergraduate courses to students without this background, as they have decided to in the case of ancient history in order to survive as a field, the question naturally arises as to whether these students should be forbidden to go on and whether the discipline can survive without relaxing these standards. At this point notions about essentialness and inessentialness take on a real edge and a real practical significance. And this significance is reinforced by the fact of market discipline. A department cannot unilaterally choose to relax or alter standards without cheapening the degree in the disciplinary market.

The same sorts of questions characteristically arise in interdisciplinary programs that seek to free themselves from essentially arbitrary limits imposed by the training regimes of the disciplines from which practitioners of every disciplinary area are drawn. Is it necessary, for example, that a specialist in social and political thought be a skilled statistician? To the extent that particular requirements and portions of disciplinary training have been seen to be the true tests of rigour, this becomes a genuine problem. The fact that people with similar interests, for example, in constitutional law in the United States, are forced to sit for exams in statistics and classical political theory in order to be qualified as political scientists and thus able to teach constitutional law outside of a law school means that the teaching of constitutional law itself is in some sense at least potentially altered by this fact of common background experience. In this case the relationship is purely a matter of historical accident, something that resulted from a decision made in the first decade of the century about what areas to annex into the category political science by the creators of the American Political Science Association. Sometimes this is quite conscious, as in the case of American anthropology departments, in which a common disciplinary identity involving linguistics, cultural anthropology, archaeology, and physical anthropology was consciously created as a matter of policy in order to alter the constituent fields by aligning them with one another.

The constraints of the market make conventional boundaries into real constraints. Philosophy graduates ought to be able to teach symbolic logic – it is a bread-and-butter course in philosophy programs – so it is routinely required so that students are not crippled when they enter the market. The original impulse behind the requirement has long vanished. The program of solving the problems of philosophy by translating it into logical notation, which once motivated logic requirements, is quite dead. But the market reality of logic and critical thinking requirements lives on. Essentialism about disciplines – claims about what 'really' is or is not a part of discipline, or about how the intellectual universe would be divided up if it were cut at the joints – is invariably bad history. As Gerald Graff has suggested, each discipline has the idea that it had a Golden Age in which all the elements went together smoothly and the purposes of the discipline were the subject of general agreement, and this idea is always a myth (1987). Disciplines are shotgun marriages, either of specialities, in the cases I have discussed here, or of multiple and often conflicting purposes, and are kept together by the reality of the market and the value of the protection of the market that has been created by employment requirements and expectations.

Considerations about what should go together – what fulfils more or less common purposes, what provides useful synergies, and so forth – are very much the kinds of considerations that have motivated interdisciplinary efforts, and of course this is exactly my point in spending so much time on the notion of disciplinarity itself. Disciplines are collectives defined in part by some common interests, but they are also internal divisions of labour in a teaching enterprise oriented to the production of persons trained in a specific way. In established disciplines the collective identity is more or less fixed and the internal division of labour is more or less variable and shifting in relation to the collective identity. Areas of study become more or less important or dominant, new areas develop and become important or even dominant, and so forth, all within the larger collective identity and internal market of the discipline.

Interdisciplinarity

Interdisciplinarity in a sense starts from the other direction, by creating novel divisions of labour in response to novel ends. This is indeed a striking difference between disciplines and interdisciplinary efforts. However they begin, disciplines in the end submit to the discipline of the protected internal markets they create. Interdisciplinary efforts can be defined negatively as being directed to ends other than the production of students for protected academic job markets. But in a positive sense this means that interdisciplinary efforts may have a great many different ends, and ends of different kinds.

One might attempt to classify these ends, but this turns out to be a difficult matter. Historically, interdisciplinary efforts have had many different ends, and typically proceed under a variety of constraints, such as the need to satisfy a particular public constituency, to secure regular funding, to provide evidence of supporting institutional goals, to provide a home for persons who are displaced from other units of the university for political reasons, to fulfil promises made to funders, and so forth. It would be difficult to give a complete list of these constraints, so various are they. And these constraints, it might appear, are the answer to the question of why interdisciplinary efforts so often fail.

One common end is to secure support in the context of a university bureaucracy. But here too there will be considerable diversity. What this way of formulating the problem suggests, rather paradoxically, is that interdisciplinarity precedes or is a more fundamental phenomenon than disciplinarity. The organization of any academic unit or any research or training collectivity is a matter of establishing a division of labour directed at some set of purposes. The creation of internal protected disciplinary markets for specialized degree holders is a phenomenon that is subsequent, both logically and temporally, to the creation of intellectual divisions of labour. What I would like to do in this section is to briefly compare some cases of types of interdisciplinary programs with respect to the 'division of labour,' the organizational strategies of those working in these areas, and the funding available to them. The circumstances of disciplinary and nondisciplinary programs obviously vary among biomedical science, physical science, the humanities, and the social sciences in part as a consequence of the differences in sources of funds, and, perhaps even more importantly, the structure of careers.

A simple example of a division of labour is the field of marine science. It has some discipline-like subfields, such as oceanography and marine geochemistry. These are not usually thought of as disciplines proper. One is applied chemistry or geology, the other a specialized form of applied physics or geophysics. The major journals for physical oceanography are the *Journal of Physical Oceanography* and the *JGR Oceans and Atmospheres* series, each of which is organized around the basic kinds of physical principles and technology involved. The authors of papers for these journals may have appointments in quite different kinds of institutes, but the appointments are typically in interdisciplinary units such as marine science. Outsiders are immediately identifiable to the editors, and much of the rejection rate for the journal involves papers by people such as engineers who submit papers that concern the technology (in a largely technology-driven field) rather than the science of interest to the members to the community. Because it is a technology-driven field this is also a field that is expensive and subsidized primarily through the subsidy of platforms, such as satellite and research ships.

Most of the participants in this research field are housed in marine science programs that are 'interdisciplinary' in organization. The interdisciplinarity of the appointments follows the platforms or types of platforms, such as satellites and research ships, in large part, and these units tend to be physically separated from universities because they are connected to data-collecting platforms that are physically separated from universities. In the case of physical oceanography, for example, the same general kind of platforms – ships – have been used for 150 years, and these platforms are extremely costly. This is a relatively stable research community with a variety of relevant funding agencies that derives its stability and autonomy from the fact that it has a large and diverse funding base; that is, the research community is not dependent on the goodwill and intentions of a particular funding agency or on a base in university general education. Some programs are outside universities; those that are in universities may grant degrees and train graduate students and even have some role in undergraduate teaching.

The constraints here are quite substantial. To keep a facility (and a ship) operating, it is necessary to have a substantial flow of grant money. To have a stable flow, it is necessary to compete not only for the kinds of grants that are risky but promise important results, but also for the kind that are predictable, pay overhead, and perhaps also enable the university to claim that the program serves some public purpose in exchange for the subsidies it gets from the university.

The patterns in biomedical fields are similar to this but different in some very striking ways. Research communities are shorter lived and careers are more mobile between research communities, and consequently highly specialized technical skills with short-term career value are important. Teams are assembled for a series of grants on some line of work in which a particular combination of skills is needed. The work is not driven by technology in the same way, as there are few expensive platforms and machines may very often be shared between laboratories or used therapeutically. The short-termness or rapidity with which biomedical research areas establish themselves make them quite different from programs driven by expensive shared technology. Biomedical research areas are much more dependent on great personalities, meaning lab chiefs with good grantsmanship skills and high professional status. Platform-based or instrument-based technology-driven physical science fields, by virtue of their sheer expense, require much more money and much more continuity in support, but create a more stable set of political and bureaucratic connections.

Another important difference in biomedical research that separates it from dependence on such things as student demand is the phenomenon of multiple appointments and the fact of high demand for medical training, and also incidentally the fact that, as a career option, failed research physicians can become practitioners. The effect of all of this is to shift the locus of discretionary fluidity in such a way that very traditional-appearing academic units are often colonized by extremely powerful research groups led by politically adept research figures, lab chiefs primarily, or department chairs who are essentially lab chiefs with administrative powers. So, in a sense, in medical schools one doesn't need interdisciplinary departments simply because the interdisciplinary structures – the labs and centres – are overwhelmingly more powerful than the disciplinary structures.

The reason for the weakness of disciplines in medicine is that departments are primarily of importance because they deliver things in traditional clinical categories that are considerably more stable, so categories like pediatrics and psychiatry persist in their importance because the patients continue to arrive in these categories. Patients are of course an important base. Practice plans – the university's medical treatment programs, which many years ago were operated as charity clinics but which, through the Medicaid and Health Insurance systems, are now extremely lucrative – are a source of money, and the power of a chair may depend on success in maintaining this base as well. (The sheer numbers in the case of certain programs are quite astonishing. Orthopaedic surgery is one of the major moneymakers for any hospital and practice plan, so a unit that does a great deal of surgery will make or break an entire teaching hospital. The chair of an orthopaedic surgery program may receive pay from a practice plan of $1 million annually.)

Elsewhere I have described the importance in the early stages of the institutionalization of support for science of one of two kinds of trust relationships: (1) those involving an individual who is simultaneously a member of the scientific community, and (2) the political or patron community that in an academic context means sometimes at least the administrative *nomenklatura* of the university, which is often a separate and quite different caste (Turner 1990, 1996b). In the case of a platform-based physical science discipline with a very stable large capital investment and independent sources of money, once the facility or unit is established, maintaining it becomes a quite different matter. In biomedical situations, in contrast, the pattern is quite different. The kind of searching for money and support that is characteristic of moments of founding is characteristic of the whole life of many such institutes and centres and as a consequence of the dependence of these areas on funding based on the perception that the area has great promise, that the area is hot, and particularly that it might produce some important breakthrough of therapeutic significance for some pressing disease.

Students constitute a potential resource base around which interdisciplinary programs may develop, and once established, this base can greatly constrain the direction of the enterprise. The student market operates under some significant constraints that are particularly important during tight academic markets, but the fundamental constraint on the graduate level is that regardless of the importance of the people involved, students without disciplinary PhDs are at an enormous disadvantage when looking for jobs in disciplinary programs. A few students at the very top of their fields may be able to escape these constraints, and in odd cases of rapidly expanding or changing disciplinary markets persons with 'interdisciplinary degrees' may find their way into developing disciplinary programs. Ordinarily, however, the disadvantages are significant and students become aware of this.

The pull of disciplinarization itself deserves some analysis, for it is clearly much stronger for strongly teaching-oriented programs than it is in the biomedical sciences, in which disciplinary categories are increasingly nominal and of local administrative significance only. Disciplines establish a clear career track from an undergraduate major to professorial appointment and thus produce the kind of self-perpetuating generational cycles that allow for a disciplinary history and so forth. Criminal justice may seem to be a rather artificial category, but it is probably less artificial than political science was and indeed still is, but the example of political science in the United States as a discipline shows that the particular combination of topics that became the 'discipline' can be quite arbitrary. Yet the existence of a common degree curriculum will have a significant effect on the experiences of all of its professors and thus distinguish them from persons who lack this experience.

Beating the Clock: Temporality and Interdisciplinarity

In what I have said here I have identified two very stable patterns of resource base: students, some of whom have academic careers and recirculate, and clients, who have more or less stable needs. Both groups of course do not necessarily exist in advance, and indeed part of the process of establishing a discipline is creating either dependent clients or a cycle of replacements. Where researchers are not dependent on these processes and relationships, disciplinarity is weak and interdisciplinary and nondisciplinary forms flourish, as in biomedical science, at least in its research aspects. Platform dependence is not quite so corrosive of disciplinarity, but rather generates specialization along the lines of the platform or instrument, so that one can have such a thing as a field of radio astronomy, for example, that employs physicists and technical experts on radar. This field was essentially the creation of a small number of physical scientists who were excellent politicians and worked to establish instruments. They required patrons both at universities and in the government simply because the instruments were so large and so expensive that they required not only huge amounts of money but novel organizational forms for their operation (Lovell 1990).

Instruments are objects that exist in a certain time horizon, limited though perhaps very long. Disciplines operate in a very different time horizon. Classics, to choose a very extreme example, owes its origins to a resource base that has long vanished: the study of Greek was an ecclesiastic requirement that played an important role in the long centuries in which such universities as Oxford and Cambridge – not to mention Harvard – were essentially trade schools for the production of ministers who needed to be able to read the New Testament in Greek,

or high school teachers who taught these languages (which were required of Ivy League university entrants until the 1920s). Even today
the field depends in part, in the United States at least, on the large
numbers of refugees from Catholic education who went to high schools
that were designed to prepare students for the priesthood. But the
disciplinarization of classics means that the field may grind on without
this base as a place for the teaching of languages meeting university
requirements, as an adjunct to literature and religious studies programs,
and so forth, and graduate degrees in classics continue to have meaning
within an internal protected market. Interdisciplinary efforts cannot protect themselves in this way, but they can sometimes escape time. Temporary circumstances, such as the present concern with ethics, have
created endowments for applied, interdisciplinary Ethics Centers, which
will last for decades, if not centuries, and free their beneficiaries from
dependence on the vagaries of student demand or client needs.

But there is no such thing as freedom from dependence and circum-
stance. If the National Endowment for the Humanities announces a
program to create and fund interdisciplinary centres, it provides incentives for giving centres a particular form, and this obviously requires
particular actions by particular bureaucrats with particular discretionary powers. These may, and indeed do, vary from organization to organization and university to university. Similarly, when the National Science Foundation decides to cut overhead costs through centres initiatives, it also creates particular incentives in this case by reducing the
universities' proportional take in the form of overhead but expanding
the quantity of overhead of a particular university. These initiatives are
also of the sort that require particular discretionary acts, and, in this
case typically, a lobbyist in Washington and legislative involvement.
Similarly, donors to Centers for Applied Ethics must be cultivated, and
the product of the centre must be the sort of effort that, at least until the
endowment is sufficient, attracts funding.[3]

Conclusion

In discussing these different patterns of organization in relation to resources, I have provided a kind of general empirical base for the beginnings at least of a more extensive consideration of the market character
of the kinds of nondisciplinary efforts that have occurred in the past
and are presently occurring, especially in science. Gibbons et al. characterize these current efforts in terms of a second stage (1994). From a

broader historical perspective, however, this analysis is questionable. Leaving aside for the moment the important question of the distinctions between interdisciplinary, transdisciplinary, and other forms of nondisciplinary activity, it is also important to insist on the obvious fact of the relatively short history of disciplinarity, the historical uniqueness of the vast expansion of university education over the last fifty years, and the combination of this expansion with the equally rapid expansion of provision for research that lasted up to 1970.

In many ways this particular combination of rapid changes in resources is historically unique and the 'stage' of disciplinarity that Gibbons et al. regard as stage one, and that many commentators regard as normal, is in fact entirely anomalous. The sheer dimensions of these changes should be sufficient to make the case for their anomalous character. The general dimensions of the changes in available resources are well known. The pattern in the United States was one of very rapid wartime expansion of funding for physics, and a somewhat longer-term but equally impressive expansion of funding for dread diseases – primarily cancer – beginning in the thirties, and a second rapid expansion of funding in the post-Sputnik period. Student demand followed a somewhat different pattern. There was very rapid expansion in the period after the Second World War followed by a crisis of overproduction in the early and mid-fifties followed by the rapid post-Sputnik, and then baby boom expansion of the universities in the sixties, and a collapse of student demand in the seventies, followed by an increasing proportion of students enrolled in vocationally oriented academic programs such as colleges of business. In addition there was, from the late thirties on, a very significant expansion of moneymaking opportunities for academic scientists, especially physical scientists, as well as, post-medicare, an enormous expansion in physicians' incomes and the transformation of academic medical provisions from charity work done by medical school clinics as part of the process of training advanced medical students into a massively lucrative medical business. The sheer complexity and magnitude of this business, and especially of teaching hospitals, overshadows almost everything else in the university from a quantitative and administrative point of view.

Traditional academic disciplines, the paradigm case being physics, responded to these changes in resources in a fairly straightforward way. As demand for physics PhDs increased in the immediate postwar period and resources for research increased, physics instruction became more oriented to the creation of specialist researchers and could do so largely unconstrained by considerations of student demand. Physics courses were required for students in the sciences, and consequently it was not important for physicists to attract majors or for that matter to pay much attention to the difficulties of teaching. Physics departments could select from the students who had the greatest capacities and focus their efforts on this élite group. The real constraints were provided by the market and especially by the market for researchers. PhD departments of course compete for prestige, and prestige is the source of their ability to place PhD students in other departments. Dominance is reinforced by the multiplier effect inherent in what Merton (1968) called the Matthew effect, so disciplinary hierarchies were, in general, fairly stable despite the fact that competition was intense.

Physicists were not entirely free to define the research agendas of funding agencies, but the massive funding for weapons research and missile defences provided substantial income for physics departments and research programs, and individual physicists could frequently support themselves nicely on consulting fees. Not surprisingly, in this situation, the internal prestige hierarchy of physics came to predominate over all sorts of other considerations, and less pure areas were ceded to engineering, which is in large part, in research terms, applied physics. A very similar story could be told about economics, a field in which mathematical modelling went from being a highly specialized, totally subsidized, and, I might add, heavily subsidized activity in the late thirties and early forties to becoming the centre of the disciplinary prestige hierarchy (Beckmann 1991: 261–3). In economics as well, lucrative consulting opportunities existed and indeed increased in the postwar period. In both cases the discipline became increasingly estranged from the demands of nondisciplinary users and increasingly remote from the 'real world.' The very possibility of such massive research subsidies as the European Organization for Nuclear Research (CERN) meant that physicists could leave to others, such as engineers or departments of finance, the parts of the enterprise that were less interesting as physics even if they were more important to users, though it must be said that both physicists and economists preserved an income stream of consulting money, and in this way retained a connection to practical problems.

This process was so advanced in the late sixties and early seventies that it was effectively impossible for physics departments to return to the status quo of the twenties and thirties when physicists were heavily involved with the production of technology and were, in many respects, indistinguishable from engineers and from what little engineer-

ing research existed at the time. Much could be said about the employment of physicists during this period, but it will suffice to say that there
were many non-academic units that did employ physicists, such as the
famous Bell labs, and these units and their leaders had high prestige in
the physics community and close relations with the leading physicists
of the day. The president of the National Academy of Sciences during
the Second World War, Frank Jewett, was a close friend of Robert
Milliken, and they both had been associated with the California Institute of Technology's highly technologically oriented science programs
of the first decades of the century. But this pattern was matched in very
complex ways by interdisciplinary programs that responded both to
contractions and the opportunities for innovation that arose because of
increased student demand. The same market forces that enabled physics and economics departments to become more demanding and selective with respect to students made it profitable for university administrators to provide alternatives, such as vocationally oriented programs,
for those students who were excluded by the more demanding, pure
fields.

The peculiar relationship between the rigidities of disciplines and the
opportunities for interdisciplinary endeavours raises some basic questions. Is interdisciplinarity simply a residual phenomenon, a product of
the opportunities that disciplines, governed by the demands of their
internal, closed markets, are unable to take up? Or could new forms of
knowledge production take over all the work? How essential are disciplinary cartels? Could one imagine a return to the science of the nineteeth
century, where they did not have much power? A simple answer is this:
disciplinary cartels are fundamentally about monopolies in the production and consumption of students destined for academic careers. These
cartels can make themselves irrelevant, and a powerful force drives
them to become irrelevant: the demands of competitition in their internal, closed market. Disciplines fossilize. But at the same time, new disciplines arise.

There are good reasons for starting a new cartel, or cartelizing an
interdisciplinary field – turning it into a discipline – as long as there is a
market for the students who are being produced, and as long as there is
something to be gained by restricting access to positions. Disciplinarization assures privileged access to this market. In the end it is nothing more than the fact of privileged access to markets. And this
provides the answer: as long as there are benefits for cartelization,
there will be disciplines. And as long as cartelization incapacitates its

beneficiaries in taking up opportunities that are of less value inside these internal markets than outside, there will be a place for 'interdisciplinarity.'

Notes

This chapter was supported by a grant from the Ethics and Value Studies Program of the National Science Foundation.

1 The disciplines of the humanities, the vast bulk of which in the United States consist of teachers of English literature who are professionally allied to the Modern Language Association, have their own history and complexities, which nevertheless are broadly similar to those of philosophy and the social sciences (cf. Graff 1987).
2 The history of sociology, dealing with many of these issues, was written in terms of the problems of disciplinary resources and their effects on disciplines in Turner and Turner (1990). My point in this paper is to show that interdisciplinary efforts are even less insulated from these problems, though they take somewhat different forms.
3 The sheer diversity of the conditions under which interdisciplinary centres operate raises some important questions about the possibility of comparing them, as Hollingsworth and Hage (1996) quite impressively does in his recent work on the organizational setting conducive to major discoveries. Many science units are responding to demands that effectively preclude major discoveries.

4

The Interdisciplinary Nature of Science: Theoretical Framework and Bibliometric-Empirical Approach

ANTHONY F.J. VAN RAAN

Contours of a Theoretical Framework of Interdisciplinarity

In this essay I discuss different aspects of the phenomenon called the 'interdisciplinarity' of science. Primarily I aim at an empirical investigation of interdisciplinarity in an *instrumental sense*: how to observe scientific activities in order to discover their interdisciplinary characteristics, and, next, to analyse these characteristics in more detail. Such observations are important as 'input knowledge' for other studies on interdisciplinarity, for instance, the more sociologically oriented work on the cooperation of researchers within interdisciplinary teams and the policy-oriented work on the stimulation of interdisciplinary research activities. But in this essay I also develop a theoretical framework. Thus, to present some basic ideas, or working hypotheses, concerning interdisciplinarity. Earlier empirical evidence is in line with these ideas, but more research is certainly necessary.

PROBLEM-DRIVEN MOTIVATION AND REPUTATION-DRIVEN REGULATION

The first working hypothesis deals with *motivation* and *reputation*. On the basis of the most fundamental characteristic of science, curiosity, science has always been and still is a highly problem-oriented enterprise that is stimulated by societal problems in many ways – much more than policy-makers try to believe. Societal problems constitute, in fact, a very profound *external* motivation of scientists. Most probably, precisely this motivation was the main driving force of the great (and only) Scientific Revolution in sixteenth-century Western Europe. Given the crucial role of reputation in science (Merton 1973), it is obvious that problem-driven, externally motivated research, *if* carried out successfully, can contribute highly to reputation in science. So there are good sociological reasons for why science, which is after all a human activity, will have strong problem-driven features.

This first working hypothesis has several further consequences. It is not only reputation *in* science but, equally important, reputation *by* science that may stimulate scientists. Here we have interesting research objectives for social-psychologically oriented studies of science.

Next, as stated above, problem-driven, externally motivated research can contribute to reputation, *if* the research is carried out successfully. This seems a rather obvious remark, but it is not. It means implicitly a hard precondition: socioeconomic problems *must also* imply interesting *scientific problems* (some more basic, like research on diseases, some more applied or technological, like semiconductor devices), otherwise they cannot contribute to scientific reputation. Absence of this *internal* motivation, appealing scientific problems, will immediately block the interests of scientists.

Third, most socioeconomic problems are *interdisciplinary* in nature. On the other hand, both scientific appeal – if present – and scientific reputation work are predominantly *disciplinary*, simply because reputation is generally coupled with the more or less established categories in which scientists are educated. Therefore, a specific discipline will mostly play the first violin in interdisciplinary work. Furthermore, this leading part of a specific discipline will be strengthened very effectively by technology, as we discuss in the next section.

The conclusion from the above scheme of thought is that there is a very tight *sociocognitive triangle* of three interacting elements: socioeconomic problems, scientifically interesting problems, and interdisciplinarity. The interactions among these three elements are *driven* by motivations, *regulated* by the reputational system in science, and *dominated* by the knowledge, craftmanship, and habits of mostly one or just a few specific disciplines.

TECHNOLOGY-DRIVEN REINFORCEMENT

The second working hypothesis concerns the role of *technology*. Apparently there is an unavoidable 'natural' and 'self-organizing' development of science towards more interdisciplinary activities, comparable with ecological systems (van Raan 1990; Noyons and Van Raan 1998). The reason is that technology – and more generally the 'extension of our human brain with relevant artifacts,' i.e., powerful instruments – acts as a bridge between the different scientific disciplines. *Without technology, domains of human knowledge would remain largely isolated.* As an example, recent developments in the neurosciences show the overwhelming role of instruments. Observations by advanced brain-scanning apparatus (based directly on fundamental physical processes) are influencing medicine and molecular biology tremendously, but also the behavioural sciences and even philosophy. Therefore we can conclude that technology continuously *reinforces* the sociocognitive triangle dramatically, mainly by the permanent creation of new instruments. And because instruments are mainly developed in specific disciplines – it is often not realized how typically disciplinary crucial instruments and apparatus are! – we have an extremely effective 'co-reinforcement' of the role of a specific discipline in the sociocognitive triangle of interdisciplinary work.

The capacity to combine brain and hands in making things we call instruments or apparatus is a unique property of the human species. Bluntly speaking, it is precisely this property that is responsible for the advancement of our human, objective knowledge, which is, given the above reasoning, increasingly interdisciplinary. Scerri (this volume) shows that eminent scientists strongly emphasize the crucial role of instruments for the progress of science, particularly the 'bridging' role between disciplines, by transferring instruments from one discipline to another.

THE DECAY OF CHATTY SCIENCE

The above ideas have further interesting consequences. From these ideas we can infer that the typical non-instrumental scientific activities such as philosophy and parts of the social and behavioural sciences and the humanities are in danger of losing their connections with the natural, basically interdisciplinary advancement of science. As a consequence, they will then lose their objective, scientific character, because they will be less and less subject to the regulating rigour of the hard disciplines that provide instrumentation. These disciplines will become more and more unscientific, moving towards ideology-based, nonsensical, *chatty* activities dominated by current fashions. These fashions are, in turn, often dictated by current politically correct opinions, thus undermining the typical scientific critical attitude.

In summary, scientific interdisciplinarity is a result of one of the main aspects of science itself, its socioeconomic, problem-driven character preconditioned by scientific motivation, regulated by the reputational system in science, and reinforced continuously – and very effectively – by technological developments. Needless to say, these technological developments are in turn influenced by scientific developments. This feedback character of the science–technology interaction is an indisputable fact. But the point here is that this feedback is dominated by sudden changes that are *not* caused predominantly by new, typically scientific, 'cognitive' discoveries, but much more by the rather contingent, thus 'stepwise,' introduction of further new instrumentation.

Bibliometric Methods of Studying Interdisciplinarity

THREE ANALYTICAL APPROACHES

Above I sketched the outlines of a theoretical framework of science and its intrinsically interdisciplinary character. This framework indicates where interesting empirical work can be done. Now we arrive at the more empirical part of our work, based on advanced bibliometric work. First we develop analytical tools in order to observe and interpret the interdisciplinary aspects of scientific research. Beyond the scope of this essay, but certainly one of the major objectives, is to test this theoretical framework to see if the working hypotheses can find support in empirical evidence.

In this section I discuss three bibliometric methods of studying the phenomenon of interdisciplinarity in science:

1 the construction of a *research activity profile:* a breakdown of the scientific work published by a research group/institute into (sub)fields, on the basis of the field-specific characteristics of the institute's own publications
2 the construction of a *research influence profile:* a breakdown of the scientific work citing the work of a research group/institute into (sub)fields, on the basis of the field-specific characteristics of the institute's citing publications
3 the construction of *bibliometric maps* of scientific fields in order to identify as objectively as possible structural relations between various subfields, as well as the relations of these subfields with other disciplines outside the central map of the field

In this essay I sketch the main lines of these approaches. For a detailed and critical discussion of the potentials and limitations of bibliometric methods, refer to a recent overview paper (van Raan 1996).

RESEARCH ACTIVITY PROFILE

For a first discussion of these three approaches, I present concrete examples.

In line with our first working hypothesis that socioeconomic problems constitute a major driving force in science, I analyse how the interaction triangle of socioeconomic problems and scientifically interesting problems and interdisciplinarity becomes visible in the scientific work of a research group/institute.

Here I focus on a typical socioeconomic problem: nutrition and food, showing that such a problem is immediately related to interdisciplinary research, and observing how this interdisciplinary research is valued by the scientific community (i.e., contributes to reputation). Such a valuation is a proof of being successfully engaged in scientifically interesting problems connected with more basics-oriented, disciplinary fields of research.

The target institute is the TNO Nutrition and Food Research Institute in The Netherlands, one of the major and most outstanding research institutes in its field in Europe. Recently, with Thed van Leeuwen, I performed an extensive bibliometric analysis of the research performance of this institute (van Raan and van Leeuwen 1999). An important part of the method consisted of breaking down the institute's publications in terms of fields defined by sets of journals. This *activity breakdown* gave a direct overview of all the (sub)fields involved in the research activities of the institute. As discussed above, this can be seen as an unambiguous indicator of interdisciplinarity. The rank-distribution function of the number of publications over (sub)fields can even be used as a measure of the degree of interdisciplinarity.

We constructed the institute's research activity profile for the period 1987–96 and for the two subperiods (1987–91, 1992–6) in order to visualize possible shifts in interdisciplinarity. In this paper I focus on the results of the entire period of 1987–96 (see Figure 4-1). The abscissa of the profile gives the size of the activity (number of publications) per (sub)field, and the colour of the bars represents the influence of the institute in the (sub)field concerned, normalized to an international standard (based on advanced citation analysis; see van Raan 1996 and legends to the figure). The institute's research relates to about forty fields

Figure 4.1
Research activity profile, TNO Nutrition and Food Research Institute, 1987–96, based on 1395 publications of the institute.

The length of the bars represents the number of publications in the (sub)field as specified on the vertical axis. The colour of the bars represents the impact level: low (white bars), average (grey bars), or high (black bars) as compared with an international standard for each (sub)field. Example: The TNO Institute published in the period 1987–96 about 130 publications (covered by the *Science Citation Index*) in the field of toxicology. These publications together (the work of the TNO Institute in toxicology) have an impact above the international (worldwide) average for the field of toxicology. For further explanation of bibliometric indicators see van Raan 1996.

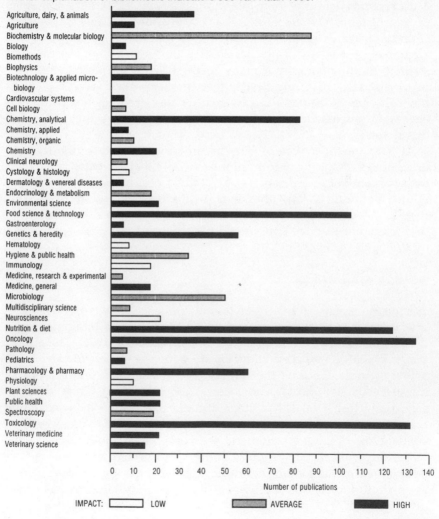

of science. No doubt, the institute's scientists perform very well in their core fields, food science and technology, and nutrition and dietary research. But they also have substantial influence in oncology, analytical chemistry, toxicology, genetics and heredity, in biochemistry and molecular biology, microbiology, pharmacology, and many other fields of science.

My main objective is to demonstrate the potential of this approach for analysing interdisciplinarity in general. If we look at the above list of research fields, we can ask another question: What is a discipline? Most research fields are quite interdisciplinary, at least to a certain level of aggregation. Therefore, it is hardly possible to 'define' interdisciplinarity. Would science be 'truly interdisciplinary' if there were, say, a complete 'amalgam' of physics and biology? Or is there already substantial interdisciplinarity if many research fields are dominated by a main discipline (e.g., physics) but at the same time have important other-discipline-oriented aspects, such as are clearly visible in the 'science map' discussed in the section 'Bibliometric Maps' that follows in this chapter?

At least the latter type of interdisciplinarity is more a rule than an exception. Perhaps the current problematization of interdisciplinarity is more a matter of mystification cultivated by post-modern ideologies or related politically correct thinking, such as the 'invention' of mode-2 research by Gibbons et al. (1994). Often claims of interdisciplinarity or 'transdisciplinarity' are supported by 'moral enthusiasm,' as described by Weingart (this volume).

RESEARCH INFLUENCE PROFILE

The measurement of the international influence of scientific work is operationalized by the concept of 'impact,' which is a bibliometrically defined measure based on citation analysis (van Raan 1996). The impact per (sub)field as indicated in the Figure 4.1 nutrition and food research activity profile concerns the impact of the institute's publications in these specific (sub)fields, regardless of the citing field. Thus, the next step is a further breakdown into (sub)fields of the scientific work citing the publications of a research group or institute (for earlier work on similar cross-disciplinary citations, see Porter and Chubin 1985).

Current work in our group is going on to design and elaborate an optimal representation of a scientific *influence profile* by a breakdown of an institute's impact on the basis of field-specific characteristics of the citing publications. Contrary to the earlier case, we are focusing on a typical mono-disciplinary institute: CERN (Geneva), the European Organization for High-Energy Research, one of the world's major high-energy physics institutes. I refer for details to Davidse and van Raan (1997). This CERN study aims at analysing the influence of basic high-energy physics research on fields other than physics, and particularly on application-oriented research. We found that about 10 per cent of the CERN physics publications were cited by publications outside physics. The most important outside-physics fields appeared to be astronomy and astrophysics, computer science, electrical and electronic engineering, and instruments and instrumentation. Similar analyses were made for two other large particle accelerator institutes, Deutsches Elektronen-Synchrotron (DESY, Hamburg) and Stanford Linear Accelerator Centre (SLAC, Stanford), for comparison. We found that accelerator institutes, particularly DESY, have developed a quite substantial interdisciplinary environment, mostly because of the application of photon and particle radiation in biological and medical fields. So I stress that our study focused on the *physics* of these institutes.

We found that the physics-to-nonphysics knowledge flow (an interdisciplinary flow), as measured by unravelling the 'citation traffic,' was about six times smaller than the physics-to-physics knowledge flow (the disciplinary flow). Nevertheless, this interdisciplinary flow is still considerable in size. Particularly, but not surprisingly, the strong relation between basic physics and engineering/instrumentation (the technological influence) plays an important role.

BIBLIOMETRIC MAPS

The third major line of our quantitative methods is *bibliometric mapping,* or cartography of research fields. Here I limit myself to the main lines and refer for a more detailed discussion to Tijssen and van Raan (1994) and Noyons and van Raan (1998). The basic idea is as follows: each year about a million scientific articles are published. For just one research field, such as materials science, the number of papers is already about 30,000 per year. How do we keep track of all these developments, particularly relations with other fields? Are cognitive structures hidden in this mass of published knowledge at a meta-level? And what can these cognitive structures tell us about interdisciplinarity?

Suppose each research field can be characterized by a list of the most important, say 100, keywords. For materials science such a list will

cover words like ceramics, polymers, semiconductors, high-tempera-
ture superconductivity, alloys, and so on. Each publication can be characterized by a subset from the total list of keywords. For all 30,000
publications we compare their keyword lists in pairs. In other words,
these 30,000 publications constitute a gigantic network in which all publications are linked by one of more common keywords. The more keywords two publications have in common, the more these publications
are related (keyword-similarity) and can be regarded as belonging to
the same research field or specialty. In mathematical terms, publications are represented as vectors in a high-dimensional word-space. In
this space they group together, or take very distant positions when they
are not related to one another.

We developed mathematical techniques to unravel these publication
networks and to successively cluster and map the underlying word-
structures ('co-word maps'). What is fascinating is that these structures
can be regarded as the cognitive or intellectual structure of science. As
discussed above, this structure is entirely based on the total relations
among all publications. Thus, the structures that are discovered are not
the result of any pre-arranged classification system whatsoever. No-
body prescribes these structures – they emerge solely from the internal
relations of the whole universe of publications. In other words, what
we make visible by our mathematical methods is the *self-organized 'ecology' of science* (van Raan 1990, Noyons and van Raan 1998). Similar
structures arise from the analysis of citation-relations ('co-citation maps').

Figure 4.2 shows the first results of our recent work: the 'freezing-
out' of the underlying patterns in about 100,000 publications in agricultural research (based on a co-citation and co-word analysis combination). We performed a two-step procedure: First, we constructed one
global overview map (shown in Figure 4.2) and, second, for each discovered cluster (which practically means field of research) we made
detailed, fine-structure maps (for details of this work, and particularly
for a presentation of the fine-structure maps, we refer to Noyons et al.
1996, as well as note 1.)[1] Figure 4.2 clearly shows the mutual relationships between agricultural research (a field undoubtedly devoted to a
whole spectrum of socioeconomic problems) and many other fields of
science. The closer the clusters (fields) are, the more related they are *in
connection with agricultural research*. We observe, next to agricultural research (general), the dominating role of biochemistry and molecular
biology as well as chemistry (general). Many other fields of science play
a role, such as microbiology, endocrinology, virology and immunology,
plant research, and biotechnology.

Figure 4.2
Bibliometric map of agricultural research, 1994, based on about 100,000 publications worldwide.

The map represents a relational structure of clusters of publications based on cluster-similarity measures. The clusters can be identified as research fields. The closer the clusters are, the more related the (sub)fields concerned. White clusters are characterized by decreasing publication activity worldwide; grey clusters by no significant decrease or increase in publication activity; black clusters by increasing activity. For further explanation see note 1.

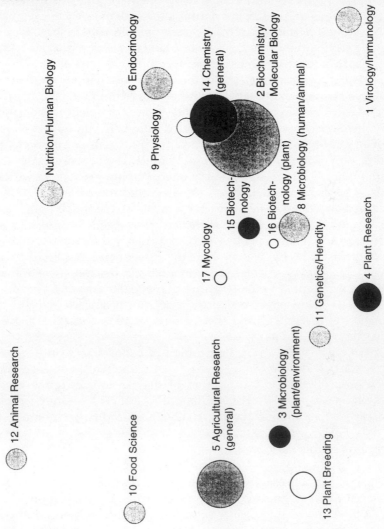

Again we make the same observation discussed earlier: science is a fascinating amalgam of 'cognitive regions' that are part of more or less established disciplines. Often these disciplines are research fields that originated from earlier interdisciplinary developments. Above all, the whole is undoubtedly interdisciplinary. As in any complex, self-organizing system, the global characteristics of the whole – such as the typical power-law distribution of the sizes of parts of the system – are not so much a direct result of the constituting individual elements, but they represent a very specific property of the system as such.

This bibliometric cartography has interesting potentials. First, it visualizes the intrinsically interdisciplinary landscape of a scientific field embedded in its surroundings. These surroundings have both a cognitive as well as a semantic meaning: the word combinations on the map are always positioned in relation to other word combinations, i.e., representatives of research fields, specialty topics, or scientific concepts. Thus a field-specific context is generated automatically by the above-described self-organizing process. Therefore, problems of interpretation of words on the map are in our opinion much less severe than as discussed by others who consider these interpretation problems a serious drawback of bibliometric mapping (Maasen, this volume).

Second, by making these maps for a series of years, we are able to observe trends and changes in structure. So we gain insight into the dynamics of the scientific endeavour, particularly the interdisciplinary developments. Clearly we observe the phenomemon described by Weingart (this volume): 'Instead of assuming a disciplinary structure that has to be adapted to the structure of the real world by approximation, it has to be recognized that the structure of knowledge and the delineation of disciplines and their subject matters constitute perceptions of the world.'

Third, we are able to put the position of major actors on the map. Thus we are creating a strategic map: who is where in science, and, more precisely, what is the position of these actors in terms of the interdisciplinary relations of the different fields? (For recent examples of bibliometric mapping including 'dynamic' examples, see note 1).

Concluding Remarks

In this paper I first presented a theoretical framework for the interdisciplinary nature of science. It can be described as a socio-cognitive triangle of three interacting elements: socio-economic problems, scientifically interesting problems, and interdisciplinarity. The dynamics of the relations between these elements of this triangular compound are driven by motivations, regulated by the reputational system in science, dominated by one or just a few disciplines, and continuously reinforced by instrumentation. As a consequence of this model, we can forecast the decay of what I call 'chatty' science.

The combination of the three bibliometric approaches – analysis of research activity, research influence, and mapping – appears to be a powerful instrument for further investigating the interdisciplinary nature of science. They form a coherent set of approaches for diagnosing important aspects of interdisciplinarity. In particular, the analysis of developments over time and of the role of major actors is important in testing the various working hypotheses that form the basis of our theoretical framework.

In this contribution I presented the main lines of our empirical 'instrumentation.' Further elaboration will address more specifically how the above empirical methods fit into the theoretical framework, that is, how the different empirical steps are related to the different parts of the theoretical framework.

This context involves further important problems. For example, the first two bibliometric methods focus on science as represented by its chief constituting elements, namely research groups or institutes. The third method addresses science – or at least major parts of it – as a whole. This dichotomy is typical for any complex system. On the one hand we have the elements with which the system is built; on the other we have the system as a whole, with its global characteristics, which are partly related to properties of the constituting elements, but partly also has its own properties.[2] This demonstrates a fundamental aspect in the empirical operationalization of a concept such as 'science,' and, in fact, of any complex system. We think that in science disciplinary fields are the constituting elements, and that interdisciplinarity is the general, large-scale property. We know that a general property of a system (e.g., the always limited amount of total space, energy, resources) can induce major effects in its constituting elements (e.g., in the way they have to interact).

Notes

1 For recent examples refer to our institute's Internet home page at http://sahara.fsw.leidenuniv.nl/cwts/cwtshome.html

2 To further illustrate this problem I will make a comparison with a physical complex system: turbulence in boiling water. Certainly several aspects of this complex system are related to the properties of the constituting elements, the water molecules. Clearly the boiling point temperature is element-dependent: for the water molecules it is 100°C, for any other molecule it will be completely different. Nevertheless, the turbulence patterns resulting from boiling will be very general and will manifest themselves in any type of liquid, regardless of the specific properties of the constituting·elements, in this case the water molecules.

5

Mapping the New Cultures and Organization of Research in Australia[1]

TIM TURPIN and SAM GARRETT-JONES

Introduction

Research institutions throughout the world are beset with pressures to fundamentally transform their activities. These pressures are emanating from within science and from institutional requirements to make science more directly useful.

Scientific research is increasingly carried out in organizational forms built around multidisciplinary, small research teams with both basic and applied research contextualized in application to defined national objectives. Immediacy and face-to-face relations are central, both in the development of new fields of research and in the transfer of knowledge across disciplinary and organizational boundaries. At the same time, universities and public research institutions are pressured to 'corporatize,' to seek commercial outcomes and to steer research according to institutionalized performance indicators.

As these two pressures intersect, a blurring at the organizational boundaries is spurring the development of interdisciplinary groupings within traditionally discipline-based teaching institutions. As a result, new forms of organizational culture are emerging. These changes in the 'production of knowledge' represent a new phase in the relation between knowledge and society where, paradoxically, 'local' knowledge and person-to-person relations are paramount in knowledge production that is otherwise global and abstract.

Scientific disciplines in the process of adapting to such change are driven in two opposing directions: towards fragmentation and specialization in order to capture or retain a professional niche, yet at the same time towards identifying their relevance for the widest possible segments of society. This is evident in the worldwide trend towards the formation of university research centres; in the trend towards universities acting commercially; in the increasing salience of horizontal links among universities, industry, and other socio-economic sectors; and in the blurring of the boundaries between basic and applied research in almost all fields of research.

Based on the work of the Centre for Research Policy (CRP) since 1991, this paper reviews trends in Australia that are driving the public research system towards more explicit social and economic outcomes, examines their effect on the organization of research, describes techniques used to map the socio-economic connections of research, and considers the implications for the practice and management of interdisciplinary research.

We focus on the socio-economically–driven coalescence of disciplines, largely ignoring the 'platform' and 'instrument/research techniques' driven interdisciplinarity described by Turner and Scerri (this volume), and the 'intellectual' and 'big motivational questions' provoked interdisciplinarity referred to by Maasen and De Mey (this volume), respectively.

Rumbles from Within

NATIONAL RESEARCH INSTITUTES

In Australia's Commonwealth Scientific and Industrial Research Organization (CSIRO), there is a marked difference in the relationship between scientists and managers in the 1990s from that which existed in the 1960s. In contrast to today's corporate approach the scientist of the 1960s was encouraged to act as the key 'driver' of research projects and programs. 'No matter what the field, the purpose, or the source of the financial support, the research staff decide, devise and direct their own research programs, and every research officer in the CSIRO is expected within a few years of the commencement of his research career to take full responsibility for his [sic] own area of research activity' (Gillespie 1964: 23).

The role of the corporate body in this context was in ensuring that the scientist did not experience undue frustration through unsympathetic administration. This contrasts starkly with the more recent view that emphasizes the importance of corporately managed organizational structures.

Through the 1980s, the CSIRO was confronted with changes in government and public expectations, as well as changes in financial and industrial commitments. In a decade of economic rationalist policies and economic downturn, the CSIRO was particularly vulnerable to severe questioning of its value to the nation (see Landsberg 1989). It was subject to growing pressure to not only demonstrate its worth, but to adopt 'business-like practices' to ensure that its resources were used with maximum effect (CSIRO 1987).

The CSIRO's response was to implement considerable structural change. In 1990, a priority-setting exercise was introduced across the entire organization to bring national economic and commercial factors into the priority-setting process. The organization has also become more strategic in terms of human resource management and more commercially oriented. Formal procedures were introduced during the 1980s to increase staff mobility and encourage closer collaboration with industry and to exploit such links through the development of more multidisciplinary projects and programs. Consequently new occupational expectations of research staff in the organization emerged. New training programs introduced during the late 1980s were designed to realign the entire business strategy and to develop a whole new set of skills and behaviours that were previously 'quite foreign to many scientists' (Blewitt 1992: 7). Reinforcing these organizational expectations, the then CSIRO Chief Executive argued that the boundary between business and public sector research should be almost indistinguishable: 'Bureaucrats and scientists acting alone are not usually the best judges of what scientific breakthroughs will be ... a seamless link with the business community is required' (Stocker 1993).

The move to develop closer funding links with industrial enterprises has occurred in other Australian research institutions. The CSIRO, the Australian Nuclear Science and Technology Organisation (ANSTO), and the Australian Institute of Marine Science (AIMS) are all now expected to obtain a significant proportion of their research expenditure (30 per cent in the CSIRO's case) from non-appropriation (government budget) sources and have introduced procedures for identifying and supporting priority areas of research. At the same time the federal government has ensured that primary industry-based research funding, collected through industry levies, is now also allocated competitively through research and development (R&D) corporations, and distributed to encourage public research organizations to be more active in commercializing research.

While the funding system has become more competitive, new group-ings and alliances have been formed that challenge traditional organi-zational boundaries. Cooperative agreements between research groups and business partners have emerged and old alliances have taken on new meaning as research managers accept the responsibility to manage the boundaries between science, industry, and commercial activities.

The increased organizational complexity of research institutes like the CSIRO has led to increased imperatives for interdependence within and beyond institutional boundaries. Occupational tasks and the career structures of research scientists and research managers in the organiza-tion have shifted dramatically. For scientists familiar with the independ-ence of the culture of 'modern science' that dominated the 1960s and 1970s, this shift is disorienting (Kash and Rycroft 1994).

As the organizational structures and the roles of scientists have changed, so too has the nature of tensions within the organization. During the 1970s and 1980s the major tension tended to be between scientists in their efforts to remain autonomous and managers imple-menting corporate demands for scientific relevance and organizational accountability. During this period the scientific values by which the work of scientists was judged became increasingly reorganized through strategic planning based on corporate expectations of relevance and accountability. As Flood (1984) observes, the strategic setting of corpo-rate objectives threatened this balance between industry and science. He describes the CSIRO of the 1980s as an organization that had changed in institutional style from one that supports autonomy to one with centralized direction, less individual freedom, increased bureaucracy, and more accountability requirements.

Our recent studies show that the organizational tensions of the 1990s are different. They are not so much associated with a 'redirection' of scientific research, a sharper focus on industrial application, or an in-creased emphasis on strategic planning. Rather, they implicate a range of 'new' commercial strategies and commercial symbols that are per-ceived to be driving and assessing the *value* of research.

During interviews we carried out with 200 scientists at the CSIRO there was a widely shared view that the research environments of the 1990s were substantially different from those of the 1980s. There was also widespread agreement that the organization and its scientists needed to adjust to these changes. The importance of industrial relevance and multidisciplinary team-based research – contentious in the 1980s – ap-peared deeply embedded in the broad expectations and organizational values articulated by the researchers we interviewed in the 1990s. These embedded values, however, stood in contrast to a markedly weak acceptance of commercial values that were described as impinging on the organization's capacity to produce scientific knowledge.

This tension in the 1990s is therefore not so much between researchers as 'autonomous scientists' and organizational demands for corporate objectives and judgments of outcomes. It is more between the scientific and socio-economic values that provide the cultural capital for 'relevant research' and the commercial values that provide the economic capital for the institutions themselves.

This is demonstrated in the struggle between the organizational and individual expectations about 'valuing' science. We asked over 100 scientists at the CSIRO to say what they preferred as the key evaluative factor for establishing industrially oriented projects and what they experienced as the current evaluative factor. More than half the respondents agreed that the key factor should be the potential of the project to contribute to national economic competitiveness. However, only 7 per cent experienced this as being the case in practice. Over 70 per cent felt that the current evaluation criterion was based simply on the capacity of the project to bring finances into their research division. Research programs are therefore experienced as being driven not by science or scientific relevance but by the notion of profit, a concept quite dislocated from the practice of science itself.

THE UNIVERSITY SYSTEM

The intrusion of commercial values and expectations has not been restricted to government research institutions. Similar events have been unfolding across the university system. In 1987 the Australian government ushered in a new era of higher education research. The reforms removed the college and university binary divide and created a Unified National System. This brought previous teaching-only institutions into the university research market-place, as well as whole new disciplines such as podiatry, nursing, occupational therapy, home economics, and other vocation-related subjects. As a result, the organizational and public expectations of academics have changed considerably.

The notion of the university as 'an assemblage of learned men, zealous for their own sciences, and rivals of each other ... brought by familiar intercourse and for the sake of intellectual peace, to adjust together the claims and relations of their respective subjects of investigation' stands in marked contrast to the expectations of higher education administrators today (de Lacey and Moens 1990: 3). Rather, the expectation of university leaders is to produce a unifiable and marketable commodity. As a senior university administrator told us: 'Our task is to homogenise the expectations of the different faculties, schools and individuals into a generally shared view about teaching and research; we need to bring disparate philosophies, ideas and expectations into a unified set of directions and objectives.'

The commercial market has entered the domain of university disciplines with a vengeance, and the organizational values, actions, and expectations within these institutions are rapidly changing. Universities are experiencing a major (and not unpainful) organizational and cultural transformation.

The university research environment, like public research institutions, has moved from one largely characterized by individual autonomy and local institutional decisions about priorities to one characterized by centralized policy and competitive institutional processes dominated by commercial market concerns. Through government policy instruments new amalgams of institutions have been steered towards developing research management plans and concentrating research effort into new organizational groupings. These groups are characteristically research 'centres,' research 'programs,' and research 'institutes' that straddle traditional departmental and institutional organizational boundaries. In a system-wide study of the Australian university research centres we identified over 800 that had been established since 1982 (Hill and Turpin 1993). This is in a national system of only 36 universities.

The trend towards the formation of research centres and multidisciplinary research has been underpinned by government policy since the early 1980s. Government funding programs have promoted collaborative research through the formation of Key Centres for Teaching and Research and Cooperative Research Centres (CRC). However, a range of other policy initiatives have both contributed and responded to the emergence of an 'enterprise culture' in Australian universities. Infrastructure funding mechanisms have promoted the sharing of major facilities, and project collaboration has been promoted through the provision of collaborative university and industry research grants. The National Health and Medical Research Council, the Australian Research Council, and the science ministry all have their own independent and competitive funding programs for supporting academic–industry collaboration. The generation of commercial capital for funding public science was increased for a period by the introduction of 'taxation havens' whereby private enterprises could invest profits in 'pooled development funds' managed by and financing university-owned commercial research companies. Further business capital investment in the public R&D system has been encouraged from the mid-1980s by a 150 per cent taxation concession for industry research (reduced to 125 per cent in 1997). Although the intention of this initiative was to increase R&D activity in the private sector, it provided an additional incentive for businesses to contract the public sector for specific research tasks (Turpin, Sullivan, and Deville 1993). Between 1981 and 1991 business sector funding for research in higher education increased by 74 per cent, and between 1991 and 1994 by a further 114 per cent (ABS 1996), indicating a considerable growth in direct industry and university research linkages.

New organizational structures known as offices of research were established to manage research within institutions. In a survey of universities, the Centre for Research Policy found that most universities had recently formulated rules for establishing, managing, and, if necessary, disbanding research centres. One of the key features of the rules was the management of multidisciplinary research and the relationship between centres and departmental structures. Thus, research-intensive business enterprises, public research institutes, and universities have increasingly sought new organizational models for collaborative arrangements (Turpin, Sullivan, and Deville 1993). The identification of performance indicators to measure research outputs is a feature of current research management concerns. Issues of quality, national relevance, and industry links are also high on university policy agendas. Like their counterparts in the public institutes, academics have felt the intrusion of commercial values to the very roots of their research experience.

Fissures in the System

The proliferation of university research centres illustrates the tensions at the boundaries of research organizations. The majority of these centres do not rely on university funding for their research activity, but draw on the host organization's institutional umbrella for basic infrastructure support and scientific status. Their structure, although governed by university rules, is not driven by traditional discipline-based university departments, but by a combination of interests that include those inherent in scientific disciplines, industry expectations, academic institutional aspirations, and commercial opportunities (Hill and Turpin 1993). The university rubric provides centres with 'a license to deal with [these] client groups,' as Turner (this volume) observes. The boundaries of disciplines, departments, working relationships, business activities and universities themselves are, in this situation, 'all up for grabs.'

In 1990 the Australian government embarked on one of its most ambitious reorganizations of science by establishing the Cooperative Research Centres program. Sixty-nine CRCs are now established. Each centre forms an organizational structure based on a contractually agreed-upon research program, typically incorporating at least one university and one business enterprise and including at least one public research institute. In one case there are eighteen separate partners and the centre has locations at six different national sites. The titles of the CRCs – such as Waste Management and Pollution Control – reflect their inter-disciplinarity and emphasis on socio-economic outcomes.

A critical question for the future is to what extent CRCs should remain linked to, or driven by, the science or industrial systems from which they grew. We observe an interesting contradiction for CRCs operating in a transdisciplinary context. On the one hand, they may be expected to achieve eventual financial autonomy, and thus forced to give more attention to short-term commercial research. To pursue the more fundamental research questions they will require access to existing basic research funding programs. Yet we question the capacity of the research councils in Australia to support both the CRCs and the basic research carried out within traditional university departments (Turpin 1997).

In this context, organizational behaviour within public research institutions and universities is appearing to be increasingly out of step with the research behaviour that takes place within them. The CSIRO responded to the imperatives of the 1980s by establishing a separate corporate commercial arm for the entire organization. Although this has now been disbanded and the business responsibilities have been devolved to the separate research divisions, the commercial activities and practices are still to a large degree centrally coordinated and controlled.

Universities are increasingly seeking to control research activities within their own institutional boundaries. In Australia this has given rise to varying forms of commercial 'companies' owned by individual universities. These enterprises intervene directly between academic researchers and the commercial world. In the aptly named *This Gown for*

Hire, Wing (1993: 6) describes how Australian vice-chancellors have grappled with the problem of integrating industrial firms with general campus activities and, in the process, given birth to a new profession of managers whose task is to 'motivate, keep motivated, and extract performance from academic staff.' Reflected here is a boundary struggle between the extended research networks of the academic and the commercial networks of the institution; at stake is the control of the research funds, the research directions, and, ultimately, the economic and social return from the research product.

Through organizational restructuring science has been relocated in organizational cultures that tend to be driven by markets rather than scientific discourse. The new missions and functions are diffuse rather than specialized, the expected skills are flexible rather than inflexible, and the internal activities are collectivized rather than individualized.

The importance of extra-organizational activities on the part of individuals and the controlling activities of research institutes and universities presents a paradox. The evidence suggests that a fundamental dislocation is emerging between the traditional organizational structures that seek to organize science and the activities that scientists are engaged in. Organizations' responses to changes in their environment have tended to focus on organizing structures and discourse to maintain control at their organizational boundaries. Yet at the same time the evidence emphasizes the critical importance of the individual as actor in inter-organizational networks that seek to transcend such boundaries. These findings are consistent with broader conclusions that personal networks and immediate personal relations are of crucial importance at the leading edge of new fields.

ORGANIZATIONAL TURBULENCE

The organizing and reorganizing activities that have taken place in science institutions during the past decade have given rise to new patterns of scientific communication. During our CSIRO study we asked respondents to record diary entries of internal and external professional contacts. Analysis showed that external contacts with industry and with universities were perceived as being far more important than internal contacts. These external contacts accounted for 40 per cent of all contacts. Internal contacts were considered more important in relation to administrative matters rather than to scientific or industrial application. Only 17 per cent of all respondents identified contacts within their own

TABLE 5.1
Multidisciplinarity in publications from Australian universities, 1991

Field of publication	Number of Journal articles (a)	Number of AOU* groups (b)	Multi-disciplinarity index**
Psychology	363	49	13.5
Education	969	49	5.1
Political science	633	44	6.9
Clinical science	3161	43	1.4
History	305	35	11.5
Economics	411	30	7.3
Genetics/Biotechnology	267	23	8.6
Organic chemistry	126	8	6.4
Inorganic chemistry	170	5	2.9

Source: Selected data from Hill and Murphy 1994, Table 3.10
*Academic Organizational Unit
**100/(a/b)

division as being their most important contacts. In contrast to the 'ivory tower' criticism leveled at the CSIRO in the past, we found that the communication patterns were, both in preferred terms and in practice, strongly externally focused and directed towards a wide range of applied and experimental activities (Turpin and Deville 1994).

System-wide surveys of the publications produced from Australian universities have shown that a considerable proportion of scientific literature is published in journals outside the field in which the original research was carried out, and, conversely, that 'academic organizational units' contribute many publications to journals outside their nominal field of research (Bourke and Butler 1993; Hill and Murphy 1994). Table 5.1 suggests, for example, that psychology journals draw from a wider range of research disciplines than do organic or inorganic chemistry journals.

Across all fields, personal networks lead the way in what researchers pay attention to and communicate (Hill and Murphy 1994). Citation analyses clearly show that new authors tend to cite previous publications from their home country rather than publications from overseas countries. Foreign citations follow with a considerable time lag.

These same sorts of communication patterns are important in the industrial context. In a study that covered all Australian universities and a sample of eighty industrial collaborators we found that university and industry links tended to be formed and maintained as a complex web of varying modes of relationships rather than a managed sequential chain of contacts. Industrialists and academics identified a rich network of participants with a wide array of activities and expected benefits. Respondents identified key researchers in each sector who acted as successful mediators at the 'interface,' whose contribution was usually based on their specific research skills as well as their experience with both industrial and academic sectors. Formal structures within the university were viewed ideally as supportive for research linkages rather than formative. In fact, in some cases we were told that research links were established *in spite* of structural difficulties rather than because of structural support (Turpin, Sullivan, and Deville 1993).

In some cases these links between academic researchers and their industrial counterparts were driven predominantly by industry, in others they were driven more by university researchers, and, in many, by a combination of both. But in all cases the importance of individual contacts was paramount. These activities are increasingly managed through hierarchical systems that claim to both protect the interests of the scientist and maintain control of the market activities (corporation). The scientists' workplace therefore includes at least four different meaningful social domains: a research knowledge domain, a research application domain, a commercial domain, and a management domain. Each is dominated by different sets of reward criteria, different sets of strategic objectives, different ways of measuring success, different modes of communication, and different forms of symbolic capital, supported by different forms of legitimating authority. The conceptual distinctions between the domains are summarized in Table 5.2.

In practice, however, most researchers in the 1990s are impelled, to varying degrees, to work across more than one of these social domains. Thus, the social boundaries between each domain are constantly negotiated by a range of actors including scientists, institutions, managers, and politicians in the course of their work. The socially defined status associated with occupational distinctions between scientists, technicians, administrative assistants, managers, and entrepreneurs was a feature of the research institutions of the 1970s and 1980s. In the 1990s, however, the distinctions are blurring. Scientists are increasingly expected to, and do in practice, manage their own activities across the different social domains (Turpin and Deville 1995). On the one hand, researchers are

TABLE 5.2
Domains of research work and associated cultural components

Cultural components	Domains of research work			
	Research	Application	Commercialization	Management
Predominant discourse	Science	Industrial	Market	Organizational
Major actors	Scientists	Industrialists	Business managers	Administrators
Predominant symbolic values	Excellence	Relevance	Money	Ownership
Predominant authority	Peers	Government/ Public opinion/ Peers	Market forces	Executive
	(Is it good science?)	(Does it work?)	(Is there profit?)	(Do we benefit?)

pressed by institutional policy to produce new science and are directed towards clearly defined socio-economic objectives. At the same time they are encouraged through various policy mechanisms to be concerned with securing and maintaining market niches for developing the commercial potential of that knowledge.

It is not surprising, therefore, that boundary struggles between these organizational domains have emerged. For example, scientists involved in our CSIRO study identified 'increased relevance to industry' as the 'most welcome change' in their organization. On the other hand, the largest category of responses concerning the 'least welcome change' was the increased emphasis on generating income.

Practical advances towards increased industrial relevance are made by scientists themselves, and through these emerging links they are extending the boundaries of research beyond traditional departmental structures. However, the management systems that have been introduced to manage the changing environment are often in conflict with these shifting boundaries.[2] At the heart of these tensions are the imposed modes of control on the researchers' activities. These modes of control are embedded at the institutional level but, importantly, they exist in abstract but powerful form beyond the institution, embedded in the symbols of the market.

Managing Interdisciplinarity

Our findings from empirical studies of the research system in Australia have significant implications for the practice and management of inter-disciplinary research and research training. These are, notably, the pressures to make science more relevant; the organization of science into small, multidisciplinary, application-oriented research teams; the blurring of organizational boundaries caused by interdisciplinary research groupings within discipline-based organizations; the increased links between research groups and socio-economic sectors; and the blurring of the boundaries between basic and applied research.

These observations lend support to international findings on changes in the organization of research and knowledge production, most notably those of Gibbons et al. (1994), with their Mode 2 (knowledge generation in the context of application) concept, and the Triple Helix (university-industry-government) model of Etzkowitz and Leydesdorff (1997). As van Raan (this volume) suggests, such 'horizontal' intersectoral research linkages are commonly, if not invariably, interdisciplinary by virtue of their focus on socio-economic problems. This point is emphasized by Ziman (1996: 74), who regards applied and industrial science as the true antecedents of Mode 2: 'The world of practice does not carve itself up neatly along the joints between the academic disciplines. In the context of application, all problems require a multidisciplinary approach ... The most radical feature of Mode 2 is that it strives to take a broader view than can be achieved from within any one discipline.'

Gibbons et al. (1994: 4–5) postulate four distinct features of trans-disciplinarity in their Mode 2 of knowledge formation. These are a distinct but evolving framework generated in the context of application that (a) is applied by the same group of practitioners that developed it (and by implication cannot be applied to a different context by a different group), and (b) cannot easily be reduced to disciplinary parts; the development of distinctive theoretical structures, methods, and practices that 'may not be located on the prevailing disciplinary map'; the communication and diffusion of the results by participation and through the movement of the original practitioners, rather than through the formal 'academic' channels of scientific papers and conferences; and the suggestion that the knowledge produced may not fit into the disciplines that contributed to the solution or be easily referred to disciplinary institutions or recorded as disciplinary contributions.

'Massification' of higher education, by diffusing technological and scientific knowledge and skills in society, has led to a greater 'social distribution' of knowledge production. By inference, this has produced greater competition between university-based research and other 'knowledge institutions' but also a greater potential for collaboration between them.

A related question concerns the future of disciplinary identities and transdisciplinary competencies. Gibbons concludes that multidisciplinary competencies can no longer be viewed as a secondary 'add-on' to the primary, largely disciplinary, identities. In future, 'a portfolio of identities and competencies will have to be managed, none of which need to be pre-eminent' (Gibbons et al. 1994: 165). Again, this reflects our experience in Australia and represents a major challenge for researchers and intermediary agencies such as research councils.

These practical issues of managing interdisciplinarity lie at the heart of recent work that CRP has carried out for the Australian Research Council (ARC). The ARC is in essence a 'traditional' university research council, allocating research and scholarship/fellowship funding on the basis of a disciplinary peer review of proposals submitted by university researchers. Like research councils in other countries, the ARC has responded to demands from government and higher education institutions to provide support for multidisciplinary research centres, major national facilities for use by researchers from a range of disciplines, and university-industry collaborative arrangements in research and training. While none of these initiatives could be described as merely 'add-ons' to the ARC's 'discipline-based' funding role, the Council is clearly grappling to achieve an appropriate balance between its discipline-focused and multidisciplinary or industry-collaborative programs. The federal government has increased significantly the funding for ARC's university–industry collaborative programs, at a time when funding for higher education research is generally tight (McGauran 1996). But the Cooperative Research Centres program – Australia's largest and most successful intersectoral and interdisciplinary collaborative research program – was set up not by the ARC, but under the prime minister's portfolio, and now resides in the science and industry department.

With the ARC as client and partner, CRP is pursuing two streams of research. The first relates to information on the types of intersectoral links that are established; their genesis, structure, and networks, and how they obtain, exchange, and disseminate knowledge; and the role played by particular types of intermediary or government programs.

The second is aimed at producing a more general 'national map' of the importance assigned by particular socio-economic sectors to different research disciplines in general, and disciplinary groups in the academic or public research sectors in particular.

Our objective is to provide empirical evidence to inform the following issues: what provokes interdisciplinarity – is it primarily a response to socio-economic application of research and to specific external markets? What 'bureaucratic circumstances' (in Turner's words, this volume) or other organizational factors influence how multidisciplinary research groupings form, are structured, and are sustained? What are the universal and national characteristics of Mode 2 knowledge formation? Is Mode 2 operation independent of research discipline, that is, are university researchers in a particular field of research more or less likely to be drawn into interdisciplinary collaboration, particularly with industry partners, than those in other fields? Are the 'basic' or 'applied' research groups more likely to be drawn into collaboration with industry and other 'users' – or is this typology of R&D activity no longer relevant? What analytical methods are effective in tracing the evolution of university–industry linkages?

Interdisciplinary Trends in the Socio-economic Connections of Academic Research

We illustrate our findings by reference to two studies completed in 1996 (Turpin et al. 1996a, b). 'Using Basic Research' aimed to demonstrate the value and the social and economic benefit of public investments in academic research, and to assist the ARC in a strategic assessment of how funds should be invested optimally across the disciplines and across interdisciplinary programs.

The study focused on assessing the status and nature of links between basic research and national socio-economic objectives through a methodology that reflected the flows of both codified and tacit knowledge. The study had as its premise that there are indeed external clients and markets for basic academic research. It explored the relationship between basic research and socio-economic activity from three different perspectives. First, the links were examined from the industrial perspective – documented through a major national survey of nearly 600 R&D-performing companies and organizations and through case-studies. The second perspective was drawn from the experiences of academic researchers. This was documented from a national survey of academic researchers and was supported with analyses of higher education research funding data and information on the employment of research-trained graduates. The third perspective was a 'technology perspective' drawn from the scientific literature cited in patents. The overall analysis was complemented with information collected through twenty case studies covering a wide range of socio-economic sectors.

What is interesting is the remarkable consistency in the conclusions drawn from the different data. For example, we found a general concordance between industry perspectives on the importance of various fields of research, and those fields that were predominant in citations to the literature in industrial patents.

INTERDISCIPLINARITY: AN INDUSTRIAL PERSPECTIVE

The key question that the surveys were designed to answer was 'What is the nature of the linkage between particular fields of research and various socio-economic objectives?' The data collected through the industry survey allowed for an analysis of the nature of the links between various fields of research (and groups of fields) and different socio-economic objectives, and of the importance placed on them by industry respondents, all of whom were R&D performers themselves.

Table 5.3 shows the importance (on a 5-point scale) that industry respondents placed on particular research fields for their general innovation activities. The question enabled data to be collected according to (a) a research field generally, (b) research carried out by universities, and (c) research carried out in government research institutes.

Respondents were classed as users or non-users of basic research, on the basis of their own R&D activities. Not surprisingly, the users placed a higher importance on research generally and across all research fields. Interestingly, the greatest difference in importance between the two groups was in the applied and biological sciences fields. This could be because links between universities and industry in these fields are more direct. Overall, the fields of research that produced the highest scores were information technology, applied sciences, and engineering.

For all fields of research, respondents placed a higher value on a field of research generally than they did on the same research field carried out in universities. However, the difference in importance (within fields of research) between university research and research generally varies. For example, in earth and biological sciences, medicine, and the humanities, university research seems to be almost as important as the

TABLE 5.3
Importance of fields of research for research users: Universities and government
research institutes

Field of research	Basic research users (importance score)			Non-basic research users (importance score)		
	All	Univ.	Govt.	All	Univ.	Govt.
Mathematical sciences	1.7	1.4	1.3	1.3	0.9	0.9
Physical sciences	1.8	1.5	1.4	1.4	1.0	1.0
Chemical sciences	2.1	1.7	1.7	1.6	1.1	1.1
Earth sciences	1.4	1.3	1.3	0.9	0.8	0.8
Information technology	2.8	2.2	2.0	2.4	1.5	1.4
Applied sciences	2.8	2.2	2.1	2.0	1.4	1.3
General engineering	2.6	1.9	1.8	2.3	1.4	1.4
Biological sciences	1.8	1.6	1.6	1.1	1.0	1.0
Agricultural sciences	1.6	1.3	1.4	1.0	0.8	0.9
Medical and health sciences	1.7	1.5	1.4	1.0	0.8	0.8
Social sciences	1.4	1.2	1.1	0.9	0.8	0.8
Humanities	1.1	1.0	0.9	0.8	0.7	0.7

Source: Turpin et al. 1996a, Table 12

research field generally. Further, for those fields where the variation between university and general research is greatest, it appears less acute among the users group. Separating the basic research users from non-users in this analysis allows us to observe in more detail the research areas in which industry is more directly reliant on university research (which is likely to be more basic). The more reliant areas appear to be earth, biological, medical, and social science. The less university-dependent areas appear to be engineering, applied, and information sciences. These areas were identified as being more important generally, so it is likely that the lesser reliance is due to a greater level of in-house research in these fields. In other words, firms are not necessarily looking to universities for support in their most important research area – a point reinforced by case-studies.

IDENTIFYING INTERDISCIPLINARY LINKS THROUGH THE MOVEMENT OF PEOPLE

The survey also sought information on the disciplinary backgrounds of doctoral researchers employed by the company. A total of 6837 PhD graduates were identified across the 594 organizations surveyed. From this sample, it was possible to identify areas where particular fields of research appeared to be closely linked with particular socio-economic (SEO) categories. This is shown in Table 5.4, where we see that chemistry graduates were mostly employed among organizations in the manufacturing SEO subdivision. Mathematical science graduates were concentrated primarily in the 'advancement of knowledge' SEO and information industry SEOs. Physics graduates were also mainly concentrated in manufacturing, but they were generally spread more widely across a range of industrial SEOs. Biological scientists were distributed mainly between plant production and health-related SEOs, and agricultural scientists primarily in plant production.

From the patterns of distribution that emerged two sorts of links can be observed: links where disciplinary research skills are widely dispersed across a range of SEOs, and links where they are concentrated in particular SEOs. The more concentrated fields include the chemical, agricultural, and medical sciences. The more dispersed fields include the mathematical, physical, earth, applied, and biological sciences.

Comparison of the organization's main fields of research investment with the field of qualification of their doctoral researchers showed that in many cases companies are employing people from a wider range of research disciplines than their current R&D would seem to require. We concluded that frequently it is the broad body of experience and knowledge the PhDs bring with them that is valued by industry. Thus, it is not that companies engage these people *for* specific research knowledge, rather *because* they have fundamental research knowledge and training.

INTERDISCIPLINARITY: A TECHNOLOGY PERSPECTIVE

Analysis of the citations to scientific literature contained in patents provides a partial indicator of codified knowledge flows between research and technology. This analysis shares the limitations of all patent-based indicators in that important but less tangible technologies such as software will be poorly represented, and newly emerging technologies and patenting companies may be deliberately disguised.

We examined Australian patents registered in the United States for the period 1984 to 1994 in order to identify which *fields* of research were providing the antecedent science for the development of particular products or technologies.[3] Seven leading product groups or subfields (i.e., those with the highest number of citations over the period) account for

83 per cent of all coded citations in the data set. Figure 5.1 presents the number of citations appearing in each field of research for selected patent product fields and subfields over the eleven-year period. The data suggest that, for example: professional and scientific instrument patents heavily cite literature in physics, chemistry, and medicine. Miscellaneous electrical machinery patents are almost wholly linked to the medical and health sciences literature (this subfield includes patents in advanced medical prosthetic devices where Australian companies are strong patentees). Drug and medicine patents predominantly cite literature in the medical and biological sciences, but also in chemistry, agricultural sciences, and physics. Organic chemical patents cite almost exclusively biological sciences, medical and health sciences, and chemistry. Electronic component patents cite information science and technology, engineering, and physical sciences.

A NATIONAL MAP OF DISCIPLINARY AND INTERDISCIPLINARY CONNECTIONS

An important conclusion to emerge from the study was that basic research investment in many fields is contributing to a wide range of socio-economic objectives – and therefore external 'clients' – beyond simply the advancement of knowledge. This conclusion is not only true for those research fields that are more applied in orientation, but also for many of the more basic fields of research.

While many industrial enterprises identified a major research field that supported their own R&D activities they also identified other fields that were connected to those activities. We used data from the study to generate a schematic 'map' or set of matrices of the primary and secondary connections between basic research and socio-economic objectives. A summary of the links that emerged consistently through all data sets is shown in Figure 5.2.

Figure 5.2 illustrates the way that some fields of research contribute quite specifically and deeply to core categories of socio-economic activity, while others contribute more broadly across a range of socio-economic activities. For example, applied and engineering sciences – fields that contribute extensively to manufacturing – are also strongly connected to energy resources and supply, construction, transport, and environment. Chemistry – another research field contributing significantly to manufacturing – is also strongly connected to mineral resources and plant and animal production and primary products. On the other hand, medicine and health, and agricultural sciences are more

TABLE 5.4
Socio-economic objective of employer by field of research of PhD-trained staff

Main socio-economic objective of employer	Field of PhD study of employees												
	Mathematics	Physics	Chemistry	Earth sciences	Applied information and communication	Science and technology	General engineering	Biology	Agriculture	Medicine	Social sciences	Humanities	n =
Defence	0.6	6.2	0.0	0.0	0.9	0.9	1.7	0.0	0.0	0.0	0.0	0.0	44
Plant production	3.1	0.0	2.1	22.5	1.3	3.5	1.2	31.0	83.4	0.0	5.0	8.9	1265
Animal production	0.6	2.8	2.1	0.0	0.5	1.5	0.4	1.5	2.8	0.8	0.0	0.0	87
Mineral resources	3.1	4.8	22.2	14.2	2.9	5.5	5.4	0.3	0.0	1.9	0.0	0.0	331
Energy resources	0.6	0.0	0.3	5.0	0.0	1.3	0.5	0.2	0.0	0.0	0.0	0.0	26
Energy supply	0.6	3.4	1.4	0.0	0.3	0.7	3.5	0.0	0.0	0.0	3.0	0.0	70
Manufacturing	13.8	24.1	54.8	1.7	51.2	37.6	46.5	11.8	2.5	8.5	1.3	13.3	1944
Construction	1.9	2.1	3.3	0.8	1.8	6.0	7.4	0.0	0.0	0.0	0.7	6.7	176
Transport	1.3	2.1	0.1	0.8	0.5	13.9	12.1	0.0	0.1	0.0	0.7	0.0	249
Information and communication services	25.8	13.1	1.8	5.0	25.4	4.8	6.6	0.4	0.1	0.4	2.3	15.6	459
Commercial services	5.7	2.8	1.1	0.8	4.9	1.6	2.4	0.2	0.1	0.0	3.4	0.0	122
Economic framework	0.0	0.7	0.0	0.0	0.1	0.1	0.3	0.0	0.0	0.0	0.0	0.0	6

													n
Health	3.8	13.8	7.4	0.0	4.8	18.0	4.0	28.3	0.0	74.8	17.1	2.2	1033
Education and training	4.4	0.7	0.1	3.3	1.3	0.5	0.4	2.1	0.0	0.6	3.4	13.3	74
Social development and community services	1.3	0.0	0.3	0.0	2.3	0.3	1.6	0.0	0.0	0.0	35.9	11.1	158
Environmental knowledge	1.9	6.2	0.7	17.5	0.0	0.3	1.5	6.1	1.3	0.0	0.0	0.0	131
Environmental aspects of economic development	1.3	6.2	1.2	20.8	0.9	1.2	2.2	3.9	3.0	0.0	0.0	0.0	157
Environmental management	0.0	0.0	0.0	1.7	0.0	0.1	0.3	0.1	0.0	0.0	0.0	0.0	7
Advancement of knowledge: Natural science	28.9	11.0	1.0	5.0	0.7	2.1	2.1	12.9	6.6	13.0	0.3	4.4	388
Social sciences/humanities	1.3	0.0	0.1	0.8	0.0	0.0	0.0	1.3	0.0	0.0	27.5	24.4	110
All SEOs	100	100	100	100	100	100	100	100	100	100	100	100	
n =	159	145	726	120	991	748	1072	1023	995	515	298	45	6837

Source: Turpin et al. 1996a, Tables 23 and 24

FIGURE 5.1
Literature citations to fields of research by leading product groups, Australian patents in the United States, 1984-94

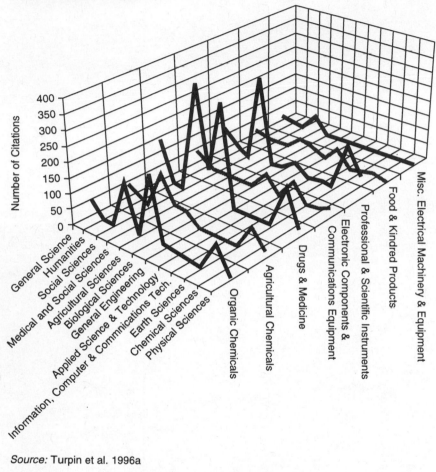

Source: Turpin et al. 1996a

deeply (but narrowly) linked to the health and the plant and animal production and primary products socio-economic categories, respectively. It is important to note, however, that these connections are not exclusive. A finer analysis showed that there are many supporting or 'spot' links that can be identified at the project level.

Some research fields contribute directly and some indirectly. Further, some fields contribute over a short span of time, and some contribute over much longer periods – much shorter in information and communication services than in health or mineral resources, for example.

In order to understand these patterns, one needs also to examine the characteristics of the linkages among universities, government R&D, and industry. Although most research–industry links are a two-way process, providing benefits to each participant, nevertheless different patterns can be observed. We find a qualitative difference between those links generated initially from industry and those that develop from innovative ideas within universities (Turpin, Sullivan, and Deville 1993), as well as in the patterns of links built around a wide industry focus and those built more around a core technology or resource. This leads us to identify four types of research–industry links: *Type 1:* Science-driven linkages built around a wide range of technologies and applications; *Type 2:* Science-driven linkages built around a leading edge in a specific area of science; *Type 3:* Industry-driven links built around a wide range of research fields and industrial applications; and *Type 4:* Industry-driven links built around maintaining a leading-edge core technology.

Some characteristics of these different types of linkages can be summarized as follows:

• **Type 1. Science-driven socio-economic linkages built around a wide range of technologies and applications:** Communication of knowledge in these types of links tends to be through a wide range of possibilities. The main focus is on maintaining access to advances in science that have as yet not been fully utilized. The emphasis is therefore on using existing science rather than generating new science (although the latter can be a consequence of the former). Universities tend to be the key organizations in these sorts of links. Scientific knowledge for these links tends to be drawn from codified sources available in the public domain. Therefore, direct collaboration between industry and universities is often built around joint ventures protected with contractual agreements. These structured arrangements tend to *follow* the link rather than create it. An important feature of these links is that they often emerge a considerable time after the basic science advances have been made. The links are made when an industrial application and science become aligned.

Figure 5.2
Summary of links between socio-economic objectives and academic research in Australia

Socio-economic objective	Main field of research											
	Mathematical sciences	Physical sciences	Chemical sciences	Earth sciences	Information and communications technology	Applied science and technology	General engineering	Biological science	Agricultural science	Medical and health sciences	Social sciences	Humanities
Economic development												
Plant and animal production and primary products			P					P	P			
Mineral resources			P	P		S	S					
Energy resources and supply			S	P		S	P				S	
Manufacturing			P		S	P	P	S				
Construction			S		S	P	P					
Transport					S	P	P					
Information and communication services	S	S			P	S	S				S	

Commercial services	s				s		s		s	
Society										
Health	s			s		s			P	P P
Education and training				s			P			P P
Social development				s					P	P
Environment	s	P	s	s	P	P		s	P P	P
Advancement of knowledge	s	P	s	s	s	s	P	s	P s	P

Source: After Turpin et al. 1996a, Table 31

Excludes SEO of Defense; P = primary links; s = secondary links

Some of the links between agricultural science and plant and animal production provide examples of this type of link.

- **Type 2: Science-driven socio-economic linkages built around a leading edge in a specific area of science:** These links are driven primarily by major advances in a particular field of science. They emerge when a new technology intersects with social and economic imperatives for whole new industry areas. Examples include biotechnology industries and waste management, which create new commercial niches to be filled by new or newly aligned commercial companies. All forms of communication are important, but a major emphasis is placed on maintaining the leading-edge science base. Therefore, basic research remains a critical activity. The latest literature is scanned rigorously, and long-term projects are maintained to press the knowledge further. The applications, however, tend to be 'fast track,' so timing is critical. The basic research activities thus tend to be science-driven, but the applied development work is market-driven. Because of the importance of maintaining the science base, collaboration between universities and research institutions plays an important role.
- **Type 3: Industry-driven socio-economic linkages built around a wide range of research fields and industrial applications:** These are the fast-moving links driven by industry and utilizing a wide range of scientific fields. Specific fields of research are valued not so much for their scientific base, but for their capacity to open up new market or socio-economic opportunities. Science, embodied in creative experts, can solve many problems and shorten the road to market. From the scientists' perspective, being involved in such activities provides resources and ideas for more distantly related basic research activities. The role of PhD graduates in these sorts of links is not connected so much to the field of research of their PhD training but more to the creative capacities they have built up. These sorts of links tend to be more associated with fast-moving industries, such as information technology. But they also involve a wide range of socio-economic activities that service other large industrial sectors. Business systems design and medical instrument manufacturing are examples.
- **Type 4: Industry-driven socio-economic linkages built around maintaining a leading-edge core technology:** Communication of knowledge in these cases is likely to be structured through joint ventures and contracted research as well as long-term informal

contacts with academics across a range of universities. New knowledge is gathered primarily through people rather than through literature or patents. Because of the crucial importance of core technology, planning can be long-term, with many projects and programs contributing to an overall long-term objective. Basic research as a training platform for research is particularly valued. In-house contributions to international knowledge are valued because they enhance organizational status. Much of the new knowledge emerges *from* structured arrangements such as contract research and joint programs, rather than leading *to* them. Advances in science tend to be generated or stimulated by the industrial requirements. Industry examples include mineral extraction and processing, steel and steel product manufacturing, and advanced medical prosthetics.

These characteristics illustrate the different ways that science is used by industry and that industry is used by science. In other words, the links are not a simple unidirectional process but embedded in a highly dynamic social process. Although, in practice, many individual cases fit somewhere between the four types of links, the typology nevertheless serves to emphasize the different patterns of strategies, objectives, and expectations that are in play.

In Figure 5.3, we see a specific Type 3 arrangement – an industry-driven collaboration drawing on public-sector research and training expertise in fields as diverse as management, economics, food technology, agriculture, and biosciences. Our example is the winegrape and wine industry in Australia. The industry involves a large number of small primary producers, a smaller number of medium to large wine producers, and an even smaller number of universities. Structured collaborative links are a major feature for all modes of cooperation. Training links and research links between the sectors have existed for some time, however, it is only recently that the various mechanisms have become integrated. Agencies such as the Grape and Wine R&D Corporation, the Wine Research Institute, the Wine Industry National Education and Training Council, and the Australian Viticulture Council play a critical role in mediating between industry and the university sector. They collect levies, distribute research funds, establish priorities, and are formative in steering long-term plans for training and R&D. A relatively new CRC for viticulture brings together the universities (one of which has its own vineyard and winery), wine producers, and related supporting industries.

Figure 5.3
The wine and winegrape industry in Australia – A Type 3 link generated through intermediary agencies

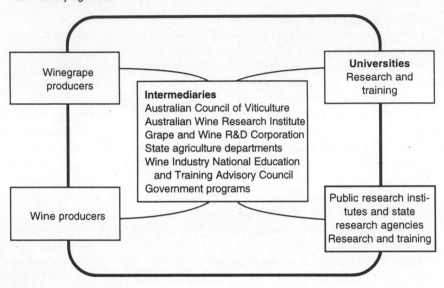

Source: Turpin et al. 1996b

Conclusions: Practising and Managing Interdisciplinarity

What are the implications of the data presented here for those interested in managing or practising interdisciplinarity, whether from the university or research institution point of view, or from that of the government policy maker or research funding council?

Managerialism and the 'enterprise culture' have turned public knowledge-producing cultures towards market-place values. New local organizational cultures with their multidisciplinary approaches, the movements of tacit knowledge and people, and the immediacy of personal face-to-face relations have thus paradoxically emerged in the foreground of knowledge creation. Local culture and local knowledge generation and capture have assumed an entirely new power within a global culture that is driven by market responsiveness.

The 'new' science institutions are driven by commercial imperatives and seek to be flexible in order to establish market niches or enclaves. They rely on formalized network structures for innovation, efficiency, and the 'competitive market edge.' Such structures are often loose-knit and complex, inherently unpredictable, and disorienting (Kash and Rycroft 1994: 39).

Paradoxically, this act of managing the network boundaries both liberates and constrains the production and dissemination of knowledge. On the one hand science escapes the cultural hegemony of academic disciplines and institutional structures. At the same time, however, science becomes subject to the vagaries of the market and the commercialization of academic pursuits (see Cohen 1993). To engage in science in this context therefore engages one in a struggle between scientific cultures – between the organizational forms that seek to own and gain economic benefit from investments in science and the working practitioners of science.

We need and are getting, whether we like it or not, new organizational forms. The proliferation of centres is creating strains and challenges, and it is not yet clear what their role in the research system will be in the long term. The formation of socio-economically oriented, interdisciplinary centres such as CRCs may well be the Australian harbingers of organizations that are neither universities nor research institutes, and neither entirely public nor private.

With the entry of the commercial market directly into the knowledge system, the symbols that steer knowledge production, such as first discovery prestige, reputational status, and attributed authority (all part of the disciplinary 'market') become *replaced* by symbols of the commercial market-place.

The present research system is certainly more competitive and less restrained by organizational boundaries than it was a decade ago. Research communication and collaboration are taking place in different organizational contexts. New forms of organized research are emerging that are directly confronting disciplinary, sectoral, and corporate research boundaries.

We are observing in Australia many of the trends in the diffusion of knowledge creation and the breaking down of single-disciplinary research and training structures that have been identified in other countries. Significant and far-reaching changes are taking place in the way that academic research is funded, carried out, and linked to other socio-economic activities. We also see industry-linked research and training activities moving within the same organizations. This has led to what we term the 'disorganization' of many of the structures that have traditionally supported academic research and their 'reorganization' in new ways, involving interaction between individuals and agencies representing government, industry, and the research sector.

This is an international, or rather multinational, trend that is not restricted to the most advanced industrial countries (Turpin, Garrett-Jones, and Rankin 1996; Turpin and Garrett-Jones 1997). Our typology of linkages can be observed in different countries, although the balance between industry-driven and science-driven linkages varies. The shift to Mode 2 knowledge production is not some independent event occurring in isolation. It is both contributing to, and a product of, structural changes at the interfaces of universities and industrial enterprises – and its interpretation requires a grasp of these processes.

Therein lies the benefit of the national 'mapping' approach, supported by specific case-studies of university–industry interaction. In contrast to our typology of linkages, we would expect the 'map' to look quite different in different countries, reflecting their national research capabilities, as well as their technological and commercial strengths.

As industry becomes more closely involved with academic research, the boundaries between many fields of research are being renegotiated. The impact is more pronounced in some fields than in others, but the net effect (in those fields most closely allied with industry) is a process of adaptation (Turpin and Garrett-Jones 1997). Whether data such as those presented here reflect a trend towards further interdisciplinary research per se, or whether the impetus to interdisciplinary research is provided predominantly through knowledge creation 'in the context of application' remains an open question. The data imply that some disciplines are more likely than others to be drawn into interdisciplinary collaboration in the context of application. Prima facie, we might expect those fields of research on our 'national map' that contribute in common to the same socio-economic objectives to be more likely to form an interdisciplinary alliance than those that contribute to different objectives.

It would therefore seem inappropriate to implement policy initiatives aimed at managing interdisciplinary activities without taking full account of the various *ways* through which academic research is linked to social and economic activities in a particular country. Policy options should be developed and considered for the impact they might have for different *types* of links and for different groupings of research disciplines.

The opportunities provided by the force of this 'new localism' is perhaps the 'big idea' that has emerged as society sets itself for the new millennium. Capturing these opportunities requires building organizational forms (frequently interdisciplinary) conducive to science, technology, innovation, and local cultures. Concurrently, there is a critical need to ensure that the integrity of science (with its disciplinary foundation) is maintained. At stake is the continued production of new knowledge, as well as the maintenance of sustainable economic and social development.

Notes

We thank our present and former colleagues in the Centre for Research Policy, especially Stephen Hill, whose work has contributed to this paper. Julie Klein, Peter Weingart, David Edge, and three anonymous referees provided helpful comments on drafts of the paper.

1 This paper summarizes and updates two papers presented at the "Interdisciplinarity" conferences at Bielefeld in 1995 and Vancouver in 1997 (see References).
2 Wasser (1990) has described this shift in activity as creating an identity crisis among universities where 'the qualitative change is so radical that the very identity of the university and the justification for even using the term itself may be called into question.' Keat (1991) has noted that British academics complain that their research 'is now being judged by intellectually facile considerations of "marketability."'
3 This is feasible only where the product group in question is sufficiently large, has a large number of citations, and where the citations are not predominantly to multidisciplinary journals ('General Science' in Figure 5.1).

PART III

NURTURING ENVIRONMENTS OF INTERDISCIPLINARITY

Scientific disciplines are both intellectual and social structures, or, one may say, the social organizations of intellectual work. This means that they are frames of reference for intellectual work, and at the same time they are, like other organizations, involved in demarcating, defending, and promoting that work vis-à-vis other organizations. That is, they are in the business of representing 'interests.' This does not preclude cooperation and, in rare cases, even fusion. But the normal experience is one of the development, over considerable periods of time, of separate cultures, distinct vocabularies, and insulated practices. What unites scientific disciplines and brings them occasionally into conflict is their common métier: they are all part of science, and they depend on the same sources for resources and public recognition. For those very reasons the generally positive connotations associated with the project of interdisciplinarity are counter-factual. Interdisciplinary research takes place where a commonality of *intellectual* interests emerges, and even then robust disciplinary social structures present obstacles because their removal is much slower and more cumbersome than the crossing of intellectual boundaries. This divergence of organizational structures and intellectual development is a continuous concern in the discourse on interdisciplinarity. It may plausibly be claimed that this prevalent view underestimates the extent to which organizational structures in fact constitute intellectual perspectives and their boundaries and the degree to which organizational attributes are inscribed into cognitive perspectives. Thus, in order to probe the potential for a crossing of both organizational and intellectual boundaries, it is necessary to examine the actual practices of interdisciplinary research, the organizational environments and intellectual work embedded in them as well as the interaction between them.

Starting at the psychological level, Rainer Bromme in his contribution points out that *empirical* attention paid to interdisciplinary work to date has been minuscule compared to the extensive and repeated *endorsement* of interdisciplinary activity. Such inattention is particularly pronounced when it comes to approaches that are psychologically informed.

Bromme develops a psychological approach to interdisciplinarity that focuses on knowledge structures. In particular, he asks what the conditions are for the possibility of effective communication and cooperation among researchers with different conceptual domains. Bromme concurs with those perspectives on cognitive development generally and interdisciplinary interaction in particular that have argued that a confrontation of diverse knowledge systems is not so much an impediment but a distinct asset for the production of 'new' knowledge. He surveys some of the relevant psychological approaches and experiments and concludes that the deliberate and conscious self-examination of one's own perspective and that of the other often is a crucial vehicle for the possible emergence of cognitive commonalties among various interlocutors.

In his paper on the genesis and development of individualized graduate interdisciplinary degree programs at the University of British Columbia, Rhodri Windsor Liscombe illustrates that interdisciplinary work not only is frequently demanded but also successfully practised. His contribution moves us more specifically towards the analysis of the broader social and institutional basis for nurturing interdisciplinarity. He concludes that the crossing of boundaries among and within disciplines in the process of generating novel knowledge requires sustained but malleable administrative and faculty support.

Marc De Mey examines, as a participant observer and using an evolutionary perspective, the recent history of cognitive science that originated about two decades ago as an offshoot of artificial intelligence research. Cognitive science is a relatively new field, organized, in this case in the form of a *centre for advanced research* at a major university in the United States, as an intellectual endeavour or a form of interdisciplinarity in action. De Mey finds general support for the notion that the adoption, intervention, and migration of procedures, perspectives, and persons unfamiliar to its practitioners often are instrumental in allowing for the possibility of cognitive displacement and therefore what soon constitutes an intellectual breakthrough. De Mey describes the organization of both teaching and research activities in cognitive science and the interdisciplinarity of the emergent field as a communication structure that is evidently superimposed on disciplinary alignments. He finds that interdisciplinary commitments are particularly strong among faculty but observes that interdisciplinarity is displayed in a surprisingly low-key way.

Shifting to the different organizational context of an institute of advanced study, Sabine Maasen analyses the social organization and intellectual work of an *interdisciplinary group* that worked on the 'biological foundations of human culture' and resided at the Center for Interdisciplinary Research in Bielefeld, Germany. The Center was set up and designed to facilitate the flexible organization, communication, and migration of ideas and scholars across more or less visible cognitive boundaries in the general pursuit of agreed-upon thematic issues. In addition to a description of the general context within which interdisciplinarity is practised at the Center, Maasen describes the steps taken to organize the research group, how it functioned during the academic year of its official lifetime, the evolving formal and informal interaction among its members, and their emerging intellectual concerns. She even carries her account to the period afterwards, when the product of the group a substantial anthology, was produced. The production of the book, *Human by Nature*, was itself a major task and lesson in interdisciplinary practice. The gist of Maasen's analysis is the reciprocity of the group's social organization and its intellectual work. The tension between 'irresistibility' and 'infliction' of interdisciplinarity is extensively documented and acts as a major metaphor of the case study.

Eric Scerri inquires into the institutional and cognitive context of interdisciplinary scientific practice in research institutes that are explicitly set up to foster and encourage such work. The specific case he examines is one of the four major Beckman Institutes that are designed to carry out interdisciplinary natural science research. The present-day Beckman Institute located at the California Institute of Technology benefits, in the first instance, from the well-established styles and traditions of interdisciplinarity at Caltech dating from the 1920s, when the astronomer George Ellery Hale recruited top faculty to Pasadena.

Scerri explores the notion that the possibility of interdisciplinary practice is fostered by what might be called a convergence in methodological assumptions, instruments, and approaches among different specialties. The fields that are represented at the Beckman Institute, which began operating in 1989, are primarily chemistry and biology. On the basis of four interviews, Scerri establishes a portrait of the academic journeys and practices of contemporary natural science 'interdisciplinarians' and describes some of the persistent institutional barriers in the form of traditional university structures to the practice of interdisciplinarity.

The final contribution to this section is by Rogers Hollingsworth and Ellen Jane Hollingsworth. Based on comparative and narrative methods, as well as a historical approach, the authors examine which *structural and cultural characteristics of research organizations* influence the making of major discoveries in twentieth-century biomedical sciences. A comparison of institutions with different success rates and at different times in their history yields a portrait of the central properties of research organizations that are associated with scientific breakthroughs. Two extensive case studies of highly integrated but small research institutes are presented in detail. The examples of the Rockefeller Institute/ University and the California Institute of Technology indicate that two concepts are significantly associated with repeated major discoveries: interdisciplinary and integrated culture across diverse fields of science, and a leadership form that gave particular attention to creating and maintaining a nurturing environment accompanied by rigorous standards of scholarship.

As research organizations respond to the growing complexity of fields of knowledge and increase in size and diversity, they tend to experience more social and cognitive differentiation, which is in turn accompanied by increases in hierarchy and bureaucratic coordination. These transformations tend to be associated with a decline in the possibility of major discoveries, although they may lead to the production of a significant number of scientific papers. Hollingsworth and Hollingsworth discuss strategies for adding diversity and enhancing integration in such large research organizations.

6

Beyond One's Own Perspective: The Psychology of Cognitive Interdisciplinarity

RAINER BROMME

Only rarely has interdisciplinary thought and behaviour been made the object of empirical-psychological research. Existing empirical studies on work in research laboratories have mostly been carried out from a microsociological perspective and are based mainly on qualitative methods. In addition, there have been surveys and case studies by researchers about experience with interdisciplinary research, as well as bibliometrical studies (Kocka 1987; Klein 1990, 1996; Weingart 1995a; Parthey 1996). In contrast, psychological studies on the conditions and processes of interdisciplinarity are virtually absent.

In what does a specifically psychological perspective on interdisciplinarity consist? In this essay, I will try to answer that question. My intention is to sketch some empirically treatable questions on the cognitive conditions and processes of interdisciplinary thought and activity.[1] The first part will discuss some obvious psychological variables, like the individual traits of the researchers involved in interdisciplinary projects. It will be shown, however, that the factors that at first glance are considered to be psychological do not really represent a viable approach to the psychological analysis of interdisciplinarity. Instead, I would like to make the *differences between disciplinary (and subdisciplinary) conceptual structures the principal point of departure.* Hence, I propose to analyse interdisciplinarity by way of a research focus on the processes of confrontation between different structures of knowledge, or perspectives.

For the sake of developing a psychological approach on interdisciplinarity, the phenomenon of interdisciplinarity will be reduced to the cognitive prerequisites and consequences of communication between interacting persons endowed with different conceptual structures. The confrontation of different perspectives is a condition for any kind of cognitive development (cf. Schön 1963), both in interdisciplinary dialogue and in individual thought. Even where individual thought tackles a new perspective, an encounter of hitherto different perspectives occurs. Nevertheless, the following analysis will be confined to the confrontation of perspectives taken by at least two persons.

Why Personality Variables Do Not Offer a Viable Approach for Psychological Studies of Interdisciplinarity

From the perspective of other disciplines, psychology is commonly expected to analyse the *personal* conditions of human activity. In order to understand why humans differ in their actions and views, why some relate well to others while some have difficulties doing so, one must get to know people's individual traits and motives. Psychology is expected to provide an analysis of such personal traits.

The debate on interdisciplinarity contains many hints that personal traits matter in interdisciplinary work. One example is the identity or ego-strength of the persons that may collaborate. Often, interdisciplinary work is like moving about in foreign territory. Participants in such work must have sufficiently strong personal identities to abide with situations where fundamental assumptions about the legitimacy of their own discipline-specific views are challenged, or where the latters' self-evidence remains at least unaccepted (cf. Schneider 1988). Furthermore, the self-assertiveness and self-confidence of scholars is supported by their being well qualified in their own disciplines, a feature consistently emphasized in the discourse on interdisciplinarity.[2]

On the other hand, however, the very specialization obtained in a long process of professional training and the identity formation connected with it can be problematic for interdisciplinary cooperation (Hübenthal 1991: 150). The essential prerequisites, these authors suggest, are to partially dissolve traditional disciplinary views and to accept new or different problem definitions. There is also the hypothesis that a strong personal identification with and commitment to one's own discipline may impede openness for the perspectives represented by other disciplines. The debate on interdisciplinarity thus calls for properties that concern the very ability to stand back from one's own attitudes and experiences. In the best of cases, both features are presumably combined in one person: a stable disciplinary identity and flexibility. There is no contradiction between these requirements – they are an expression of the necessary tension to which an individual is exposed in interdisciplinary work.[3]

Among the personal traits of a scholar that are deemed to be conducive to interdisciplinary research are 'reliability, flexibility, patience, resilience, sensitivity to others, risk-taking, a thick skin, and a preference for diversity and new social roles' (Klein 1990: 183). In addition, personality traits that are requirements for dealing with representatives of other disciplines (or, for that matter, inhabitants of other territories) are tolerance for ambiguity, willingness to learn new things, and ability to engage in divergent thinking. Curiosity and courage are also important, as are modesty and the ability to subordinate one's own personality and views to new goals that are at least partly controlled by outsiders (foreigners). In his report on his experience with an interdisciplinary project at the Bielefeld Center for Interdisciplinary Research (ZiF), Klaus Immelmann (1987: 86) named the necessity of abandoning 'imposing behavior.'[4]

Two critical objections come to mind upon considering this list of personal traits. The first concerns the stability and predictive validity of these personal traits. The second relates to the specificity of these traits for interdisciplinarity.

The theoretical constructs of 'cognitive flexibility,' 'rigidity,' and 'tolerance of ambiguity' were developed in personality research to describe stable interindividual differences (traits) between persons and thus also to predict differences in behaviour. To this purpose, questionnaires were constructed to measure how marked a trait is in a person. What emerged, however, is that the actual behaviour that is assumed to reflect traits is very dependent on situation and on context. Therefore the predictive value of interindividual trait differences for interindividual behavioural variance is relatively low. This is a significant result that contradicts everyday folk psychology. Actually, people in everyday life tend to systematically underestimate the situation-specific variability and temporal instability of behaviour preferences in themselves and others (Norem 1989; Mischel 1990).

A second objection against a trait-oriented approach to the psychology of interdisciplinarity follows from its lack of specificity for interdisciplinary communication and cooperation. Would it be possible to make decisions on how to compose interdisciplinary teams on the basis of personality tests? It is obvious that traits such as tolerance of ambiguity or creativity are not exclusively or specifically required for interdisciplinary work. Interpersonal communicative skills (ability to listen, tolerance, etc.) will always be necessary if several individuals are to cooperate successfully. Similarly, open-mindedness for new information and tolerance of ambiguity are prerequisites for every advance in learning. The concepts of the personality trait approach are simply not sufficiently specific for a psychological analysis of the preconditions for and the processes of interdisciplinary communication and cooperation.

The conclusion is that looking for stable *personal* conditions (personal traits) for interdisciplinary thought and activity does not represent a viable approach for psychological research into interdisciplinary. Nevertheless, neither the phenomenological nor the practical significance of flexibility and ambiguity tolerance for interdisciplinary communication and cooperation can be disputed. This essay will attempt to reconstruct these dimensions by taking the *conceptual structures* of researchers as a point of departure for understanding interdisciplinarity.[5]

The psychological approach to interdisciplinarity sketched here, however, has been prompted not only by the above difficulties encountered with the trait approach in psychology. It is also founded in the assumption that communication between different conceptual structures is the core of interdisciplinarity itself (see also Maasen, Weingart, this volume). Communication between individuals endowed with different conceptual structures is not simply a precondition for attaining interdisciplinary insights, but is an essential component. If such processes are analysed with psychological methods and concepts, such an approach, while remaining discipline-specific (and one-sided thus far) is also concerned with a prime topic of the discourse on interdisciplinarity: the question of how new insights emerge from interdisciplinary research. This is why I designate the psychological analysis of the confrontation of different conceptual structures the *psychology of cognitive interdisciplinarity*.

The Interaction between Different Perspectives: Interdisciplinarity's Cognitive Core

The concepts of curiosity and ambiguity and the tension within a personal identity (which is both stable and flexible) already point towards the cognitive core of interdisciplinarity: the semantic (sometimes also syntactic) *diversity of the knowledge systems* introduced into the interdisciplinary interaction by the participants. This diversity is both motive ('overcoming specialization,' cf. Klein 1990) and condition for attaining the productive border-crossings of which interdisciplinary research consists in its most productive sense (Weingart 1995b).

While the knowledge offered by the participants should be different, it should also show enough interfaces to permit linkage or at least contact with the concepts and methods resulting from an interdisciplinary discourse. This also means that the boundary between disciplinary and interdisciplinary is flexible, because it depends on the participants' specific knowledge systems.[6]

'Knowledge' in this context does not only comprise special methods or concepts, but also the epistemic styles typical for a discipline or a domain of research activities. Referring to a certain discourse in social as well as in developmental psychology, this kind of knowledge will be called 'perspective' in what follows (Markova, Graumann, and Froppa 1995).

We will use the difference of perspectives as a point of departure for the psychological study of interdisciplinarity. The next two sections will be concerned with the question of how mutual communication and comprehension are possible at all in the presence of different perspectives. In the final section, this question will in a sense be reversed by asking why the difference of perspectives can in fact favour the creation of new knowledge.

Communication and Difference of Perspectives: The Theory of 'Common Ground'

In everyday communication, interaction partners encounter different perspectives. As everyday perception of facts and events depends on the categories we bring to a certain situation, the question of how mutual comprehension in the case of different perspectives is possible arises here as well.

The 'common ground' theory tries to find an answer to this question (Clark 1992, 1996). As the significance of subjective construction for perceiving, seeing, and acting became evident in cognitive psychology, it also became clear that successful communication by individuals having different perspectives is a phenomenon requiring explanation. The common ground theory postulates that every act of communication presumes a common cognitive frame of reference between the partners of interaction called the common ground. The theory postulates further that all contributions to the process of mutual understanding serve to establish or ascertain and continually maintain this common ground.

In the following analysis, the description of common ground theory is reduced to the situation of an encounter between two active individuals. Basically, however, common ground theory also applies to written communication (e-mail is a quite recent example), to communication among more than two individuals, and to asymmetrical communication, as in a lecture.

The common ground theory assumes that any verbal encounter represents an act of cooperation: When we communicate, we do so to attain a certain goal, to respond to – in most cases – an unspoken question (cf. von Stutterheim and Klein 1989).[7] All contributions to communication are formulated and understood on the basis of background assumptions we make about the situation in question, the object of conversation and its goal: 'Two people's common ground is, in effect, the sum of their mutual, common, or joint knowledge, beliefs, and suppositions' (Clark 1996: 93). This also includes assumptions about the interlocutor's situation and views. If I tell a secretary, 'Please prepare the letter for me,' I assume that we both know which letter is meant, where it is supposed to be prepared, when this should be done, and so on. One's own assumptions on which the conversation is based are designated as *one's own perspective* and that of the other person as *perspective of the other*. The common ground also contains a reflexive element; that is, we know that we have a certain perspective about the object and the context of the conversation while knowing that the interlocutor has his or her view as well. These assumptions about the view of the partner of communication are called the *presumed perspective of the other*. The logically iterative continuation 'A knows that B knows that A knows' normally is not significant for planning and realizing verbalizations. Reflexivity is usually confined to one step; it is part of one's own self-awareness and one's integration into the social environment.

CATEGORIES OF PEOPLE AS SOURCES OF INFORMATION ABOUT COMMON GROUND

How do people attain a common ground if they meet for the first time or, if they are already acquainted, have not yet talked about the topic of conversation? Clark (1996) distinguishes between two sources of information in such a context: first, the stereotypical presumptions that are activated on the basis of one's own categorization of the interlocutor (communal common ground), and second, the immediate personal experience within the conversation (personal common ground).

The communal common ground is based on categories concerning the interlocutor's cultural, social, vocational, and local background; his or her gender, age, education, and profession; and social roles that are intuitively assessed. These categories result in assumptions about the communal common ground, such as which expertise can be assumed, which language can be used, and so on. Talking about a conflict within my department to a colleague from another university, I use different formulations from those I use when talking about the same episode to my neighbour who has nothing to do with universities in his vocational life. Stereotypical information is usually correlated, making the intuitive 'computational effort' necessary for choosing and forming hypotheses about the knowledge that can serve as common ground in conversation smaller than might be supposed from the long and nevertheless incomplete list of stereotypical information.

Kingsbury (1968, quoted in Krauss and Fussell 1991) has empirically demonstrated the effect of stereotypical information about the conversation partner in an experiment that can be replicated by anyone. He had a trained subject ask for directions to a well-known Boston department store. Depending on the accent (home vs. foreign accent) and on phrasing that betrayed whether the person asking for directions was a Boston resident or not, the answers differed in length and detail; that is, the directions given were based on different assumptions about the common ground of familiarity with the city.

The categories just named that determine how people are perceived (gender, expertise, background, etc.) refer to differences between groups of individuals. More general, ontological assumptions are also assumed as communal common ground in every conversation. These concern, among other things, the distinction between animate and inanimate objects, between causes and events, and between word/sign and the signified. Only a conflictual situation will reveal that all contributions are based on generally shared ontological assumptions. This can be observed, for example, in communication with children who, up to a certain age, differ from adults in drawing the boundary between the animate and the inanimate world (see Keil 1989).

As far as personal knowledge is concerned, our assumptions about what our interlocutor knows (i.e., the presumed perspective of the other) are to a large part based on what we know ourselves and on what we believe to know. When I am scanning my memory for certain information, for instance, I am able to assess rather well beforehand whether I really have this knowledge, even if I have not yet reactivated the information itself. This 'feeling of knowing' also is the basis of assumptions about which information we may expect in other people (Jameson et al. 1993). Krauss and Fussell (1991) have presented images of public figures in the United States to students, asking them to judge how many of their fellow students would be able to identify these persons. In addition, Krauss and Fussell empirically established how many students actually knew these public figures. A rather high correlation between the presumed perspective of the other and the actual social distribution of this information was found, as well as a tendency among subjects to overestimate the distribution of information they knew themselves. This is the so-called 'false consensus effect' (Ross, Greene, and House 1977).

THE PROCESS OF GROUNDING

The stereotypical assumptions brought to the situation by the interlocutors constitute only the starting point for establishing the common ground. The most important basis for developing the common ground are current common experiences and common activity (personal common ground). When I realize that my office neighbour hears the same students in the corridor, I may presume that this perception belongs to our common ground. I may for instance remark, 'They are loud today' and be sure that he knows whom I mean (but not that he shares my sensation). If we both tell the students to calm down a bit, this event will belong to the common ground of our experiences. The particular history of jointly seen episodes and jointly executed actions forms the basis of knowledge for the momentary formation of assumptions about the common ground.

The sources of information just described form the knowledge basis for getting at the required concrete and specific assumptions about the common ground pertaining to the particular topic of conversation or for establishing this common ground from scratch. Clark (1996) designates the establishment of common ground as 'grounding.' If interlocutors, for instance, agree on a concept's referential context, this is a process of grounding. This happens, for instance, as the result of activities designed to point out objects.

In oral, direct communication, we have a comprehensive repertoire of signs at our disposal to agree on the actual status of the common ground used mutually to inform one another whether the flow of conversation can be continued or whether 'repair measures' must be undertaken to re-establish the common ground. This is done by changing emphasis, by using assertive terms like 'ugh,' 'yeah,' by repeating parts of phrases while changing the accent to a question or exclamation mark, by making speech pauses, and by varying the length of our verbalizations until we signal that we expect the other person to take a turn.

Clark's theory of common ground has not remained without criticism. In particular, it has been questioned whether it is necessary that the common ground assumptions of the interlocutors actually agree. Everyday communication is often very imprecise, but it still works if we understand approximately what the interlocutor means (Johnson-Laird 1982; Sperber and Wilson 1986). Besides, it has as yet not been empirically shown how strong the presumptions about the common ground really influence the adaptation of verbalizations during conversation to the listener, the so-called 'audience design' or 'recipient design' of the contributions to communication (Krauss and Fussell 1990).

Against these objections, it may nevertheless be noted that a certain measure of common ground is indispensable, because a complete explication of the intended meaning of a verbalization in interaction is both logically and psychologically impossible. Whether a real interpersonal agreement of the assumptions about common ground is required or whether the subjective conviction (the illusion of common ground) is sufficient also depends on the purpose of communication. If the purpose, for instance, is to coordinate activities, the common ground assumptions must at least partially agree. The potentially positive function of differences in perspectives and possible modes of coping with the illusion of common ground are discussed later in this essay.

The Theory of Common Ground as a Psychological Approach to Interdisciplinarity

The reports from interdisciplinary work groups contain many hints at initial difficulties of communication, and at the sometimes considerable amount of time that passes until a feeling of mutual understanding has been reached (see Hollingsworth and Hollingsworth, Klein, Maasen, and Scerri, all in this volume). Frequently, developing a common language and introducing colleagues from other disciplines to one's own perspective are described as the key problems of interdisciplinary cooperation. These descriptions can be interpreted as indications of the problems that arise in creating a common ground of interaction. The reports about problems of understanding in interdisciplinary work groups show that the agreed-upon research topic as a rule does not suffice as common ground for further communication, since a large part of scientific work consists in the theoretical reconstruction and hence in the produc-

tion of the problems under study – in other words, in the continuous
theoretical and methodical reconstruction of the object of research (see
also Weingart, this volume).

If the distinctiveness of perspectives in the scientists concerned is the
very constitutive feature of interdisciplinarity, then we must empirically examine the process of developing a common ground, that is,
investigate grounding and its cognitive prerequisites. The theory of common ground, however, has been developed for everyday interactions
and not for scientific communication, and must thus be tested as to
whether it works as a heuristic for a psychology of interdisciplinary
thought and activity. What empirical questions arise from this heuristic?

PRESUMPTIONS ABOUT THE STYLE OF THOUGHT WITHIN THE OTHER DISCIPLINE:
ONE'S OWN PERSPECTIVE ON THE OTHER

Inquiring into the stereotypical representations and previous knowledge about the other disciplines with which scientists enter into interdisciplinary work situations offers a first approach for empirical analyses. The assumptions about the epistemic style (Weingart 1995b) or
style of thought ('denkstil' in German; see Fleck [1935] 1979) of the
other disciplines involved seem to be particularly promising. What do
the participants know about the other disciplines' mode of work and of
arguing, what is deemed to be in need of justification, what is considered presupposed, which type of data and proof are accepted, and how
important historical change is within the other discipline?

A proven method of mutually establishing such representations about
the other disciplines is the qualitatively oriented interview (see
Hollingsworth and Hollingsworth, and Scerri, this volume). One of the
difficulties of such an approach is that the epistemic style a discipline honours is itself no homogeneous corpus of knowledge (cf.
Klein, this volume). Therefore the normative pattern that is necessary
as background to understand the more personal, sometimes idiosyn-
cratic 'versions' of a discipline's epistemic style is difficult to reconstruct. Epistemic style also comprises the practice of obtaining scientific
insights, not only their normative theory. On the other hand, it is possible to conduct such interviews, as they can be confined to such aspects of another discipline that might potentially be critical for the intended cooperation.[8]

Which aspects of epistemic style are of particular interest here? First,
we are interested in those components of epistemic style that found or

reflect differences in the social status of scientific disciplines. Summing up studies on the social psychology of interdisciplinary cooperation, Klein (1990: 127) reports: 'Teamwork has been compromised by the disdain scientists have for engineers, mathematicians for physicists, pure scientists for applied scientists, physical scientists for social scientists and humanists and vice versa.' As a discipline's epistemic style contains a significance guiding both activity and cognition and thus also a normative component, it may well be expected that it contributes to stereotypes of this kind.[9] This again affects how open-minded a researcher will be about data, proofs, and refutations obtained on the basis of other epistemic styles.

We have a second interest in the assumptions about duration and conditions of the learning processes typical for the discipline concerned or, in other words, its implicit theory of learning and education. If a discipline, for instance, stresses the role of intuitively obtained insights over empirical experience, this is sometimes accompanied by notions of giftedness, that is, by a widespread presumption that the partner in cooperation coming from another discipline must be similarly 'gifted' in a particular way (say, mathematically) to be able to understand the concepts alien to his or her own field.

Third, we are interested in the metatheoretical conceptions about interdisciplinarity itself. The discourse on interdisciplinarity (in this volume as well) contains views according to which successful interdisciplinarity depends on a large number of personal and institutional margin conditions and is thus bound to be a special case that cannot be significantly influenced, as well as the view that there is in principle no difference between problems of interdisciplinary communication on the one hand, and problems and features of the discourses taking place within the disciplines concerned on the other. These views are again influenced by the epistemic style of the discipline concerned, and it is reasonable to expect that they are significant for interdisciplinary communication.

Empirical analysis both of one's own perspective and of the presumed perspective of the other is a way of getting beyond understanding the differences in status and obstacles to communication merely as a problem arising from the individual psychologies of the participating scientists. It is useful to be able to empirically reconstruct the extent to which stereotypes about other people as well as lack of open-mindedness in oneself is enhanced or maintained by one's own epistemic styles. To the individuals involved, personal stereotypes often appear as individual attitudes and biases (resulting from traits) that can only be countered by an appropriate selection of researchers. The proposal sketched here aims at clarifying empirically the extent to which personal stereotypes about other disciplines are also based on epistemic style assumptions in interdisciplinary communication.

ASSUMPTIONS ABOUT THE SOCIAL DISTRIBUTION OF ONE'S OWN KNOWLEDGE: THE PRESUMED PERSPECTIVE OF THE OTHER

As described above, we base our everyday-life hypotheses about common ground on our own feeling of knowing while tending to overestimate the distribution of our own knowledge and our own beliefs (the false consensus effect). The presumed exclusive character of his or her own professional knowledge, however, is part of the scientist's self-awareness as a specialist. This raises the intriguing empirical question as to what perspective is presumed in the other: What presumptions do the members of an interdisciplinary team have about the social distribution of their own knowledge among colleagues coming from other disciplines?

It may be assumed that there are discipline-typical conceptions about the degree of exclusiveness of access to the disciplinary knowledge in question, and that these conceptions are also influenced by the public discourse about the role of the discipline in question within a given culture. Thus, disciplines like mathematics or philosophy with basic elements of knowledge are considered to be part of general education; these basic elements are part of the standard curriculum in schools. For other disciplines, such as engineering or linguistics, this is not true. Besides, considerable interpersonal differences are to be expected according to the degree of personal experience with the other's perspective.

An interesting question is whether there is a false consensus effect in spite of the exclusiveness that is constitutive for scientific knowledge. We have started a series of studies aiming for an answer to this question. Up to now we have obtained mixed results: Interviewing professionally experienced architects, we found examples of substantial overestimation as well as a few examples of underestimation of the distribution of architectural knowledge among laymen (Bromme and Rambow 1995). This result is surprising, since the exclusiveness of professional knowledge is constitutive for the concept of 'expert' not only in the relationship between disciplines, but also in that between expert and lay knowledge (Stehr 1994; Bromme and Tillema 1995).

Grounding and Developing a Common Language

The empirical survey of the actual and of the presumed perspective of the other sketched in the previous sections concerns only the cognitive prerequisites (the communal common ground) for an emerging development of a common understanding between the various interlocutors, that is, for the grounding process. Another empirical question is how the personal common ground is negotiated between partners of interaction that have different cognitive perspectives. To a considerable degree, the burden of such negotiation is on verbal and non-verbal signals of understanding well known from everyday communication. While these are of practical importance in interdisciplinary communication, they are of no further interest in our context here.

In everyday communication, a part of grounding consists in negotiating a shared referential context for the concepts used, and under some circumstances also in developing a new terminology (Isaacs and Clark 1987; Garrod and Doherty 1994). Newly established work groups spend some time developing a group-specific language of their own in order to inform one another about the meaning of disciplinary concepts and to facilitate certain terminological clarification. In interdisciplinary communication, differences in common ground are frequently 'discovered' only when the partners of cooperation find out that they use the same concepts with different meanings, or that they use different codings (terms, symbol systems) for approximately the same concepts.[10] The discourse on interdisciplinarity contains many examples of the fact that participants experience this discovery as a burden, and cope with it as a process of mutual misunderstanding.

The elaboration of a common, group-specific language is an empirical phenomenon that suggests other empirical investigations.

First, we need to know how the development of a language used for mutual information about the respective disciplinary perspective is revealing, that is; how signals about the establishment of a common ground are exchanged.

Second, it is important to analyze the cognitive function of the emergence of new terminology, that is, the process within which terms originally only introduced for purposes of fixing references and thus assuring a minimal common ground are gradually filled with intensional meaning. If the development of a group-specific disciplinary language leads to new theoretical concepts, this is an example of the possible cognitive effects of grounding. In the next section, this process will be examined in more detail.

Third, the communicative function of a new terminology for the process of establishing a new field (if interdisciplinarity results in the development of new disciplines) must be analysed. It is fascinating to investigate the reinterpretations of already established terminology as well as the formation of new, group-specific concepts that can transmute into a disciplinary language of their own in relation to outsiders.

On the Uses of Differences in Perspective

It is obvious that a successful agreement on a common terminology in interdisciplinary communication does not dissolve the differences in the disciplinary perspectives. This would not even be desirable. However, this raises the question of how interaction is possible in case of – at least partly – different assumptions about the common ground. I will attempt to sketch an answer by means of the concept of *linguistic division of labour*.

In the above presentation of the theory of common ground, it has already been pointed out that the assumptions of the interlocutors on the common ground need not agree. Up to a certain degree, an *illusion*[11] *about the common ground* will suffice. Several empirical studies have shown that speakers like to shift the burden of understanding to the listeners. Phrasing occurs without regard for special assumptions about the audience, while setting trust in the feedback that will provide occasions for corrections (cf. Krauss and Fussell 1991; Horton and Keysar 1996). Schober (1993) found that individuals will speak in a mode less adapted to their audience if they recognize that the listeners will be able to give feedback than if this opportunity is clearly excluded.

The common ground can also be composed of knowledge that is distributed among the participants of an interaction. It need not be cognitively represented to the same extent and the same content in every participant. Common ground is also socially distributed knowledge (Hutchins 1995). The socially distributed character of common ground explains why interdisciplinary communication cannot (and should not) dissolve the differences between the participants' perspectives but may even benefit from these differences and, as a result, retain such assymetries in knowledge. Common ground can also comprise agreement on what is not part of the shared knowledge and therefore will fall among the responsibilities of the partners in interaction.

Metaphors as Tools for a Linguistic Division of Labour

The discourse on interdisciplinarity emphasizes the role of metaphors to explain how new insights can arise from the interaction between different perspectives (Klein 1990; Bono 1995). The principle of borrowing is described as one of the fundamental cognitive mechanisms on the basis of which novel insights are produced in interdisciplinary communication.

In agreement with recent approaches in cognitive psychology to metaphors (Lakoff 1987; Gibbs 1994; for a critical position on this view of metaphor: Murphy 1996), metaphors are conceived of, in this context, primarily not as linguistic means but rather as cognitive units of categorical perception, not primarily as tools for illustrating messages but rather as fundamental categories of experience. It is thus clear that metaphors assume a central role not only in interdisciplinary research but also within single disciplines in that they are not only necessary for the 'large-scale' revolution of theories, but also indispensable in everyday research work (cf. Knorr-Cetina 1981).

In our context, the focus should be on a certain variant of metaphors that has been emphasized by Lakoff (1987): metonymies. From a linguistic point of view, metonymies are not metaphors, but the two are distinct types of synecdoches. It is reasonable under cognitive aspects, however, to treat metonymies as variants of metaphors. In case of a metonymy, certain aspects of meaning of a more comprehensive concept are used as placeholders for the whole concept. For example, in the statement 'Bosnia must not become a second Vietnam for the American army,' Vietnam stands for a complex historical event.

The use of metaphors in their metonymic function helps to explain how communication is possible in interdisciplinary research even in the presence of distinct theoretical perspectives. The different perspectives each of the participants attaches to the jointly used metaphor need not be dissolved even in long-term cooperation. Each of the participants may work with his or her own use of the concept, and there is no compulsion to totally integrate or unify the meanings of concepts.

In his analysis of 'meaning of meaning' Putnam (1975) has pointed out that our intuitive assumptions about a concept's meaning are based on our knowing that there is a linguistic division of labour. We know that a part of the meaning of the concepts we use is rather more precisely or differently defined – that is, known by specialists – and that we lack their knowledge. Nevertheless, we can use these concepts without difficulty, and we can as a rule defer to the specialists by consulting an encyclopaedia or an expert. Putnam illustrates this point by means of the concept of water. We know that there is a certain chemical definition for water and that it has physical properties that experts can explain, but we do not need to know all these meanings in order to use the concept (Malt 1994).

The *communicative implications of the 'linguistic division of labour'* have not yet been analyzed. It must be clarified empirically, for example, whether individuals can anticipate how certain concepts can be used when they are at odds with another person's perspective. Especially for well-defined concepts (from science, technology, or mathematics) it must be established whether experts are able to anticipate that these concepts may have an at least partly divergent meaning for non-specialists. We have carried out an empirical study on this subject that demonstrates how data on this question can be obtained (Bromme, Rambow, and Wiedmann 1998).

In the first step our study contributed to a question that is discussed in psychological research on concepts. Can differences in typicality like those found in everyday concepts also be established in the case of precisely defined natural science concepts? Thirty-two chemists from laboratories of a university chemistry department were asked to assess instances of the concept 'acid' on a scale judging how typical the examples are for the general concept of acid. It was shown that hydrochloric or sulphuric acid is considered to be very typical. With respect to other concrete examples, however, there is agreement that there are less typical samples.[12]

In a second trial, our subjects (laboratory chemists!) were asked to rate the samples once more, this time from the presumed perspective of a chemistry teacher. The judgments changed in a systematic manner. Certain acid samples remained highly typical for the notion of acid, but depending on the theoretical type of acid there were also changes. These changes agreed with the practical significance of the acids for a chemistry teacher's work. Our results indicate that the subjects of our study had an intuitive understanding of the fact that different extensional aspects of the concept of acid are significant for chemists working within different vocational contexts. The study shows also how the influence of vocational perspective on certain extensional aspects of meaning can be measured, and that this is not only possible for concepts belonging to the humanities, for which a certain fuzziness of meaning might well be expected, but also for natural science concepts.

Concluding Remark

These experimental designs have been discussed for yet another, more practical reason. They are also suited to prompting the participants to reflect on their communication with other colleagues. As soon as somebody inquires into the presumed perspective of another on one's own specialized domain of knowledge, such an interview may prompt reflection on one's self as an expert or as a specialist. As soon as one obtains data on false consensus bias, communicating the data afterwards to the interviewed, this of course will influence their assumptions about the social distribution of their own knowledge. At least some of the empirical designs that have been sketched above can also be transformed into instruments for reflecting on and perhaps improving communication between inhabitants of different cognitive territories. *The difference in perspectives is not only an impediment to understanding, but at the same time a condition of successful interdisciplinary communication.*

Notes

Many thanks for helpful comments to Julie Klein, Matthias Nückles, Riklef Rambow, Elmar Stahl, and Nico Stehr.

1 In this overview of psychological conditions of interdisciplinarity, I shall also refer to my own personal experience during sixteen years of work as a psychologist at an interdisciplinary research institute for mathematics education, where my interaction was mainly with mathematicians, but also with social scientists and philosophers of science.
2 It is a recurring point of emphasis in the discourse on interdisciplinarity that researchers doing successful work in interdisciplinary research projects must at first develop outstanding excellence in their own field, and this also means a specialized one. Recently, however, some other views have been held. While it remains undisputed that a high personal qualification is required, this is not necessarily seen in a specialization that has been

acquired over a long time, but rather in a so-called 'profound' flexibility of disciplinary identities (cf. Gibbons et al. 1994; Turpin and Garret-Jones, this volume). This difference of views is due to the fact that Gibbons et al. for instance, are primarily concerned with a scientific activity oriented towards practice (Mode 2 research), an orientation that has in part different cognitive prerequisites than basic (Mode 1) research (cf. Bromme and Tillema 1995).

3 See also Hollingsworth and Hollingsworth, Maasen and Scerri (all in this volume), who use similar notions to characterize both intellectual openmindedness and necessary excellence within one's own field.

4 Since Immelmann is a behavioural biologist, it can be assumed that the notion of 'imposing behavior' is based on some experiences within interdisciplinary work that reminded him of his observations of Canada geese and duck behaviour.

5 A similar shift from a trait-oriented focus to a cognitively oriented focus on conceptual structures as it is proposed here for the psychology of interdisciplinarity can be observed in psychological research on individual creativity (cf. Ward, Smith, and Vaid 1997).

6 The boundary is flexible for the very reason that there is already such a considerable differentiation and specialization within most of the traditional disciplines, as well as conceptual and methodological heterogeneity, that border crossing becomes necessary where representatives of the various subdisciplines intend to communicate (cf. Klein 1996 and this volume; Weingart, this volume). The boundary is also flexible because it repeatedly happens in the history of science that interdisciplinary approaches develop the typical social, institutional, and cognitive characteristics of disciplines such as described, for instance, for 'cognitive science' by De Mey (this volume).

7 Of course, talking to each other has additional functions in social interaction besides exchanging information. For example, talking may serve to regulate the social relationship between the partners of interaction. We may, however, do without these other dimensions here.

8 A rewarding source of information for the construction of questionnaires are the reports by scholars who are or have been members of two disciplines (cf. Kingsbury [1987] for interesting observations about the differences in the ways of thinking between psychologists and psychiatrists). As far as fundamental representations about the epistemological principles of the natural sciences are concerned, the survey inventories on 'science attitudes' developed in the context of research on science teaching also

offer suggestions for constructing appropriate survey tools (Ledermann 1992).

9   The stereotypes underlying such or other differences in status are of course not only founded in the assumptions about the presumed or actual epistemic style of the respectively other and foreign discipline, but also reflect the social importance of disciplines and subdisciplines within a society. Accordingly, they are also subject to historical change. Just think of the presently occurring change in the status of biochemistry, which seems to supplement or replace physics as the leading science.

10 Latour and Woolgar (1979: 11) describe an example that illustrates the fact that this already occurs within subdisciplines.

1   The concept of the 'illusion of common ground,' however, must not be taken literally here. What is meant is an assumption about the common ground that is based on knowledge about the linguistic division of labour and thus about the differences of meaning inherent in the concepts used. Such a reflexive illusion of common ground may serve to recognize the differences of meaning without perceiving them as mutual misunderstandings that must be dissolved before successful exchange can take place.

12 The result is revealing in itself, because it shows that an abstract and theoretically clearly defined concept like 'acid' is subjectively seen in close connection with certain of its instances, but in a more distant relation to other instances. This is remarkable for the fact that the abstract definition of acid of course holds in the same way for all of the samples used. From a logical point of view there should be no samples that are more typical or less typical in the light of a general and at the same time precise definition that holds true for all instances.

7

Practising Interdisciplinary Studies

RHODRI WINDSOR LISCOMBE

Introduction

This paper recounts the genesis and evolution of graduate interdisciplinary degree programs at the University of British Columbia. In addition to recording the organizational narrative with particular reference
to the Individual Interdisciplinary Studies Graduate Program (IISGP), it
reconstructs briefly the pedagogical discourses and administrative policies that have informed and affected the enterprise from its establishment in 1971 to the present. The description of the objectives and operation of the program includes discussion of the conceptualization of
interdisciplinarity as well as of its support within the university context. The strengths and weaknesses of the program are also examined in
company with problematic or contested features, and the potential for
future development. Consequently the paper is best defined as a historical analysis of situated interdisciplinary practice, moving from its
general accommodation within the university structure to its specific
embedding through an individually configured process of study. The
critique of interdisciplinarity theory is thus framed in terms of practical
outcomes and modes of facilitation. The thesis of this paper – or more
precisely the propositions concluded from observing the operation of
an interdisciplinary program at one university – is that the crossing of
disciplinary boundaries and uncovering of previously uncharted
knowledges require sustained but flexible administrative support and
that such support be conceptualized rather than preconceived, proactive but with fluid rather than fixed outcomes, attained through
multidisciplinary exploration and even disciplinary contestation. In addition, while configured (in the IISGP) around individual initiative,

interdisciplinarity needs to be nurtured through the active collaborative and critical participation of faculty supervisors.

Intentions and Objectives

The Individual Interdisciplinary Studies Graduate Program at the University of British Columbia was established in 1971.[1] At the outset it was conceived as a practical response to the desire for liberalization in the academic organization of knowledge and to facilitate a growing number of students who wished to combine more than one disciplinary field in pursuit of their research. Those faculty who initiated interdisciplinary studies appreciated the significant realignment of traditional disciplines, especially in the pure and applied sciences, but also including subjects in the humanities such as geography or comparative literature. The rapid pace of new research and changing methodology brought new focii of academic study that demonstrated the intellectual validity of integrative, innovative reconfiguration of knowledge and subject areas that would lead to the development of institutes, centres, and other new programs such as Canadian studies.[2] Furthermore, the IISGP was regarded as a means to effect more radical linkages between those three increasingly disconnected knowledge domains defined most readily by C.P. Snow as the (pure) sciences, arts (humanities), and social sciences (Snow 1964). The program was situated in the newly expanding Faculty of Graduate Studies to embed this approach in research rather than undergraduate teaching. Although not a radical innovation, the program was the first to be set up in Canada.[3]

This decision reflected both the culture of the university in the late 1960s and also the interest of those faculty most involved in establishing interdisciplinary studies. The pedagogy of UBC represented an intermixing of chiefly Scots and United States values and traditions, summarized by Dr John Stager (assistant to Acting Dean Ben Moyls at the inception of the IISGP) as 'deep and narrow' versus 'broad and thin.'[4] This resulted in a somewhat less strict alliance of academic discipline with department than in many North American universities, but also an awareness of developments in the major United States institutions, especially those on the West Coast, such as Stanford or Berkeley universities, where new subject alignments were being developed to accommodate the impact of new knowledges or techniques. Dr Moyls, for example, was a mathematician conscious of the need to redirect his discipline to exploit such new directions. Indeed, he accepted the invitation of the dean of Graduate Studies, Dr Ian McTaggart Cowan, to become his assistant in 1967 in order to advance the creation of an Institute of Applied Mathematics at UBC. Dr Cowan himself had been appointed dean in 1966 by the then President, Dr J. MacDonald, to promote graduate studies and to extend graduate research on the basis of his establishment of an interdisciplinary Fisheries Centre when head of the Department of Biology. The activity of Drs Cowan and Moyls in broadening the reach of their respective disciplines – and Dr Cowan's contribution to the burgeoning interdisciplinary field of ecology – was matched by Dr Stager's work on the sociocultural dimensions of his own subject, geography.

Their interests obviously represented a wider consensus, given the ease with which the IISGP came into being.[5] The faculty who formed this consensus appreciated the value of expanding graduate research and its pedagogical parameters. One instance is recorded in a proposal for a Centre for Materials Research endorsed by the dean of Graduate Studies and accepted by the Committee of Deans at their meeting of 26 June 1969: 'A very large committee representing the departments on campus is seeking a Negotiated Development Grant to proceed with interdisciplinary research and graduate student training in the area of hydrology.'[6] They were among those who acknowledged that the current administrative/pedagogical structure could not enable, let alone promote, many potentially valuable areas of research or study. That realization emerged both from their awareness of the professional discourse within their own fields and also from students interested in emergent and non-conventional areas, or in pursuing more broadly based studies. One increasingly popular area was environmental interconnectedness.[7] Environmental ecology coincided with the era of student revolt – marked at UBC by a student sit-in of the Faculty Club in late October 1968 – with opposition to the contemporaneous use of toxic chemicals in the Vietnam War, and with the inception of the IISGP.

The decision to establish the IISGP, however, was essentially a pedagogical, not a political, decision.[8] The program was one of a number of liberalizing strategies promoted from within the ranks of the faculty and supported by the dean of Graduate Studies and his associates. Student cases rather than student agitation were their motivation, not least since student representation was then absent from each level of academic regulation at UBC. Their intentions and attitudes are well encapsulated in the outline for a seminar on Urban Regional Planning in Developing Countries included with the proposal for a School of Community and Regional Planning successfully forwarded by Graduate Studies to the Senate Curriculum Committee in December 1969: 'This course together with formal offerings in other Departments in this University will fill a void and serve to provide an opportunity for in-depth study by Graduate Students cutting across Departments ... ' (UBC Box 39, File 5).

Such rhetoric explains the situation of pedagogically experimental or synthesizing programs – including the IISGP – in the graduate arena. Graduate Studies made a quantum leap in course offerings between 1970–1 and 1978–9; from generalized PhD or EdD degrees with specific offerings at the masters level in architecture, English, forestry, law, nursing, and physical education to a broad swath of doctoral and masters degrees in the majority of departments, supplemented by those offered through the increasing range of institutes and centres. Moreover the academic conduct of graduate programs at UBC during the 1970s was relatively flexible in terms of required courses, units, and comprehensive or candidacy examinations. Those latter were decided by each graduate student's supervisory committee, enabling the type of experimental inclusionary and integrative approach embedded in interdisciplinary research. The receptivity of interdisciplinarity to the contemporary pedagogical and administrative organization at the graduate level is demonstrated by this passage from the record of the Senate Curriculum Committee for 20 January 1971: '[An] interdisciplinary programme in transportation seems to be emerging, though not in a consciously planned way. The departments concerned are careful to consult with one another concerning possible overlap of courses, but little attention appears to have been given to overall programme structure, or possible gaps in the total offerings relating to transportation.'[9] The note of caution expressed by the committee is, again, less an issue of theoretical definition than structural arrangement.

Consequently the defining concepts of the IISGP corresponded with existing UBC practice and were relatively straightforwardly inserted within the evolving graduate agenda. Here is the original definition of interdisciplinary studies from the 1971–2 *Calendar* (page 204):

The Faculty of Graduate Studies encourages the realignment of traditional disciplines into new patterns, crossing department and faculty boundaries where this will foster the development of new areas of learning.

Where such interdisciplinary arrangements, by virtue of major special facilities, regional orientation or patterns of approach, take on the character of departments they may be established as Schools or Institutes within the Faculty.

Less formal arrangements may be termed Areas and the graduate study and research in these will be under the coordination of special committees of the Faculty.

Where the programme of an individual graduate student does not fit into established departmental boundaries, the Dean of the Faculty may set up an ad hoc committee to plan and guide the entire programme, including the administration of the comprehensive examination and overall direction of the thesis.

The interdisciplinary enterprise was to be an option *and* a springboard for new or reconstituted subject entities. It was channelled through the research initiative of individual graduate students directed by a supervisory committee of qualified faculty. From that derived what might best be termed a self-regulating academic scenario: graduate student and faculty had to demonstrate personal commitment and intellectual focus around a legitimate research issue or problem. Interdisciplinarity was to be mapped by individual explorations motivated by intellectual inquiry sustained by the expertise available on campus or within the academic orbit of the university. It was to be rigorous but non-programmatic, collaborative but not institutionalized, differentiated but not conventionalized.

This strategy of facilitating interdisciplinary studies through faculty commitment and departmental initiatives effectively circumvented most criticism within the university.[10] Those sceptical about the intellectual efficacy of either new inter- or cross-disciplinary subject areas or individual interdisciplinarity – and such contestation existed at UBC, partly motivated by the association of interdisciplinarity with vaguely construed holistic thought and the intrusion of social scientific theory upon many of the traditional humanities[11] – were pacified by the fact that the selection and monitoring of graduate students remained primarily with the departments. Indeed, every graduate student in the Individual Interdisciplinary Program over the first decade of its existence was enrolled only after initial admission into a department and one year's assessed/examined work under its authority. Moreover, the IISGP approach continued to be defined as an option secondary to attachment to an institute or centre into the 1980s. In 1979–80, the *Calendar* description reiterated this view through a number of telling amendments to the 1970–1 text reprinted above. Thus, at the end of the opening paragraph of the 1979–80 version this sentence was inserted: 'A major function of the various institutes [and Centres] of the Faculty consists in promoting interdisciplinary research' (page 147). There is more than a hint here of the subversion or natural relapse of supposed interdisciplinarity into new orthodoxies (and administrative entities) detected by Stanley Fish in 1994. And the influence of more conventional pedagogical and administrative structuring seems manifest in subsequent revisions; a now doubtless deliberately modest apologia for interdisciplinarity to diffuse potential opposition towards its further growth:

> Degree programs are also available in interdisciplinary studies. In some
> cases, an interdisciplinary area has been authorized to offer and adminis-
> ter formal degree programs (e.g. Genetics, Comparative Literature, etc.).
> Where an established degree program exists, a student may request
> admission into a special interdisciplinary program administered by an *ad*
> *hoc* committee representing the various disciplines involved. All arrange-
> ments involving special interdisciplinary programs must be approved by
> the Dean. The Dean will review annually the progress of all students in
> special interdisciplinary programs.
>   Some inter-departmental or inter-faculty groupings offer guidance in
> setting up interdisciplinary programs [Applied Mathematics, Commerce,
> Hydrology, Resource Ecology and Planning, and Urban Studies].

Five years later that last parenthetical phrase was replaced by direct reference to 'Institutes, Centres, Committees.'[12] Not until July 1996 was the IISGP established as an entirely distinct program, under the direction of a part-time Chair and an Advisory Committee of five senior faculty.[13]

During the first decade of its operation, opposition to the IISGP thus apparently resided less in matters of pedagogy than in university bureaucracy. And the target was primarily the Faculty of Graduate Studies alone. A substantial number of faculty plus the major departments regarded Graduate Studies as the imposition of an unnecessary new strata of administration as well as interference in their monitoring of academic standards.[14] Nonetheless, those senior faculty associated with the promulgation of the interdisciplinary options recall a clear demarcation in attitude across the campus. Departments with some stake in the environmental and applied fields, or those affected by speedy redefinition or enlargement of the parameters of their subject fields, tended to be positive (for example, anthropology and sociology, forestry, geography, and political science), whereas those that claimed a well-defined pedagogical rationale tended to be negative (for example, economics). Another somewhat irrational factor was the established power of departments that, despite internal recognition of fundamental repositioning within the nature and objectives of their knowledge domains, resisted administrative change (for example, chemistry and physics). But if the resistance was inconsistent, and relatively subdued and non-specific to Interdisciplinary Studies, the academic culture of UBC remained conservative with little radicalization among either faculty or departmental grouping.

Such an apolemical and 'live and let live' environment for interdisciplinarity has persisted at UBC. However, a critique has also endured, if anything increasing with the advent of (1) more specialized or politicized interdisciplinary centres such as Women's Studies, (2) renewed talk of thorough-going reconstruction of the undergraduate curriculum around the interdisciplinary Arts One and Science One models, (3) the interdisciplinary and multifaceted cantilevering outward of many disciplines/departments, especially in the humanities, and (4) increasing cuts to university funding. So new variations recur on earlier critiques of interdisciplinarity with regard to the embedding of disciplinary study in interdisciplinary research, academic competence prerequisite to research beyond the recognized or supposed boundaries, and even to the ability of existing discipline/departmental structures to better facilitate such non-conventional research. On the other hand, opponents also argue that interdisciplinarity can only occur through a systemic reorganization of the undergraduate curriculum or the evolving creation of institutes or centres constituted around particular fields of study with a demonstrable interdisciplinary pedigree and relevance – the environmental and comparative literature areas still being the most readily accepted. Apart from legitimate anxieties about imprecision of thought or investigation and claims to growing inclusivity within existing disciplinary entities, an underlying misgiving remains the potential erosion of departmental funding and authority. In turn, the issue of interdisciplinarity has sustained a series of ongoing arguments about the relative balance of graduate to undergraduate support and the mission of a large provincial (rather than privately endowed) university.

The Individual Interdisciplinary Studies Graduate Program

The academic construction of interdisciplinarity at UBC around an emergent subject/issue area or as an individual, case-by-case process has thereby circumvented the preponderance of faculty opposition. Moreover, by being directed towards the facilitation of experimental research this construction avoided implication with contentious and probably fruitless discussions about substantive alteration to curriculum and bureaucratic organization. By placing the initial onus in the IISGP on the graduate student, faculty and thus indirectly departments have been drawn into the practice of interdisciplinarity. This type of interdisciplinarity could be justified readily by virtue of being clearly focused and modest in scope if not in essential research objective.

Similarly, an individual program steered a pragmatic course between mere 'adhoccery' on the one hand and orthodoxy on the other. Prospective students had to prove the intellectual and procedural validity of their topic – both course and research work – with at least four qualified faculty as well as a broadly-based selection committee (originally comprising the dean and associate deans of Graduate Studies but since 1996 an Advisory Committee of, on average, eight senior faculty and the IISGP Chair). Consequently the topics or sites of interdisciplinarity were neither predetermined nor fixed. In this respect the IISGP corresponded and continued to correspond with generally accepted attributes of interdisciplinary research. By most definitions the program implies exploration beyond the already prescribed or bounded intellectual territory: it can be at or beyond the supposed margin, beneath or adjunct to the presumed core of disciplinary study; it can seek to appropriate concepts or theory and methods from one to another disciplinary domain; it can integrate or critically interrelate materials from several fields; and it can reconfigure or reposition knowledge as well as its pursuit.[15]

THE CONCEPTUAL TERRITORY

Most attempts to be definitive about interdisciplinarity either as an exact ideological or operational quantity have failed. The current debates about terminology underscore the properly slippery nature of this liberalizing and reconstructive approach to the comprehension, arrangement, and explication of knowledge. If 'interdisciplinary' remains the main term, convincing arguments have been advanced recently for the substitution of 'transdisciplinary.' And 'multi-' and 'cross-disciplinary' continue in usage, although these terms seem more applicable to the course work and problem definition stages of most IISGP degrees (i.e., as preparation for the integration of knowledges in the research process and their articulation in a thesis).[16] That is because the interdisciplinary approach can reside predominantly in the space of interchange across disciplinary boundaries or in the creation of means to transfer aspects of one discipline or academic territory into another, and because the very pace and compound nature of present research appears to diminish the cohering or reintegration of knowledges it reveals or promises. For example, medical research, be it positioned about fundamental questions of genetic structure or peripheral (though not less significant) matters of health care, increasingly entails the interrelation of so-called pure science with ethical, political, and sociocultural issues.[17] Similarly reductionist study paradigms increasingly have to be measured against broader visions or other models of knowledge because of their growing impact in a rapidly compressing global environment.

However defined, the practice of interdisciplinary is necessary not only for instrumental purposes but also for cognitive (including ethical) reasons; indeed, an argument can be made that cognitive displacement is one of the crucial prerequisites for the enlargement of knowledge. Many fields of study and disciplines have benefitted from the internal contestation sparked by the induction or intrusion of theories and methodologies developed elsewhere. The proliferation of new branches in the pure and applied sciences is especially evident. Equally important has been the impact upon the traditional humanities of social scientific thought and research, typified by the considerable broadening and re-invigoration of such an esoteric 'discipline' as art history consequent upon the appropriation of the structuralist and post-structuralist discourses. Art, literature, physics, computer science, engineering, and even such hybrids as biogenetics – once supposedly mainly self-referential about distinct disciplinary-generated foci – obviously share relationships through material form and non-material influence let alone through social and environmental impact. Yet those relationships are elusive to codification, frequently established at the initial stage of individual investigation, and subverted if constrained under new terminologies.[18]

Clearly the diversity of conceptualization and modalities of interdisciplinarity provide a justification for the situating of interdisciplinary research in subject-issue centres/institutes or in an individual program such as the IISGP.

OBJECTIVES AND ORGANIZATION

The Individual Interdisciplinary Studies Graduate Program at UBC is thus interdisciplinary neither by default nor by avoidance. From its inception the IISGP followed a proactive concept of interdisciplinarity, one that deliberately privileged individual initiative as the means to validate and exercise such integrative research. In this respect the program has remained responsive to the new ideas and information that construct both knowledge and its organization and application – whether thereo-critically or functionally. The limited scale of operation has diminished anxiety within the university community about the intellectual qualification of prospective IISGP graduate students, the academic substance of their programs, and career prospects. Being placed under the authority of the dean of Graduate Studies, the overall academic criteria and protocols became well-established. As the program evolved from 1971 the entrance requirements have remained rigorous but flexible. A major revision occurred during the 1980s that involved the institution of direct application into the IISGP as well as by transfer on the specific recommendation of a department.[19]

The process of refinement based on experience has continued, especially under the remit of Drs John Grace and Frieda Granot (the former and current deans of Graduate Studies) to the present IISGP chair and Advisory Committee. The least changed features of the program are first, the reposing of responsibility for academic direction with a faculty supervisory committee (and general oversight by the IISGP chair and Committee), and second, the absence of the predetermined course requirements imposed by most departments and degree-granting units. Instead the graduate students, in negotiation with their supervisory committee, have been empowered to formulate a schedule of course work and candidacy (comprehensive) examinations relevant to their acquisition of appropriate discipline-based knowledge or methods, and subsequent pursuit of their chosen research topic. In that sense the IISGP has always stressed the collaborative nature of learning and its primary emphasis on discovery.

REQUIREMENTS AND PROCEDURES

The selection process cannot be described as easy. Prior to making an application the prospective IISGP graduate students have, from the outset of the program, been required to confirm first-rate performance in prior academic studies and then to embark on a lengthy and challenging quest. They must be able to identify and articulate an area of study that clearly ventures beyond the parameters of relevant departmental or institute/centre graduate programs at the MA, MSc, and PhD levels. Even including students who approach the program through 'umbrella' units – those that handle graduate work through the administrative and collegiate aegis of the IISGP (the Institute of Health Promotion, Social Work and Bio-Resource Engineering) – all candidates are asked to contact the chair. At the first interview they are invited to explain their reasons for contemplating the IISGP and thus to make an initial defence of the interdisciplinarity of their project with regard to intellectual content and course work integration. At this stage the resolve of candidates has been, and continues to be, challenged by discussion of alternative departmental/centre/institute offerings as an additional process of self-selection and academic monitoring.[20] This clarifies the thinking of the applicant, and is also intended to assure the wider university community that the IISGP neither seeks to poach good graduates nor to accept those who balk at departmental requirements or are not quite acceptable elsewhere. That policy has been followed by the present chair who, in addition, has through meetings with deans and heads indicated that the IISGP cannot be regarded as an academic longstop for problem students.

Thereafter the potential applicant to the IISGP must devise a sufficiently persuasive research topic and associated campaign of study to win the support of three qualified faculty for the MA/MSc, and four for the PhD (at least one being a full professor or senior associate with a proven record of research and publication). The chair of each supervisory committee is usually from the department or academic unit representing the main or core disciplinary area of the research topic; in turn that department becomes the 'home department' to the respective graduate student and his or her means to obtain (highly valuable) support facilities such as office space and experience as a teaching assistant. This is no easy task due to the inconsistent recognition of such service by departments until very recently, and to the increasing teaching/administrative load carried by most faculty. Furthermore, faculty have to agree to serve collaboratively with colleagues from one, or more usually two, different departments and thus agree to extend their own understanding while renouncing some of their authority, especially with regard to the candidacy (comprehensive) examination. The program also actively encourages the participation, either as a full member or in an advisory capacity, of appropriately qualified faculty from other universities (predominantly in BC but including those in the United States, Britain, and Europe). Conversely the enhanced responsibility accorded to the graduate can be problematic for some students and represents an additional self-selecting component.

The hurdle of assembling a supportive supervisory committee passed, the applicants advance to the task of compiling a well-argued and written statement of their research and course work. They have always been, and still are, advised strongly to develop this in consultation with the IISGP chair, as well as members of their preliminary supervisory committee. Until the revision in 1996 of the application procedure, the statement of research usually comprised a fifty-to-sixty page document setting out the research problem(s), explicating how the various disciplines were to be integrated or cross-modelled or interrelated, and describing the contribution of the research to the existing field of study (supported by a full bibliography) and the likely outcome(s). The statement of research also included a preliminary schedule of course work, justification of off-campus research, and details of relevant professional experience, not forgetting the usual letters of reference of academic ability and transcripts. However arduous, there was no guarantee of straightforward acceptance, since the document was distributed for adjudication to the associate deans, themselves representing a wide spectrum of intellectual interest.

Admittedly, the 1996 revisions have simplified and codified the application process and form. Stage I requires a ten-page maximum (not including bibliography and relevant work experience) Statement of Proposed Research Topic, a provisional 'signed-on' supervisory committee, letters of reference, and transcripts. At this point the application file is distributed to members of the IISGP Advisory Committee, who are invited not only to render a decision about entry into the Program but also to identify areas of possible weakness. Their decision and comments, together with those of the chair, are communicated to the applicants and members of their supervisory committees. If accepted into the program the graduate student then has four months to complete Stage II of the application. This involves the members of the supervisory committee signing a standard form acknowledging their acceptance of the revised Statement of Research Topic, schedule of associated course work, and a preliminary scheme for the candidacy (comprehensive) examination. This document is intended to protect both the graduate student and the members of the committee by establishing research and study objectives at the outset of work. It is also designed to reinforce the objectives of empowering the graduate student and encouraging pedagogical innovation. Perhaps only then will the graduate entering the IISGP appreciate the last and continuing *difficultas* to be surmounted – the lack of a fixed academic abode.

That has been counteracted by the location of the IISGP at Green College UBC, effected in 1996 by Dean Grace, in cooperation with the principal of Green College, Dr Richard Ericson (a charter member of the newly created Advisory Committee). This has instilled a greater sense of community among the IISGP graduates, enhancing their academic attachment to a 'home' department (albeit generally less secure than for those registered in a conventional departmental graduate program). This link is reinforced by the chair attending at least one meeting of the graduate student's supervisory committee, and availability for counselling or intervention when required. In addition the chair has arranged meetings between the Advisory Committee and graduate students, partly to clarify matters relating to the important issues of legitimacy of interdisciplinarity (i.e., not merely a cobbling together of faculty or courses across departmental nomenclature) and the assessment of progress. Other meetings have also taken place with representatives of those academic units that use the program, in order to assure the pursuit of comparable research aims.

STRENGTHS AND WEAKNESSES

The range of research topics, and of their attendant knowledge areas and thereo-critical approaches, has expanded over the course of the IISGP's existence. During the first decade the preponderance of theses concerned environmental/ecological issues that related such fields as forestry, economics, biology, and sociology. Other lines of graduate interdisciplinary research sought to enlarge the interpretation and implementation of health care or the applications of applied science to more environmentally benign agriculture. While the ecological and broader environmental (planning) fields would be marshalled into centres and institutes with separate graduate programs, not forgetting the concurrent opening of an Institute of Health Care and Epidemiology, the IISGP still acts as the administrative umbrella for the doctoral students enrolled in bio-resources engineering and for a large proportion of those who apply for advanced graduate work with the Institute of Health

Promotion. This latter association persists because of the pace of change in the academic exploration and professional organization of societal health, reflecting a growing interdisciplinarity in the pedagogy of medical education; one member of the IISGP Advisory Committee is the Coordinator of Health Sciences at the university (Dr John Gilbert). Those developments and the diversity of and in research topics pursued by IISGP graduate students is best illustrated by reference to the diverse areas of knowledge (disciplines) and methodologies cited by those enrolled in the programs.

The fields of study intersected by those fifty-eight graduate students enrolled in March 1997 are remarkably wide. Within the quite extensive group studying health issues – partly through avenues mapped by health promotion, health care, rehabilitation sciences, human kinetics, family practice, nursing, and medicine – some are seeking to address significant gender and ethnic aspects, others new perceptions and processes of healing, and still others both the profound and the practical dimensions of the treatment of severely injured or terminally ill people. In each case the research work is pushing the boundaries of knowledge-gathering and knowledge-framing, especially by broadening the conceptualization of medicine and health care together with their ethical responsibilities.

At an entirely different locus are those seeking to reveal the ideological topography of contemporary culture through varying paths of analysis and thereo-critical paradigms, several revisiting the legacy of fundamental tenets of Enlightenment thought. The tangential impact of early Modern European philosophy upon indigenous cultures or colonial spaces is being examined through First Nations women's stories, ethnic resistance to hegemonic cultural policy, and the previously unperceived critique of postwar middle-class assumptions in the books of the Canadian West Coast author Ethel Wilson. Another student explores the management of scientific knowledge by the academy, private corporations, and government bureaucracy through the application of post-structuralist critique and qualitative research based on models in sociology and educational theory. Nor have IISGP graduates failed to exploit the mobile, discursive, and comparative potential of computational technology. Indeed, the first Canadian doctoral student to be allowed to present her thesis in CD-ROM format is enrolled in the program. IISGP graduates are experimenting with the synthesis of several computer programs in order to chart the organizational, psychological, and systems theory aspects of major change to the structure of an institution.

Another is also using hypertext applications to enable the reconstruction and contextualization of a significant medieval text. These students' pioneering application of computational systems and thinking will be sustained by a recent applicant who intends to rejuvenate archaeological and architectural historical research through virtual reality techniques combined with cultural studies theory.

This pattern of diversity recurs. In one batch of applicants to the IISGP from 1997, for example, four have topics around biomedical ethics, variously crossing over into theological as well as philosophical definitions of the body and individuality, the cultural traditions of medical practice, and the legal dimensions of treatment. Another will concentrate on legal rhetoric, but now as differently articulated by established authority and by First Nations peoples in the litigation of land claims in Canada. The problem of contested forest policy in South America, and especially how to assemble the empirical data needed to establish principles for the use of the resource, is the objective of another applicant. By contrast, two other graduates have identified quite different intellectual topographies that demand the interrelation, integration, and interaction of knowledges. One will mobilize history, historiography, film theory, and literary theory and criticism to illuminate the evolving cultural meaning of filmic adaptations of celebrated narratives of colonial United States. The other seeks to perform an interdisciplinary analysis of 'problems of the mind' as they relate to chiefly postmodern debates concerning the concept of 'subjectivity.'

The variety of IIGSP thesis topics, and the corresponding interdisciplinary course and research work, underscores the major strength – or successful defining feature – of the program: flexibility of intellectual no less than programmatic construction. That is, of course, a consequence of the decision to validate individual graduate student initiative as well as emergent research/subject areas through centres and institutes. It is, too, a function of the empowering (not reification, due to a rigorous application process) of experimental thinking and effectively directed intellectual enthusiasm. Such enthusiasm tends to be a factor of individual interest, exemplified by the desire of one current graduate to clarify the effect of legal and financial protocols on the definition of forestry practices. But the impetus can also originate in new realizations or perceptions about the academic and 'real' worlds, demonstrated by the recent batch of applications centred on the ethical implications of high-technology and non-scientific (holistic) medical assessment or treatments. However, the impressive record of graduate work and career achievement[21] cannot obscure the continuing appearance of potential applicants with interesting speculations but ill-formed ideas and weak justification of interdisciplinarity, usually comprising a loose association of faculty from different departments rather than different knowledge areas. And some faculty and students still assume that the program is an easy option or catch-all. A less negative *lacuna* is the relative absence of applicants seeking to illuminate wider perspectives around or intersections between the creative arts and pure sciences.

The enthusiasm and tenacity of the graduate students in the IISGP has counteracted the major deficiencies of the current program: the absence of sufficient funding, let alone designated graduate fellowships; the want of teaching assistantships assigned to the Program; and the lack of common room, seminar, and office space with online communication capability. Those financial, pedagogical, and physical facilities would probably further reduce disjunctions in their progress to graduation. Common room and associated space would afford the material means to improve the frequency and hence contribution of supervisory committee meetings (enabling regular attendance by the chair). Moreover, discussions between the Advisory Committee and umbrella groups as well as the graduates in the Program would be enhanced with a corresponding additional stimulus to the ongoing critique of the conceptualization and practice of interdisciplinarity. Enhanced support services would augment linkages between the IISGP and compatible academic units in Canadian, American, and international universities through the existing Internet home page (http://www.interchange.ubc.ca/iisgp).

FUTURE DIRECTIONS

The location of the IISGP at Green College has enabled the expansion of a regular pro-seminar that originated in 1995.[22] The monthly seminars, supplemented by thematic workshops and lectures plus an annual graduate symposium, provide an intellectual and, no less importantly, social focus where graduates exchange ideas and insights on their practice of interdisciplinarity. Materials from these events and especially the symposium are placed on the IISGP website. The symposium will be promoted as an international site for the conceptualization and practice of interdisciplinarity at the graduate level.

Another major new initiative will be the development of an associated Interdisciplinary seminar, co-sponsored with Green College, to be conducted around the theory and *praxis* of knowledge – by faculty and graduate students both associated with and outside the IISGP. The purpose is to sustain a dynamic and varied demonstration of the practice of interdisciplinarity.

It is hoped that the thematic interdisciplinary seminar will attract graduates from those less well-represented poles of academic territory, although the IISGP does not actively recruit either students or subjects. The absence of recruitment or research area promotion, and the resulting stress on student motivation, has effected a minimal drop-out rate after acceptance into the IISGP. The dedication of the program to the nurture of individual interdisciplinary research ensures the viability and variety of future intellectual endeavour. The driving force of the Individual Interdisciplinary Studies Graduate Program at the University of British Columbia is the facilitation and encouragement of adventurous, rigorous, and critically integrative approaches to the creation, definition, and articulation of knowledges.

Notes

I am most grateful to Drs Nico Stehr, Peter Weingart, and Sabine Maasen for their critique and advice; this paper also owes much to the speakers at the 1997 Royal Society of Canada International Conference on Interdisciplinarity.

1 An interdisciplinary studies option was first offered by the University of British Columbia in the 1971–2 academic year: *Calendar – Graduate Studies* (UBC 1971: 184). The historical account that follows is based on interviews with Drs Ben Moyls and John Stager, respectively acting dean and assistant dean of Graduate Studies under Dr Ian McTaggart Cowan (who was on leave 1969–71 when the Interdisciplinary Studies option was passed through the Committee of Deans and Senate). Further information was supplied by Drs Kenneth MacCrimmon, Laurie Ricou, and Donald Stephens, who were responsible for this interdisciplinary program at various stages thereafter.
2 For example, the 1971–8 UBC *Calendars* list a series of newly founded centres and institutes – notably the Animal Resource Centre (from 1978 the Institute for Animal Resource Ecology) and Centre for Human Settlements – together with a range of new subject area concentrations including bioresource engineering, comparative literature, creative writing, genetics, health care and epidemiology, industrial relations, and international relations (see especially 1978–9 *Calendar*: 144 ff.).

3 Other individual interdisciplinary programs, listed in the *National Guide to College and University Programs* (Hull, PQ: Government of Canada, Occupational and Career Development Division, 1996), are found at York (Individualized [Liberal] Studies) and at Concordia (Individually Structured Program).

4 Interview 24 June 1997.

5 The main documentary records are Senate Minutes and Senate Records, specifically the Senate Curriculum Committee (UBC Special Collections ([= UBC Sec. Coll.]), Senate Fonds, Box 39, File 5) and Committee of Deans (UBC Sp. Coll., Senate Fonds, Box 40, Files 10/11). However, because the IISGP required no specific course structure or revisions to existing graduate offerings, there is no distinct reference to its establishment in the Senate Minutes (UBC Sp. Coll., Senate Minutes, Box 6 File 6–2). This new option must, however, have been accorded some kind of general approval on or before 14 January 1970 when Dr Moyls successfully presented to Senate course changes for Graduate Studies (UBC Sp. Coll., Senate Minutes, File 6-2: 5178).

6 UBC, Sp. Coll., Senate Fonds, Box 40, File 10, noting that National Research Council funding would cease in 1971 after five years. The other new programs promoted by Graduate Studies were a climate committee, comparative literature, industrial relations, and international studies.

7 One student who considered entering the IISGP but eventually completed his doctoral studies with forestry was Patrick Moore, co-founder of Greenpeace. Dr Moyls recalls Patrick Moore's oral defence, contested by representatives of more conservative attitudes to the comprehension of the ecology sciences, as one of especial vigour.

8 The Committee of Deans on 9 March 1971, for one instance, discussed a memorandum from T.S. Myers, Director of Information Services at UBC, regarding appropriate charges under the Criminal Code to suppress student unrest, and a letter from the Head of the Department of Religious Studies, the Rev William Nicholls, warning of the dangers to the university community of student disruption especially as a consequence of improper 'experimental education' and uncritical application of Gestalt theory.

9 The report of the Curriculum Committee received the endorsement of the Senate on 24 January 1971 (UBC, Sp. Coll., Box 39, File 5).

10 This assessment is based on interviews with Drs Moyls, Stager, and Stephens.

11 The institutional and intellectual resistance to interdisciplinarity, or rather arguments for the organization and articulation of knowledge around disciplines, is examined in several essays in Messer-Davidson, Shumway, and Sylvan (1993). See also Salter and Hearn (1996). In the context of UBC,

and more particularly over recent years as financial constraints have grown, the main reservations about interdisciplinarity voiced to this author concern the preservation of materials intrinsic to the comprehension of the knowledge embodied in the 'discipline,' the necessity of achieving certain levels of understanding within a clearly specified and recognized area of study as a prior qualification to integrate information and ideas around novel issues or questions, the existence of essential concepts and expressions within the canon established through the disciplinary process, and the diffusion of scarce resources – including faculty energy – at a time when the disciplinary departments are encountering increasing funding reductions.

12 At this juncture the incumbent Dean of Graduate Studies, Dr Peter Neufeld, sanctioned a semi-formal association between Bio-Resources Engineering and the IISGP, whereby the former could select graduate students on a quasi-independent basis. This was the reason for the provisional entry option into the IISGP that remains on the admission document. All other departments or institutes that use the IISGP as the means to graduate doctoral students conform with the other entry options: direct application or admission by transfer.

13 This substantial redefinition was achieved by Dr John Grace, dean of Graduate Studies 1991–6, who also encouraged a major campus-wide exercise to foster interdisciplinary study and research in 1994.

14 All those interviewed for this paper concurred that the Faculty of Graduate Studies had been assigned a primary role by President Macdonald (and his successors) in the attainment of consistently high levels of academic performance across all departments offering graduate degrees.

15 An excellent review, with a comprehensive bibliography, is Julie Thompson Klein (1996: 226–7).

16 For example, S.J. Kline argues for the superior merit of 'multidisciplinarity' in *Conceptual Foundations for Multidisciplinary Thinking* (1995).

17 An example of the interrelation of scientific, philosophical, and social knowledges around medicine is the area of biogenetics, for which the IISGP currently has five graduate students either enrolled or applying to enter the program.

18 See especially Fish (1994), 'Being Interdisciplinary Is So Hard to Do.' One example might be cultural studies, said to have been created inadvertently by Raymond Williams and Stuart Hall to be an essentially fluid and inclusionary interdisciplinary analysis, now increasingly formulated into an intellectual territory, even an orthodoxy, with designated gatekeepers and voices; I owe this suggestion to Dr Sharon Fuller.

19 During this period the IISGP was administered by Associate Deans Kenneth MacCrimmon and Sheldon Cherry.
20 Dr Laurie Ricou, who, encouraged by Dr Grace, signally contributed to the consolidation of the IISGP when associate Dean during 1991–6, always challenged the resolve of applicants to the Program by advising prospective candidates to investigate all reasonable alternatives. This author had the advantage of Dr Ricou's advice and example before assuming the post of chair of the IISGP, including being present at the interviews of two prospective applicants.
21 The chair and graduate Secretary of the IISGP have started to distribute career-tracking forms to graduating students of the Program.
22 The pro-seminar was instituted by Dr Ricou, and included such valuable intellectual and communal exercises as the presentation of the research objectives of one graduate student by another in a different area of study.

8

Cognitive Science as an Interdisciplinary Endeavour

MARC DE MEY

A possible site where one might find interdisciplinarity at work is the still-fashionable cognitive science. The Program in Cognitive Science and the Institute of Cognitive Studies at the University of California at Berkeley belong to the major initiatives in this area. In 1981, the Sloan Foundation mounted a large-scale program in cognitive science, selecting two American universities to launch this new branch of science. On the East Coast, the Massachusetts Institute of Technology was selected for this leading role, and on the Pacific Coast, UC Berkeley was assigned this role.[1]

In the case of UC Berkeley, cognitive science has been made especially accessible and traceable through the publication of a series of interviews with leading cognitive scientists. In residence as visiting scholars at UC Berkeley, Peter Baumgartner and Sabine Payr met with prominent members of the cognitive science community, many of whom were at that university or in the area (UC San Francisco or Stanford). The report of their interviews (Baumgartner and Payr 1995) is a wealthy source of information on the status of cognitive science in its promises and its problems, as seen by major members of that community. As Wilenski (1995: 268) points out in that volume, UC Berkeley has wisely chosen a prudent step-by-step deployment rather than plunging into everything at once. Thus, it is possible to distinguish some of the stages through which the undertaking has evolved. Where is the current locus of interdisciplinarity in the UC Berkeley cognitive endeavour? What various shapes has interdisciplinarity already taken, and what is the payoff of the forms that have been experimented with?

Before focusing on the Berkeleyan practice, we should see whether there is a theoretical framework situating interdisciplinarity in a wider context. Such a framework will allow us to derive some conceptual standards against which observed practice can be judged and progress can be assessed. Evolutionary concepts might turn out to be quite suggestive in this respect.

The Notion of Scientific Discipline According to an Evolutionary Model

In the pursuit of themes introduced by Thomas Kuhn's *The Structure of Scientific Revolutions* (1962), there have been suggestions for an analysis of scientific development along evolutionary lines. Initially, Toulmin (1972) announced an ambitious project that would deal with scientific disciplines more or less as biological species. This project would trace scientific ramifications according to paths of productive mutations or recombinations of disciplines. The project was not followed through to a degree that one could really assess the value of evolutionary concepts for science policy along eugenic lines. The most general and most ambitious biological model with an amazingly wide span was undoubtedly Donald Campbell's (1959) comparative psychology of knowledge processes. The biological approach of Campbell, a student of Edward Tolman at UC Berkeley's Department of Psychology in the 1930s, can be considered the American counterpart to Jean Piaget's *biologie de la connaissance*. Piaget's and Campbell's work was inspired by James Mark Baldwin's functionalist study of the mind. According to this approach, the appearance of mind in man is nothing more than another invention of biological evolution, to be viewed just like any other mechanism of biological adaptation.

Life keeps exploring new opportunities by generating new forms, from random mutations at the level of primitive organisms to scientific theories on the level of more complex organisms such as humans. One of the earliest and possibly most basic discoveries of evolution is that of sexual reproduction.[2] As level two in Campbell's hierarchical classification, sexual reproduction is superior to level one (random mutation and natural selection) because of its capacity to provide for more radical innovation without endangering the achieved characteristics too much. Recombination of parental patterns generates a wider diversity than single variations on one parental pattern. An indication of the capacity of sexual reproduction as an exploratory device is provided by Ernst Mayr's (1963) estimate of diversity within the different species of organisms according to their reproduction strategy. Mayr estimates the number of animal species to be about five times higher than the number of plant species. He attributes the greater diversification in animals to the capacity of sexual reproduction to discover new ecological niches. Sexual recombination dominant in animals produces a wider range of variations. Cloning and occasional mutations that are characteristic for reproduction in a substantial number of plant species produce a more narrow range of variations. Sexual reproduction turns out to be more radically innovative than asexual reproduction. Radical innovativeness pays off in terms of greater diversity. In turn, greater diversity indicates an increase in life's capacity to exploit ecological conditions that, according to Campbell, would correspond to embodied knowledge.

However, Mayr also notices that the increased capacity for variation only pays off if coupled with a strategy of active protection of newly discovered ecological niches. Securing the opportunities of a newly discovered viable pattern occurs through 'speciation,' which comes down to a form of inbreeding among the first generations of the successful variant. Mating rituals that are, in general, quite complicated are in fact isolation mechanisms that carefully restrict sexual interaction to the members of the newly developing species. They speed up the acquisition and cultivation of the new specificity, ultimately resulting in a new species identity.

The mathematics of biological evolution and, more specifically, the analysis of speciation as a component of the strategy of sexual reproduction suggest a model for interdisciplinarity that comes close to the findings of John Law (1973), namely that successful interdisciplinarity leads to the establishment of new disciplines. Law found that X-ray protein crystallography became a new specialty as the result of interdisciplinary collaboration between X-ray crystallography and protein researchers. The collaboration rapidly displayed disciplinary characteristics of its own.

Both the 'biology of discovery' and the history of science case studies seem to suggest there are specific and rather delicate requirements for interdisciplinarity to be successful. On the one hand, there is the need for the production of innovations based upon daring new combinations. This requires a degree of openness and penetrability of disciplines, allowing researchers to become acquainted with one anothers' concepts and techniques. On the other hand, there is the requirement of promptly closing up exploratory variation upon reaching the first indications of a combinatorial 'hit' to maximize success. This comes down to isolating and cultivating the new breed more or less by a strategy of inbreeding or even cloning. The paradox of interdisciplinarity resulting in disciplinarity is probably not merely the result of territorial jargon, as Julie Klein (1990) suggests, but possibly a basic feature of knowledge production in general. Should cognitive science be situated along this line of development? Is it still at the stage of exploration in which openness seems most promising? Or is there an indication of increased 'speciation' that would entail a rapid shift towards organization along disciplinary lines?

The Diffuse Character of Interdisciplinarity in UC Berkeley Cognitive Science

As a participant observer of cognitive science in the UC Berkeley setting, one is confronted with interdisciplinarity at many more levels than the evolutionary viewpoint, or even common sense, would have one expect. While interdisciplinarity is associated with bringing together various groups, these can obviously be assembled at different levels in the various strata of the university hierarchy. Hollingsworth and Hollingsworth (this volume) refer to the fragmented organization of biomedical research at Berkeley as a possible cause of the lack of major breakthroughs in those areas. The diversity in points of interdisciplinary contact suggests a similar qualification for cognitive science, though there is a clear stratification behind it. In fact, one actually meets with four types of practitioners according to the following levels: the undergraduate, the graduate, the established staff member, and the free-floating professor.

UNDERGRADUATE MULTIDISCIPLINARY AND INTERDISCIPLINARY ACTIVITY

In the current context (spring 1997), while the Sloan Foundation support has ended, UC Berkeley nevertheless has an undergraduate interdisciplinary studies program in cognitive science that attracts a respectable number of students. To some, this might already be a first surprising element. What is the plausibility of cultivating interdisciplinarity already at the undergraduate level? Shouldn't it be the other way around: have students first acquire a solid basis in a specific discipline as an undergraduate before engaging in any interdisciplinarity at higher levels?

Confronted with a certain popularity of interdisciplinary options in undergraduate education, one becomes aware of the deeper penetration of interdisciplinarity in the organization of American college and university education in general. The segmentation between undergraduate and graduate education is, at least for certain fields, almost institutionally linked to an interdisciplinary orientation. In the mid-1960s, when the cognitive orientation was becoming influential within psychology as a discipline, the requirements for entering the graduate program in psychology at Harvard strongly discouraged candidates with a psychology major in undergraduate education. Rather, they recommended that students should have a major in mathematics or physics. If consistently enforced, such rules produce educational trajectories that have a built-in interdisciplinary orientation through the hybrid combination of the undergraduate with the graduate specialization. However, the interdisciplinary undergraduate programs cultivate that kind of hybridization in a very explicit manner at even earlier levels. What types of students choose these kinds of programs, and what do they expect to gain from them?

When talking with undergraduate cognitive science majors, at least three groups can be identified:

- One group aims quite early at a graduate program in psychology or education and chooses cognitive science as a very appropriate and straightforward undergraduate preparation.
- Another group of students is interested in the sciences and starts out taking a substantial part of their courses in physics, mathematics, chemistry, and computer science. However, they are eager to see these fields applied to challenging and, in their understanding, intrinsically interesting questions, such as the nature of the mind. They persevere in their study of the natural sciences because they can combine it with applications to fascinating 'soft' subjects that are still full of attractive scientific and philosophical challenges. It is not that the sciences are too difficult for these students, but they are not sufficiently motivated, unless there is the opportunity of applying the sciences in the study of such genuinely intriguing questions as the physics of the mind.
- The third group is somewhat related, having started with hard sciences as their first choice but having backed out because of the high demands of the disciplines involved. They have chosen cognitive science not so much because of its fascinating topics, but because of its being more in line with their abilities and generally including a more friendly working climate.

Noticing that interdisciplinarity is not merely popular among the cognitive science majors alone, one wonders if this kind of interdisciplinary orientation is simply an extension of a sound and well-rounded secondary school education. In many aspects, such an education resembles forms of gymnasium education in Europe that prepare students for study at a university. Former Dean of Undergraduate Interdisciplinary Studies at Berkeley, American literature professor Don McQuade, notices the eagerness of students to master more than one discipline. Where there are no interdisciplinary programs that suit their taste, undergraduates may end up choosing two majors. Despite some reluctance on the part of the various departments involved, if students are clever enough to fulfil the requirements for both majors, they might even end up participating in two graduation ceremonies. Thus, a substantial number of undergraduate students seem to cherish multi-disciplinarity, if not interdisciplinarity. The introduction of cognitive science at the undergraduate level is thus in line with a large segment of students' preference to explore as many fields as possible. There can be no doubt that a substantial part of these students want to postpone the choice of a professional specialization until they can make a fair evaluation of what they like most and what they are best at.

In view of its potential for creative discovery, is undergraduate education the main lever to manipulate if science policy wishes to boost the scientific activity in an interdisciplinary field? If one wants to have the number of potential Keplers[3] as high as possible, is this the level at which to begin cultivating openness for various trades?

INTERDISCIPLINARY GRADUATE RESEARCH TRAINING PROGRAM

Besides the undergraduate interdisciplinary program, the Institute of Cognitive Studies at Berkeley has, in recent years, developed a graduate research program in cognitive science. As indicated above, contrary to some other universities in the United States, UC Berkeley has no full graduate degree program in cognitive science. The graduate research program in cognitive science currently has a special focus on *spatial cognition*. It is a training program supported by the National Science Foundation that allows students in computer science, education, linguistics, or psychology to pursue a highly specialized program of courses and research projects. Capitalizing upon the in-house expertise, the program is organized around spatial cognition, guaranteeing students close and intensive collaboration with top specialists for a net number of years. The National Science Foundation grant supports students for two years, but extension to three and possibly four years may be considered. The number of students that can be accepted and supported in this program is restricted to between five and ten. NSF support imposes strong requirements for the scientific background of the accepted graduates. Philosophy majors or art historians would not have a chance of being accepted, although the theme of 'spatial cognition' obviously could be of interest to them, and their field is in a position to contribute.

The case of Kepler qualifies as a convincing example, and the whole subfield of perspective studies within art history illustrates a wealth of data and ideas relevant to spatial cognition. However, in the United States, interdisciplinary endeavours that bridge the programs of the NSF and the National Endowment for the Humanities are very restricted. The two foundations support different groups, which might handicap cognitive science since both contributions of the humanities and of the sciences are manifestly of importance to the study of the mind. Here, the structure of the funding system might constitute an obstacle to genuine interdisciplinarity for this particular domain.

To grasp the peculiar nature and the success of this form of interdisciplinary research, one needs to study both the interaction of these graduate students with their mentors as well as the outcome of the undertaking: their doctoral dissertations. This is a recent program only started in 1994. The first results should become available for assessment in the near future.

FOUNDING FATHERS' INTERDISCIPLINARITY

The level at which one would expect interdisciplinarity to be most pronounced is at the faculty level. Somewhat surprisingly, the UC Berkeley faculty displays interdisciplinarity only in a conspicuously restrained sense. As there is no specific department of cognitive science, participating staff members have a basic appointment in a department that represents a specific discipline: psychology, computer science, optometry, and so on. Affinity to the discipline of one's own graduate education, together with loyalty to the department with which one works, seems to have a strong influence upon the degree of commitment to interdisciplinary endeavours. When offering opportunities for growth and expansion, interdisciplinary projects are enthusiastically supported, but they are not allowed to endanger the intellectual integrity or the departmental autonomy and strength in staff or financial resources of the parental disciplines.

Cognitive science, particularly when accompanied by generous financial support, is gladly accepted as a meaningful and needed collaborative effort of various disciplines dealing with the mind, if in addition to disciplinary support. In general, participating staff members are very eager to preserve the disciplinary identity. They remain on the payroll of their respective departments, and they keep their main offices there, while they utilize office space at the interdisciplinary location as well. Regarding student education, participating faculty emphasize solid command of a basic discipline before extending interdisciplinary activity to a second discipline. There is explicit distrust of interdisciplinary scholars who are a bit of everything but masters of no constituent disciplines. These scholars are considered to have an adverse and detrimental effect that ultimately endangers the whole venture. The current Director of the UC Berkeley Institute for Cognitive Studies, Stephen Palmer, is deeply concerned with 'the danger of being jack of all trades and master of none' (Palmer 1995: 167). This emphasis on disciplinary identity among those who also turn out to be the strongest and most devoted partners in the interdisciplinary project might seem rather remarkable. After all, they are mostly professors with tenure who would not take too big a professional risk by moving off to exotic research paths.

Why are the founding fathers so anxious to maintain their own discipline while at the same time preaching the promises of new combinations? Most of them remain loyal to the discipline of their own graduate education in a way that only a strong imprinting mechanism can provoke. Is this ultimately a subconscious resistance to interdisciplinarity, or simply an insistence on disciplinary integrity to safeguard successful interdisciplinarity?

A FREE-FLOATING PROFESSOR'S INTERDISCIPLINARITY

The founding of an interdisciplinary educational program and research institute is not entirely an internal undertaking within the university. An important source of innovation can come from visiting scholars, who constitute a regular component within endeavours of that scope. Obviously, a wide range of scholars qualify for participation. Foreign colleagues and staff members work along with graduate students, following disciplinary lines that are loyal to methods of one of the constituent disciplines. UC Berkeley has a steady influx of such visitors, from those who stay only for a few days to those who stay for years. Within the pattern of such longer visits, there is apparently room for individual interdisciplinary expansion as well. I happened to share an office with a colleague from the department of mathematics of a first-rate American university. He was no longer entirely satisfied with teaching advanced mathematics, partly because of his science students' utilitarian interest rather than intellectual motivation. Intensive teacher–student interaction is most rewarding when the incentive for study is intellectual excitement for both participants. He was looking for domains where he could use his mathematical skills to solve problems in areas where recent empirical research had a rich yield in new and challenging findings and where the research community was clearly driven by intellectual excitement. With this background, he has moved into cognitive science, and more specifically into vision science, the interdisciplinary science of visual perception that currently constitutes one of the fastest developing and most successful subfield.[4] This professor submits proposals to the NSF for exploratory mathematical research in this area and, on the basis of his reputation as a mathematician, obtains sufficient grants to be temporarily freed from teaching. He is able to join groups in various locations, where he can pursue research on the topic of his personal interest. As his grants allow him to be a full-time researcher on the payroll of his own project, his university has no problem paying for a temporary replacement. With a substantial overhead from the projects going to the university, his home institution is actually making a profit out of this situation. The colleague who takes over his teaching duties is usually a younger and less expensive instructor.

Here we are confronted with a scientist buying himself free from disciplinary teaching duties. He is able to move unencumbered when he sees challenging research problems in other disciplines that he feels eager about applying his abilities to. This research requires him to assimilate substantial amounts of new knowledge, neuro-science findings in this case, that functions as exciting new data for creating and trying out new formalisms. Maybe mathematicians have more opportunities of this kind because of the nature of their trade. On the whole, these trajectories are not uncommon, partly resulting from and partly producing the success of cognitive studies. Brilliant scientists, having obtained celebrity status in their own discipline, can freely move to new challenges, like Nobel-Prize-winning Francis Crick, who, having disentangled the genetic code, can now take on the human mind.[5]

Which of these roles provides for the most productive interdisciplinary research:

- The curious and opportunistic undergraduate securing his well-rounded education?
- The well-focused graduate student possibly bridging disciplinary gaps in innovative graduate research?
- The established faculty who, seeing new organizational opportunities, create new programs for careful exploration and expansion that, nevertheless, remain close to disciplinary standards?
- The solitary scientific nomad moving around with his or her valuable set of skills settling within interdisciplinary groups that cultivate problems that he or she thinks are worth tackling?

Confronted with this kind of diversity of contexts and domains of interdisciplinarity, promoted from freshman level onward to postdoctoral research, one feels indeed the need for a theoretical scheme that allows one to assess these various forms of disciplinarity and interdisciplinarity in terms of their ultimate relevance for valuable discovery. Does the evolution theory – inspired concept of scientific discipline permit the assessment of this diversity? Can one determine where and in what shape interdisciplinarity is promising or paying off? Can one see where it is risky or wasteful, and strict adherence to disciplinary themes and rules would seem to be more appropriate?

The Current Status of Cognitive Science and Its UCB Brand

When applied to scientific disciplines, the speciation model is only a loose metaphor that is not necessarily applicable to all levels of aggregation within the whole of scientific activity. An interdisciplinary field can also be conceived of as a communication structure superimposed upon a number of disciplines with the purpose of enhancing their fruitful interaction, without at any stage becoming a rival of any one of the disciplines involved. Its biological counterpart would then be an entire ecosystem rather than a single species. In the mind of the promoters of cognitive science as an interdisciplinary endeavour, this is the most important objective. The Berkeley Institute is certainly based upon that scheme: a coalition among psychology, linguistics, computer science, philosophy, and physiology with the aim of understanding the nature of the mind. Zadeh (1995) considers cognitive science a precursor for a whole range of new and disciplinary sciences of cognition still evolving. It would be embryonic to several sciences of the mind. But some characteristics of the more restricted speciation-type interdisciplinarity may already have been reached by now. To assess both the value of the coalition model and the novel discipline, we should observe the UCB endeavour in the light of cognitive science on the broader scientific scene.

Cognitive science originated as an offshoot of artificial intelligence (AI) research around 1975. When it originated around the 1950s, AI was most eager to reproduce human intelligence, but then it became ambivalent towards this ambition when various forms of intelligence turned out to be conceivable without their being human. At first, humans seemed the most successful embodiment of intelligence. As a consequence, the bond between the study of human intelligence and machine intelligence was very strong. Later on, the intelligence of humans turned out to be less easy to capture or copy. Researchers of AI saw opportunities for developing intelligent machines that would not necessarily have anything in common with human beings. The cognitive science offshoot incorporated those researchers whose main focus remained an understanding of the human mind. They see AI as an important field for understanding intelligence in general. AI models are viewed as sources of inspiration for studying human mental processes, but a machine copy realized in digital computers is not directly their goal.

At the present time, it seems fair to say that the intellectual paths of AI and cognitive science further diverge. Due to several grandiose ambitions of the past that have not been fulfilled, AI is forced into a more defensive position. Cognitive science, conversely, has found encouragement in a closer association with a strong partner that is full of promise for the future: neuroscience. Impressive progress is indeed being made in the *empirical* study of the human brain. This is especially true now that computers drive sophisticated research instruments (such as PET-scanners) and are not merely being used as models of the brain. Also, much more importance is attached to the differences between the nervous system and computers. Previously, ignoring the structure of the hardware, computers were considered to come quite close to brains. Now, the sensitivity towards differences between computers and brains in both structure and operation is much more pronounced. Compared with computer chips, neurons as major components of nervous systems are extremely slow. The impressive capacities of nervous systems have to derive from a drastic difference in design with a considerable amount of parallel processing, in contrast to the common sequentially operating computers. This tends to make the more flexible neural network concepts more attractive than the crisp symbolic model approach that AI researchers first thought would be used to unravel the mysteries of the mind. However, cognitive science, as well as AI, still harbours adherents to representationalism, the older line of research, as well as to neural networks, the more recent fashion. It would be very misleading to think of the whole AI community as enlisted in the symbol-processing camp (traditional AI) and the cognitive science community as belonging to the neural network group. The divide is deeper along the philosophical dimension of the ambitious technological goal of early AI.

The philosophy partners in the UCB cognitive science coalition, Dreyfus (1995) and Searle (1995), belong to the leading opponents of AI as a viable approach to the study of human intelligence or the human mind. They point to 'intentionality' as an essential attribute of minds that is totally lacking in computers. UCB artificial intelligence researchers, such as Russell (Russell and Norvig 1995) and Wilenski (1995), do not concern themselves much with these hermetic philosophical concepts of their colleagues. The lack of intentionality is doing no harm to their straightforward AI undertakings. The issue, for example, is to make intelligent machines that take over traffic and vehicle control from those absent-minded humans who cause accidents. Who would bother with the problem of whether the intelligence of such machines is comparable to that of humans? These are Byzantine questions. Can an airplane fly? If flying means to move through the air by moving wings up and down the way birds do, the answer is no. If it simply means to move through the air on proper power, the answer is yes. Airplane designers or engineers might gain useful insights from studying birds' flight, but their main motivation is to make flying machines and not to imitate birds as closely as possible. Since a machine doesn't have to become a bird in order to fly, it doesn't need to obtain a mind to become intelligent.

The defense of the AI community seems reasonable, but one should not entirely do away with the motivating force of a daring goal coupled with a specific date for achieving it. AI evolved around Turing's (1950) claim that within fifty years machines would be world champions in chess, translate from one language into another, and do many intelligent tasks better than humans. In the spring of 1997, UCB Extension organized a course called 'Turing's Prophecy: Where Is AI after 50 Years?' The general feeling was that although some computer projects come quite close to the goal set by Turing, there is an unmistakable disappointment. If the world champion of chess were by now to be, and even occasionally already is, a computer program, it is understood that it will not beat the human opponent on his or her own terms. In an analysis of Turing's test and the ideology of artificial intelligence, Halpern (1990: 18) has indicated 'the unimportance of merely getting an answer to the problem – as contrasted to the growth of insight that would normally be gained en route to an answer. In giving us the answer without deeper understanding, by magic, the computer left us feeling that we were both cheated and cheating, as if we'd gotten to the top of Everest by helicopter.' The disappointment is even more generally phrased in Halpern's concluding paragraph: 'The computer will not really be playing chess, proving theorems, or doing chemistry, but merely executing the appropriate algorithm quickly enough to seem miraculous to humans. The results may be invaluable; the means will be dismissed as just another example of how man spins off specialized machinery to deal with problems he has (in principle) solved, so as to free himself for the mental play he calls "thinking" (Halpern 1990: 18). This sounds almost like error 4 in the analysis of the results of a scientific project: 'we have solved the wrong problem.' The motivating force has clearly been that challenge of demystifying the mind, although it has apparently contained, deeply hidden in the unconscious, the secret hope of failing.

Cognitive science has taken over the fascination with the mind from AI but runs the same risk: to achieve its goals only to discover, ultimately, that something else was at stake. As with AI, in the meantime, substantial progress might be made. The mobilizing force produced by the atmosphere of a frontal attack on the mystery of the mind can be instrumental in obtaining the means for pursuing many research projects with, in addition, the potential of gaining important serendipitous findings. Apparently the UC Berkeley Institute of Cognitive Studies has an appropriate strategy to preserve a productive tension between inspiring general goals and tangible and technical research questions. While the participating philosophers set standards for the demystification of the mind, thereby in fact preserving and cultivating the mystery, other participants engage in interdisciplinary collaborative research on very specific questions (spatial cognition) while maintaining high disciplinary standards in a cosmopolitan atmosphere. Since this could be the recipe for fruitful interdisciplinarity, it is worthwhile to list the characteristics that seem important.

A GENERAL CHALLENGE AS MOTIVATING FORCE AND BINDING GLUE FOR THE WHOLE ENDEAVOUR

Major contributions to the broad questions of cognitive studies have come mainly from the cognitive science group's own internal critics, the philosophers Dreyfus and Searle. It is interesting to note that the professional philosophers here fulfil a tempering role. They warn against an overenthusiastic and overconfident application of the cognitive science major paradigms of symbolic representation and neural nets while the non-philosophers of the group tend to focus upon specific empirical, formal, and technical questions. Occasional contributions, such as those brought in by Stuart Russell (Russell and Norvig 1995), indicate sensibility for the global questions and do not declare the philosophical questions, such as 'the nature of the mind' or 'the nature of consciousness,' meaningless. One should be aware of the high degree of tolerance required for maintaining this type of collaboration in which one group of participants declares, in a playful attitude, the contributions of the other participants either meaningless or impossible. It is a delicate manoeuvring between solid scientific criticism and enthusiastic belief in scientific promises. Zadeh (1995) quotes the Jules Verne principle, 'Scientific progress is driven by exaggerated expectations.' Philosophers should not too light-heartedly dismiss the motivating beliefs that drive their colleagues in empirical research and possibly also the sponsors of such research. An unattainable research goal does not necessarily engender corrupt findings, and serendipity is too much a part of science to be ignored. A continual reformulation of goals is part of the scientific process. Bureaucratic control of rigidly fixed goals might induce the premature closure of a line of potentially rewarding research. In that respect, the UC Berkeley philosophers may seem to walk risky paths, but they preserve the challenge and keep the debate even more lively by challenging each other.

EASY PERMEABILITY OF BOUNDARIES

Students and staff of the Berkeley Institute for Cognitive Studies have ample opportunities to attend talks and conferences in the various fields involved. These involve reports from researchers within UC Berkeley, as well as visiting researchers from across the United States and around the world. The level of intensity and the frequency (several a week!) with which such talks are organized creates, in addition to the specific communications they contain, a cosmopolitan atmosphere of intellectual excitement. Frequently the researchers who offer a lecture are the top specialists. Regularly attending students, visitors, and staff have the feeling of watching from a front row seat the developments of the entire interdisciplinary field. Aside from the valuable information obtained, this incites a motivation to join as an active contributor to a worldwide dynamic interdisciplinary community.

Beside the cosmopolitan contacts organized by the interdisciplinary institute itself, the campus of a leading university might bring in contributors from beyond the scope of current preoccupation. In the spring of 1997, widely attended lectures were organized at UC Berkeley around the theme of 'cognitive archaeology' by one of the leading authorities, Professor Renfrew of the University of Cambridge. Although his pioneering efforts have been known for several years (Renfrew 1983, 1993), the qualification of 'cognitive' applied to archaeology should seem a rather exotic extension of this term, even for mainstream cognitive scientists. It actually makes a lot of sense, and it may soon expand into a genuine component of the larger interdisciplinary endeavour. Mithen's (1996) book *The Prehistory of the Mind, The Cognitive Origins of Art, Religion and Science*, indicates the range and potential of this extension and the capacity of the cognitive orientation to induce new currents in more remote fields. Similar considerations apply to 'cognitive ethology,' the related field of animal cognition and consciousness. To hear about these potentially relevant but still peripheral developments, researchers need to be at a rather large dynamic university or near a centre for interdisciplinarity that maintains an intensive visitors' program. One wonders whether more secluded centres for interdisciplinary research are capable of providing that kind of nurturing environment.

As an example of a fruitful inspiration and interaction that came about in an apparently more secluded centre, we might look at Miller, Galanter, and Pribram's *Plans and the Structure of Behaviour* (1960). This book was very influential in the shift towards a cognitive orientation in American psychology. In fact, it also set the scene for cognitive science, but the momentum it incited was temporarily absorbed by AI. The book came about at the Stanford Center for Advanced Study in the

Behavioral Sciences in Palo Alto, California. While witnessing to what extent the healthy metabolism of an interdisciplinary endeavour depends on a big busy university (with all participating departments active in top-level research), one questions how a centre that cultivates seclusion can maintain at the same time the highly needed cosmopolitan atmosphere. Maybe such a shift from a metropolitan university to a centre of seclusion accompanies the onset of 'speciation.' But in the case of the authors working together at the Stanford Center, with their proximity to Stanford and the accessibility of the larger San Francisco area, they very much remain in touch with the various dynamic universities in the area and the steady flow of visitors these institutions receive. Nevertheless, at some stage, the extra seclusion of a centre might be welcomed when interactions converge and, as a result, give shape to a specific research program.

TIGHT COLLABORATION IN WELL-DEFINED INTERDISCIPLINARY PROJECTS

The most important locus of interdisciplinarity is the graduate research training program. It is the graduate research trainee who takes on a specific research question that is of central interest to two or more of the participating disciplines. The notion of 'tightness,' as used here, applies in particular to the continued adherence to high disciplinary standards as exhibited by the founding members. While the graduate research trainee is allowed to study a topic relevant to more than one discipline, an undertone of rivalry remains with respect to methods and methodological values. In principle, the successful PhD thesis of the graduate student could constitute the bridging event and might solidify a bond between fields of supervisors still in competition. It may even ultimately provide a founding achievement for a new discipline in the making. In practice, it has not yet reached that stage. The various terms used by the mentors to describe the cooperation between participating disciplines still stress, to a variable degree, the disciplinary autonomy. The inderdisciplinary endeavour of cognitive science is variously called an 'aggregate,' an 'amalgamation,' or a 'coalition.'

The most appropriate label is probably that of Wilensky (1995: 28), who describes the collaboration within cognitive science subdisciplines as a 'race.' Stating that 'it does not matter who is getting there first,' he indirectly underlines the reliance on specific disciplinary methods. The various disciplines face a common goal, but they opt for different approaches to take up the challenge. A graduate trainee or an individual mentor is allowed a double or triple identity, and his or her successful achievements will be celebrated as cognitive science successes. But many achievements of this kind would be needed to dissolve the boundaries between disciplines. In the meantime, progress follows a multiped-gait-pattern, with participating disciplines making a stride forward, each in turn, while the others catch up. The overall impression that such a loose collaboration produces is surprising. Despite a degree of competition and even suspicion among disciplines, there is also an atmosphere of enthusiasm, and even excitement, that makes participants very tolerant and generous. The hard-headed computer scientist might remain sceptical towards philosophy and claim it is at best irrelevant to her trade, the neuroscientist might confidently rely on results of laboratory research with animals, and the psychologist might keep trying to increase his scientific respectability by obsessive adherence to methodological rigidity. It does not matter that such rivalry and competition exist as long as communication among the disciplines is preserved. Successful bridging events will come about in dissertations that contain the spark for new evolving specialties.

Conclusion

In the light of the evolutionary metaphor, cognitive science has not yet reached the stage of 'speciation.' There is no new unified standard of concepts and methods transmitted by means of a generally accepted educational program. Can we expect that cognitive science will soon become an autonomous discipline?

As the case of the Institute of Cognitive Science at UC Berkeley indicates, neither the philosophical challenge (understanding the nature of the mind), nor new research techniques or findings (computers, PET-scans) are, on their own, sufficient to induce the mobilization of forces one witnesses in prospering cognitive science enterprises. It is the synergetic interaction among a broad scope of general challenges formulated by philosophers and the contributions of scientists in several quite specific fields that induce a dense communication network with a high output of data and ideas. A nurturing environment for interdisciplinarity should therefore aim at such enhanced scientific metabolism by cultivating interaction among the disciplines at the various levels discussed. The Berkeley experience indicates that a high degree of internal debate and rivalry is not detrimental to the interdisciplinary atmosphere. In fact, the pursuit of controversial philosophical goals can evoke productive discussion and innovative research.

To extend this pattern of interdisciplinary interaction, care should be taken not to link the solution of the philosophical issue to a specific achievement. As the case of AI illustrates with its major goal tied to the Turing test, the endeavour loses its momentum when the goal is reached, and the community of practitioners is left with a feeling of both having cheated and having been cheated. To uphold the high rate of scientific metabolism, the solution of the ultimate question should not be within easy reach. It is the paradox of cognitive science that its ultimate success will also be its ultimate defeat: the mind discovering its own secret. The kind of interdisciplinarity we encounter is easier to maintain as long as there is the promise of demystifying the mind but not the actual fulfilment of that promise. Nevertheless, other developments may open up new perspectives for cognitive science.

Up to now, cognitive science has been driven by philosophical discussion and theoretical advances in various disciplines. The push of intellectual excitement and new frontiers is very much alive as expansions like cognitive archaeology and cognitive ethology show. However, analysts of economic development predict that in the next century, only one resource will remain pivotal for the world economy: knowledge (Sakaiya 1991; Drucker 1993). Control of knowledge in its production, accessibility, and applications will constitute the core of economic activity. Cognitive science deals with how the human brain produces that very valuable product. Could the equally demystifying forces of global economical development, which are quite different from intellectual excitement, pull cognitive science into the shape of a new monolithic discipline?

Notes

With thanks to Amir Assadi, Linda Daetwyler, Susan Ervin-Tripp, George Lakoff, Don McQuade, Rafael Nunez, Stephen Palmer, and Dan Slobin for very instructive talks and ample information.

1 As holder of the P.P. Rubens chair at the University of California at Berkeley, I had the privilege of partaking more or less as a participant observer in

this reputed cognitive science community during the spring semester of 1997.
2 The distinctions explored here aim at a refined analysis of Weingart's (this volume) suggestion that organizational representation of interdisciplinarity can be traced in evolutionary terms: 'Evolutionarily minded observers may think of a variation/selection mechanism' (p. 36).
3 In the Bielefeld meeting leading up to the Vancouver conference, we referred to Kepler's discovery of the retinal image (1604) as a prototypical interdisciplinary achievement. Kepler came to a new paradigm for understanding the eye by applying artistic methods based on a radically different paradigm. His free use of methods of various fields (including art) typifies productive transgression of disciplinary boundaries (see Straker 1970).
4 For an overview of the cognitive science approach to the study of vision, see Palmer in 1999.
5 Francis Crick has also been a visiting scholar at the UC Berkeley Institute of Cognitive Studies.

9

Inducing Interdisciplinarity: Irresistible Infliction? The Example of a Research Group at the Center for Interdisciplinary Research (ZiF), Bielefeld, Germany

SABINE MAASEN

Introduction

My paper rests on the assumption that the tasks involved in organizing interdisciplinarity inevitably deal with balancing. This holds for aspects as different as the disciplines and scholars involved and the methods and degrees of organizational input, as well as for producing the results and evaluating them. That interdisciplinary endeavours can be irresistible and inflictive at the same time may be a truism for those who have already had a chance to participate in such projects, organize them, or study them. A closer look at one example, however, may both show the intricacies of such a project in more detail and point to crucial moments where organizational measures can help to advance fruitful *multi*-disciplinary communication, possibly resulting in some *inter*disciplinary activity.

The example the subtitle of this essay refers to is a research group that worked on 'Biological Foundations of Human Culture.' It resided at the Center for Interdisciplinary Research (ZiF), Bielefeld, Germany, in the academic year of 1991–2. I will first give a general account of interdisciplinarity as practised at the ZiF and then address the exact location from which the observations reported derive. Following, I will give an outline of the above-mentioned research group, structured along the most critical events of organizational demand: the search for and invitation of pertinent scholars, installation of a group, and production of immediate and (hopefully!) long-range effects. Finally, the lesson this particular research group teaches with respect to the practice of interdisciplinarity will be incorporated into the general account given in the last section. Basically, this lesson amounts to the insight that this case is not so much a success story called 'Evolutionary Social Sciences Finally Established.' Rather, this endeavour has resulted in some interactions at some intersections of some interfields in the interspheres of biology and the social sciences – a patchwork procedure that has been inflictive, but irresistible nonetheless. Thus, interspersed throughout the text are 'irresistible inflictions': generalized dilemmas of interdisciplinarity.

A Simplified Model of Interdisciplinarity at the ZiF and a Thesis

First of all, interdisciplinarity presupposes (a) a realization that certain topics cannot adequately be approached by a single discipline and (b) an identification of various disciplinary activities that converge on topics that – at first sight – might be capable of being conceptualized as a joint problem. This type of interdisciplinarity can then be described as the act of transferring insights from different disciplines into a *set* of problems and a *set* of methods for approaching them. In the course of conceptually relating problems and methods, a certain something we call 'inter' may emerge with respect to the overall topic in question.

Interdisciplinarity thus understood, however, is a result that – in *most* cases – can only be approximated and is *always* a transitory one. If it occurs it is a stage within a process of communication between a variety of specialized discourses. In its extreme forms, this type of communication may lead either to the emergence of a new 'inter-field' (e.g., biochemistry, cf. Darden and Maull 1977) or to the cessation of communication altogether – and virtually everything in between may happen as well. Centers like the ZiF proceed on the assumption that while the results of multidisciplinary communication cannot be controlled, one can see to it that this type of communication occurs and that interdisciplinarities have the chance to emerge.

Within the three type system outlined by George Reynolds, the present case represents the second type: 'multidisciplinary problems that are basically intellectual rather than policy-action in nature, but that cannot be successfully undertaken within the boundaries of a single discipline' (Reynolds in Sigma Xi 1988: 21). Unlike problems of the first kind, which are addressed by a single discipline, the second type of discourse is intellectually more demanding. And unlike the third kind of problem, which is distinctly multidisciplinary, socioeconomically driven, and calls for a quick technological fix, the second type of discourse is less oriented towards 'solutions.'[1] This, however, is irresistible infliction number 1: Unrestrained debates on an issue may prove to be a vice or a virtue depending on the participants' willingness to arrive at a basic understanding, or even innovative notions, *without* the need to 'solve' a given socioeconomic problem.

Throughout this paper I will highlight several modifications the case of the research group adds to the simplified picture of interdisciplinarity outlined above. Basically, I will show that while establishing the research group at the ZiF was meant to be a further step towards one interdiscipline called 'Evolutionary Social Science,' the actual accomplishment was different, though not at all disappointing: What we set up was a series of intersectional discourses loosely coupled to the research group, the latter providing both the organizational and the intellectual framework. Thus, we learned something about 'practising interdisciplinarity,' too: The somewhat naïve picture of an all-encompassing interdisciplinarity was replaced by a more realistic, 'do-able' concept of a patchwork of intersections.

Intermediate Perspective

Whenever a research group is set up at the ZiF, the head of the group is assigned a scientific assistant for the whole period covering preparation for the year, organization of the group's activities during their residence at the ZiF, as well as the time thereafter devoted to finishing and editing manuscripts. Usually, this period lasts about four to five years. Serving as an interface between all factions and all kinds of activities, the ZiF deems this kind of position a particular necessity for organizing a research group.

As a scientific assistant for the group on Biological Foundations of Human Culture, I had what I would call an *intermediate* perspective on the issue of inducing interdisciplinary activities: Not only did I participate in this group and assist in its organization, but I was also located between the research group and its head as well as between the Fellows and the administration. From the observatory called scientific assistance, I study the microcosm of one group at one center, the tensions created, and the measures taken to balance them. This report is thus meant to give some flesh to the bones of more abstract notions of interdisciplinarity. It will illustrate how interdisciplinarity can be valued both positively and negatively, sometimes even simultaneously. Presented in terms of 'irresistible inflictions' this paper will corroborate the major theme of this volume, 'interdisciplinarity – the paradoxical discourse' (cf. Weingart, this volume), by pointing to the practices attempting interdisciplinarity *malgré tout*.[2]

Interdisciplinarity *In Vivo*: The Idea Called Research Group and an Illustration

THE IDEA

The ZiF was designed to advance interdisciplinary research by institutional reintegration. Its designer, Helmut Schelsky, meant to counter the overwhelming trend towards subdisciplinary fragmentation by providing highly specialized scholars with the opportunity to communicate extensively with one another. Thus, it was the institution that gave residence to and in part organized interdisciplinary communication that was new, not the idea of interdisciplinarity itself. Specifically, the ZiF's agenda is to reintegrate already existing interdisciplinary activities that, before meeting at the Center, take place mostly between and outside of universities (cf. Lübbe 1987: 30–1). This is the cornerstone of the ZiF's specialty called the 'research group': each year a group of about 20 Fellows already working at the borders of their own fields resides at the ZiF to work on a joint project.[3] In brief, the concept of research groups was established as an incentive to advance *sustained multidisciplinary cooperation*. Each element is believed to be crucial for interdisciplinarity to emerge; the explanation will begin with the last one:

- *Cooperation:* Unlike other Centers for Advanced Studies, a ZiF fellowship is not granted to provide an individual scholar with the opportunity to pursue his or own research interests. Rather, scholars are invited to collaborate with others from different fields or disciplines to work on a joint topic. The kinds of cooperation vary: lecture, discussion group, *jour fixe* for the group as a whole as well as conferences featuring outside guests. Moreover, as the group not only works at the ZiF but also lives in the apartments built around it, there is hardly a chance to avoid informal opportunities of talking to one another, even while doing laundry.
- *Multidisciplinary:* With respect to the kind and degree of scholarly exchange, every research group seems to run through several stages.[4] After an initial stage in which the group members introduce their work and discuss joint interests, the project gets an ever-more

distinct profile. Dyadic cooperations and discussion groups become established in order to find overlapping research topics. In addition, the group invites outside guests to give lectures or organizes workshops. The last weeks of a research group are generally dedicated to discussing first drafts of manuscripts for the final publication. Multidisciplinary exchange then reaches its peak: Fellows may argue about one paragraph throughout a whole session. Here is where one or more *inter*disciplinarities are about to emerge.

- *Sustained:* First, the concept is to encourage never-ending efforts to truly cooperate during the year. It is an ongoing exercise in open-mindedness and a discursive attitude, despite severe controversies[5] – an exercise the merits of which hopefully outlast the participants' residence at the ZiF. Second, it is difficult to prove that research groups have a long-lasting intellectual impact on their members, let alone on the disciplines they involve and address. Yet, there are some indicators, the more spectacular ones being those cases where a team of Fellows discovers a special issue for themselves and publishes it with a huge resonance in the disciplines addressed (cf. Gigerenzer et al. 1989).[6]

In short, the ZiF considers sustained multidisciplinary cooperation crucial in order to eventually induce interdisciplinary. Interdisciplinarity, thus understood, is as much an academic enterprise as it is a general intellectual challenge. Whatever the results, the ZiF deems every research group a worthwhile endeavour, because, as a rule, every group contributes to reinforcing the scholars' activity at the margins of their own disciplines.[7]

Interdisciplinarity, according to my thesis, is primarily a matter of preparing the grounds for communication among a variety of specialized discourses to occur. Thus, interdisciplinarity depends on its organization at every stage of the process involving both the scientific organizers as well as the administration: Without an ongoing support system to provide such resources as a conference office, computer assistance, and word processing, as well as bureaucratic assistance, an enterprise called 'research group' would just not be possible. The following illustration thus touches and argues on three different levels of interdisciplinary practice: the scholarly, the social, and the administrative level. It is on and between these interacting levels that interdisciplinarity comes about – in both its irresistible and its inflictive aspects, that is.

Initiatives and intentions

The idea for a research group very often has a long history. Initial ideas for the group on Biological Foundations of Human Culture appeared as early as 1977–8. Being a member of the Advisory Committee at the ZiF, the convener of the group, a sociologist, took an interest in a research group on Comparative Study of Behaviour in Man and Animal, yet criticized it for not including members of the social sciences. In the course of his own studies concerning eugenics he came across modern behavioural genetics and sociobiology. During a fellowship at Harvard he met with both advocates and opponents of these research fields; back in Germany he encountered hostility towards any consideration of the biological foundations of human culture among fellow social scientists and held some misgivings himself. Although there was as yet no clear-cut project, the challenge presented to the social sciences by advances in evolutionary biology and anthropology became all too obvious: It suggested the establishment of an interdisciplinary research group at the ZiF.

Basically, the idea that emerged during these years had two aspects. On the one hand social scientists, instead of dismissing biologically oriented approaches altogether, should rather seek to understand them first. Are social scientists confronted with competing approaches to basic social institutions such as the family or issues related to social change? On the other hand – given the ideological rift between biology and the social sciences – a metaperspective was called for to study the emergence of biologically oriented approaches in the social sciences from a sociology of science point of view. Do these theories reflect upon their historical and political contexts as well as upon methodological questions, and if so, how? (cf. Weingart 1989a).

These questions were transformed into a fully elaborated proposal. It covered a broad spectrum of topics that enlarged and changed through the process of finding the pertinent scholars (cf. Weingart, 1989b). Among the topics to be discussed were the following:

- *analogous approaches* explaining social institutions and cultural change in evolutionary terms
- *limitational approaches* based on the assumption that the development of culture decouples humans from genetic evolution, thus limiting the domain of natural selection to subhuman species

- *co-evolutionary approaches* that acknowledge the difference between biological and cultural mechanisms of change but assume a connection between them as well as an evolutionary pattern of cultural change
- *sociological theories of change*, both with and without making use of an evolutionary framework

A smaller part of activities should take up the historical issues concerning the relationship between biology and the social sciences as well as methodological issues concerning the 'biologicalization' of social phenomena.

In 1990, the ZiF's board of directors granted this project. Although typical of a ZiF project, which normally convenes a broad array of disciplines, the number of issues addressed by the group on Biological Foundations of Human Culture was atypically high. This is irresistible infliction number 2: To organize a research group is a huge effort and thus is usually done only once. One is tempted to cover just about everything and can invite many interesting scholars working on different aspects of a topic for an extended period of time. The project, however, should neither be too broad nor too narrow: it should allow for extended interactions on various issues without permitting individual scholars to escape into their niches. What are the right dimensions?[8]

Irresistible infliction number 3 is a correlate of number 2: Every organizer of a research group wants to convene highly reputed scholars from various fields. This ideal case is hardly ever achieved for at least two reasons. First, in order to find these scholars for all the areas involved, one needs to perform an extensive search and rating. Mostly, however, the convener relies on personal knowledge as well as on pertinent literature, on preparatory communications, or on advice from peers. Second, in some cases scholars working at the margins of their fields are either not known or not acknowledged. For both reasons, it is very difficult to convene a group consisting of excellent scholars of heterogeneous areas of research. Therefore, it is all the more important to undertake such an endeavour only when the core fields are sufficiently advanced and the respective scholars are well-known and reputed (cf. Dogan and Pahre 1990).

During the planning stage we not only used the techniques just mentioned, but also organized two preparatory conferences. This helped to assess both the prospective Fellow's intellectual fit and the social cohesion of the group to be established. For one has to keep in mind that a research group is very demanding in terms of group dynamics: Over a period of nine months its members have to communicate on a daily basis, organize lectures and conferences, and settle conflicts or tolerate different opinions, world-views, and cultural backgrounds. This calls as much for intellectual open-mindedness as for sociability. If you downplay the relevance of the latter, you are bound to experience irresistible infliction number 4, which comes in two variants: (a) He/she is a very interesting scholar but ...; (b) he/she is a very nice person but ... Both are detrimental to sustained cooperation.[9]

With respect to scholarly cohesion, the two preparatory conferences had different goals: While the first conference had been rather broad with respect to both the fields represented and the issues discussed and was designed to select among both, the second encouraged the scholars to specify their own research interests and joint research foci. Both resulted in four areas of research: first, methodological reflection, notably on reductionism and anthropomorphism; second, reflection on the sociopolitical contexts of biological reasoning in the social sciences; third, discussion of a few material issues such as societal core institutions, or the study of aggression and bonding behaviour; and fourth, comparative analysis of (co-)evolutionary models and their applicability to the social sciences.

Yet, there were more mundane selective forces: the willingness or ability of scholars to come at all, the length of time they could spend at the ZiF, whether sabbatical leave could be used, the needs of accompanying families. In the end, we settled on twelve Fellows who represented the core group and another eighteen Fellows who participated on different schedules (e.g., three months or two days per week).[10] It is a common experience that it has become increasingly difficult to have scholars move to a different place for a whole year. Even if they deem it highly attractive, their universities, their immediate collaborators, and their families might think differently. Irresistible infliction number 5, then, is that inviting a scholar in fact means dealing with many more people and institutions than just the one individual.

Intensive interactions

Every research group begins with an opening conference and ends with a concluding conference. In between, however, the groups may have completely different forms of interaction. For instance, if it is dealing with predominantly scientific matters, a group might be found in the laboratories located at the university. Recently, groups have adopted so-called e-mail conferences. Our group used the more traditional methods of intellectual interaction. In addition to a weekly meeting of the research group as a whole, discussion groups emerged that met regularly. Outside guests were invited either for individual lectures (eight) or for conferences (six), each organized by two members of the research group with the help of both the scientific assistants and the staff. Generally, organizing conferences together proved to stimulate further inter-talks, particularly between the organizers.

By touching upon the different ways of collaboratively working, namely, *jour fixe*, discussion groups, and workshops and conferences, the following paragraphs will also introduce in passing some of the issues the group discussed during the year.

Jour fixe. The weekly meeting of the group as a whole was designed to be a forum at which each Fellow would introduce his or her work, to integrate newly arrived guests, and to announce forthcoming events. Normally, these meetings took from 9:00 a.m. until 12:30 p.m. and ended with a lunch provided by the Center's staff.[11]

Over a period of about four months the group educated itself on fields and issues as different as sociological analyses of the sociobiology controversy, co-evolutionary approaches and models of dual inheritance, primate intelligence, and so on. Yet, these lectures were not only subjects of the group's education but also objects of controversy. Although we were never able to settle a debate between individual Fellows, we always intended to identify positions and the exact points of disagreement. The long-standing controversy between Darwinian psychologists and Darwinian anthropologists may serve as one example: It is all about 'adaptive behaviour.'

Human behaviour is often adaptive in the biological sense of favouring survival and reproduction. A long tradition of functionalism in the social sciences appeals to the intuition that variation in human sociocultural institutions is adaptive. The huge range of environments to which people have managed to spread and their oft-dominant role in these environments speaks in favour of this intuition. Biology offers a precise definition of adaptation drawn from evolutionary theory and a considerable number of specific models predicting how people forage, choose their mates, compose their families, and so forth, drawn from evolutionary ecology. Mechanisms of phenotypic flexibility – learning, intelligence, culturally acquired techniques – allow humans to solve an unprecedentedly diverse array of adaptive problems. It is likely that mechanisms of phenotypic flexibility first arose because they were usually successful at solving adaptive problems, such as foraging on a wide variety of resources in a wide variety of environments. At this point, the Darwinian psychologists argue that much behaviour in complex modern societies is maladaptive, because it is based on psychological mechanisms adapted to the Pleistocene past. The goal of Darwinian psychologists is to map the evolved architecture of the human mind, which, they argue, is composed of a large number of functionally specialized information-processing devices, that is, cognitive adaptations. The proposed domain specificity is what separates evolutionary psychology from studies of human social evolution, which implicitly assumes that 'fitness-maximization' is a mentally (though not consciously) represented goal, the mind being composed of domain-general mechanisms that 'figure out' fitness-maximizing behaviour in any environment – even evolutionarily novel ones.

Although the controversy should have been tempered by the same adjective both fields have attached to them (Darwinian), it instead uncovered the highly discipline-specific application of Darwinian tools (cf. Klein, this volume). Most debates were best characterized by the biblical metaphor of the Tower of Babel (cf. also Dogan and Pahre 1990): Different disciplinary language games did not easily map onto one another, nor did the usage of joint concepts help much. In some cases, the same concepts meant very different things to different fields. Irresistible infliction number 6 thus is that interaction between representatives of different *hybrid fields* means multiplying the controversies by debating seemingly joint concepts.

Stepping aside, one should note that this experience does not necessarily hamper interdisciplinary communication. On the contrary: abundant up-to-date knowledge studies show that transferring concepts can be fruitful *just because* they – in the process of being transferred – become enriched with discipline-specific knowledge, thus becoming meaningful for yet another discourse (cf. Black 1962; Hesse 1972; Bono 1990; Maasen 1995). At the same time, concepts used by several disciplines act as sites and media of exchange (Bono 1990): To advance cross-disciplinary communication, discipline-specific notions have to be spelled out. Here, the institution of a research group is a perfect forum: The Fellows, sitting face-to-face for several months, have to explain different notions of, say, 'adaptive behaviour,' thereby learning about novel ways to make use of a concept that seemed so familiar to each of the discussants.[12] The flip side of multiplying controversies by using allegedly joint concepts thus are fruitful exchanges about the two-faced medium of intellectual communication: joint concepts/heterogeneous meanings.[13] Unfortunately, the usages of evolutionary terminology were mostly discussed in terms of 'right/wrong' instead of 'adequate' or 'innovative.' Irresistible infliction number 7: One has to balance the scholarly need for utmost clarification with the willingness to interact even with those colleagues whose approaches seem to be 'wrong/inappropriate.'

Compared with the group meetings, discussion groups tended to be more efficient at this task, partly because they were smaller and dealt with a more focused array of overlapping issues.

Discussion groups. Half a year was busy with intensive exchange within discussion groups and their reports back to the group as a whole. Within these groups it was often the respective initiator who took on a kind of leadership and 'imprinted' it with some guiding ideas.[14] This leads us to irresistible infliction number 8: While one should attempt to reintegrate the different discussions at a certain stage, one should actively encourage specialized discussion groups to emerge even if this means dividing the group for a while. In a way, the division of scientific labour in a research group is replaced by the division of *intersectional* labour. Interests, competencies, and time constraints still make new specializations necessary.

The discussion groups listed below not only show how the research group started to decompose the overall project, but also indicate the different approaches to the latter.

Models, conceptual changes, and analogies. This group convened representatives of philosophy of biology, history of science, psychology, and sociology to reflect upon interdisciplinary research itself. Group members discussed issues such as the division of scientific labour, reductionism, and instances of anthropomorphism. Moreover, they developed a model of multidisciplinary explanations called Integrative Pluralism. This group, in particular, encountered irresistible infliction number 9: While reaching a more sophisticated level of discussion in a smaller circle, they increasingly lost touch with the concern of the larger group. Although considered very important by most Fellows, this subissue tended to be esoteric. Later, it formed a separate chapter within the book and otherwise appeared only indirectly in the structure of the book.

Representations. This group focused on the so-called 'units of selection,' and hence on the elements that store and transmit culture or cultural knowledge respectively. Most prominently, the group dealt with the concept called 'meme' introduced by Richard Dawkins (1982), thus analogizing the biological gene and the respective cultural unit.

Transmissions. This group dealt specifically with teaching and learning in various species. Soon, Representations and Transmissions united and became the most multidisciplinary group. It concerned itself mainly with the question of whether certain types of transmission are either part of the general evolutionary process or if they can be modeled in analogous fashion. Epidemiological models from population genetics were assessed for their ability to account for the diffusion of representations as well (cf. Sperber 1985).

Social intelligence. Primatologists, ethnologists, psychologists, as well as a historian of science discussed the following question: Did human intelligence, nowadays expressed mainly in technical domains, evolve from social intelligence, that is, from basic attention to group organization and the behavioural responses required by it? This group, too, could have had many more linkages to the group as a whole than it actually realized. Irresistible infliction number 10 yields the same results as number 9, albeit for opposite reasons: In this case, it was the group members' tendency to keep to themselves, thereby maintaining a high standard of in-group communication but putting less effort into the time-consuming task of explaining themselves to colleagues who were unfamiliar with their topic.

Kinship and social institutions. Kinship relations are, in a way, the test case for different accounts, such as sociobioligial, coevolutionary, and nonbiological – that is, sociological – ones, as they are institutions of reproductive behaviour and thus subject to both biological and social regulations. Social relations in primates and reproductive strategies in premodern rural populations have been two of the topics under discussion.

Initially, this discussion group was meant to be a cornerstone of the research group. However, it turned out that comparative analysis of different accounts of societal core institutions were possible only when all accounts were more developed. This was true for both biological and sociological approaches. If anything, it became apparent that, with respect to clear-cut units of analysis, both were not on as firm a ground as previously believed.

In summarizing, it should be emphasized that *the* 'common ground' of sociological and biological explanations of human culture is as yet not in sight. Instead there are several common grounds that have been either established or strengthened, in each case focusing on a certain topic or certain methods.

Workshops and conferences. When it turned out that some of the areas deemed crucial had not been involved, the research group decided to organize a few workshops and conferences, inviting speakers who would fill the gaps.[15] The issues dealt with were as follows:

Models of cultural evolution and theories of social change. A smaller group of scholars compared evolutionarily oriented concepts of cultural change with traditional sociological ones and subjected them to highly controversial discussion.[16]

Biological and cultural aspects of language development. Here, scholars presenting neuropsychological, palaeoanthropological, neurolinguistic, and phylo- and ontogenetic studies of language development complemented the Fellows' expertise. Like the next topic, this conference brought together a broad array of up-to-date knowledge so that it seemed advisable to publish the papers as a collection. The scientific organizers of both conferences made it their business to edit these proceedings with special regard to the linkages between the respective subissue and the general theme of the research group.

Non-verbal communication and the genesis of culture. This issue seemed to provide the 'missing link' between natural evolution and cultural development. The scholars invited inquired into the non-verbal behaviour of different species. Here, as before, members of the research group were invited to comment on the contributions and to integrate these comments into the group's discussion preceding the conference.

Methodology and models in evolutionary economics. This workshop was very much oriented towards model-building and unfortunately was attractive to only a few specialists.

Evolutionary foundations of law. A funding agency, the Volkswagen Foundation, had just established a special grant program on Behavioural Foundations of Law. It was very interested in promoting this program with the help of an introductory conference on historical, psychological, and sociobiological aspects of law and justice and, thus, coinitiated the conference. In this case, in other words, two instances of institutionalizing intersections of biology and law converged just in time.

The transfer of images and metaphors between biology and the social sciences. In 1992, the annual meeting of the Yearbook Sociology of Science was held at the ZiF. The research group presented an ideal intellectual framework for studies in the areas of sociology and history of science, inquiring into basic terms such as 'organism' and 'struggle for existence': How did these terms transgress disciplinary boundaries? How did this affect the terms as well as the disciplines making use of them? Amazingly, this rather abstract discussion united both outside guests and the research group to a high degree, partly due its connections to the work of most scholars present, and partly due to the timing. At the end of the academic year a baseline of mutual understanding had been established, inspiring even more connections.[17]

In addition to the conference proceedings about thirty preprints appeared throughout the year that informed a wider audience on the research group's work.[18] Furthermore, most of the Fellows had given lectures at various universities and thus, in passing, introduced the research group to other audiences. Additionally, the ZiF asks every group to organize a so-called ZiF-Colloquium specially designed to keep the ZiF in touch with both the University of Bielefeld as well as a broader non-academic audience. All of the aforementioned opportunities created ever-new environments for scholarly exchange and helped to keep the research group from being a self-contained endeavour.

Immediate results

Producing a visible result of multidisciplinary work,[19] that is, a cooperatively authored book, proved to be a great challenge: It partly enticed, partly forced the Fellows to create a web of intersectional activities. The first months of intensive discussions in various settings had uncovered some bridges between some of the approaches, yet collecting them in a quasi-monograph seemed to be impossible. This is irresistible infliction number 11: On the one hand you want to represent all approaches, including competing ones or those that do not even relate to one another; on the other hand you want to have as convincing and integrated a book as possible. Knowing that this ideal could only be approximated, the group developed three mechanisms for coming as close as possible.

1 We set up a structure for the book that allowed for displaying both compatible and competing approaches on different levels of analyses. This resulted first in two parts covering evolutionarily oriented approaches, one dealing with homological approaches, that is, those that treat human beings as just another unique species, and the other dealing with analogical approaches, that is, those that use evolutionary theory as a "tool-box" for analyses in sociocultural domains. Both parts were to be preceded by a lengthy part exploring the contexts of biological thinking in the social sciences: historical and theoretical, social and political, as well as methodological contexts.

   The book as a whole was to be interspersed with introductions into sections so as to lead the reader through the landscape of different approaches. It should begin with a substantial introduction displaying the major dualisms the project had to face and that the book intended to challenge (e.g., Nature vs. Nurture, Reduction vs. Autonomy). In addition to this, each part was to be introduced separately.

2 We set up a structure for the authors. We agreed on eleven chapters to which three or more authors made a contribution. All but one group of authors were composed multidisciplinarily. Each group chose a lead author who was both its coordinator as well as the liaison with the editors.

3 We assigned a multidisciplinary group of four editors: an ecologist, a philosopher of science, and two sociologists. Each of them had prime responsibility for three or four chapters. Yet, in all cases of difficulty – and there were many – the 'ed-group' as a whole decided how to solve the problem.

Of course, there were additional challenges, such as finding and agreeing on a title; inviting the group back for an editorial conference and settling – once everything was in writing – unbridgeable conflicts; finding a publisher and coping with twenty-five reactions to the reviews, all of which were mixed in their assessments; and finding another publisher and coping with twenty-five kinds of impatience.

The first item – finding and agreeing on a title – is worth returning to. It had to be attractive yet informative, appeal to all the disciplines involved, and be detectable by any kind of database library research. *Human by Nature – Between Biology and the Social Sciences* (Weingart et al. 1997) was the winner, although some fellows still feel some discomfort with 'Human by Nature': Does it not sound as if we believe in a human nature? No, we do not – and we hope that the little 'by' indicates that.

Interdisciplinarity: Some Interactions at Some Intersections of Some Inter-Fields

The simplified model of interdisciplinarity (cf. the section at the start of this essay) has several implications, one of them being that the results of sustained multidisciplinary cooperation can vary considerably. The model 'may lead either to the emergence of a new "inter-field" ... or to the cessation of communication altogether – and virtually everything in between may happen as well' (p. 174). The research group on Biological Foundations of Human Culture, in my view, is a strong case for 'something in between.'

Yet, before defending the thesis that there is, as yet, no interdiscipline, one should acknowledge that the views on this matter seem to differ. For instance, those authors working on homological reasoning in the social sciences are of the opinion that we are already entitled to speak of a hybrid field called 'evolutionary social sciences.' Is there a way of reconciling these apparently opposing views? I think there is. Hybridization, according to Dogan and Pahre, comes in two basic types: institutionalized (as a formal discipline) and informal (as a topic under multidisciplinary discussion). The latter type is most likely to remain a topic that is discussed by several disciplines without ever becoming an institutionalized hybrid field (cf. Dogan and Pahre 1990: 63).

The informal type of hybridization, indeed, seems to apply to the current status of 'evolutionary social sciences': It is a conglomerate of intense interactions at some intersections of some subfields we convened. As yet, it is not established as a formal discipline, and it probably never will be. Rather, this hybridization consists of a variety of specialized discourses on a series of related topics on different levels of reasoning (analogical, homological, metatheoretical reflections). Thus, the state of affairs is certainly best described with hybridization type two, denoting a state of 'inter'-activities that is fluid, fruitful, *and* still showing some frozen borders.

There are two reasons for this mixed or informal state of hybridization. First, the project on Biological Foundations of Human Culture comprised intersectional discourses that before being convened at the ZiF differed as to the level of institutionalization. Philosophy of biology and history of science are well-established subdisciplines, and evolutionary psychology is certainly on the verge of becoming one (cf. Cosmides and Tooby 1987; Gigerenzer and Hug 1992); systems theory is an approach established in several (sub-) disciplines; least institutionalized are discourses such as evolutionary sociology. Second, the group convened scholars who, before coming to the ZiF, worked on different interdisciplinary research routines. In most cases, the scholars had pursued their intersectional research individually. In three cases, we invited a 'firm,' that is, a long-standing cooperation between two scholars.[20] None of our Fellows, however, was embedded in intersectional networks at their home institutions. Rather, they communicated with colleagues of other institutions, and it was only at the ZiF that they experienced a long-term environment that enabled them to establish a working intersection right on campus.

Being confronted with this mixed state of hybridization, the group considered a pluralistic perspective a prerequisite of the project. As a consequence, we, for instance, have not bridged the gap between those scholars who argue on an analogical and those who argue on a homological level. Rather, we documented the diversity of arguments and related them by drawing a map. The map is captured by the overall structure of the book.

However, there is more than cartography. On a very basic level, the group arrived at the understanding that any fundamentalist language should be avoided – one should adhere to neither biological nor sociological reductionism. For instance, the group's title Biological *Foundations* of Human Culture was accepted as a provocative one, yet not as a title for the final publication. Moreover, *within* the parts, and even more so *within* individual chapters, the work has been very intense and mutually influential. This effect seems to be in resonance with social psychological studies on optimal group size in cooperative work (cf. Epton, Payne, and Pearson 1984: 72)[21] as well as with Rogers Hollingsworth's study on nurturing environments for innovative work (cf. Hollingsworth and Hollingsworth, this volume). Different fields were best attached by a joint material issue, such as kinship; another hinge was the comparative analysis of 'units of selection.' In other words, the research group as a whole assembled a *set of intersectional activities*. These intersectional activities emerged typically in considerably advanced areas of study. The final results reflect several types of fruitful interaction: the fully integrated chapter, the multidisciplinary overview, the discussion among different approaches.

The amount and quality of scholarly exchange was, as has been said earlier, above all a matter of organizing it. Yet, here, too, the activities have to be balanced. One might say that the 'magic' of organized self-organization leads to the best results. Notably the facilities of the ZiF (e.g., various conference rooms, offices, a swimming pool, and a nearby forest) and its routines in supporting the group did much to facilitate formal and informal communications. Moreover, the institution of a research group (serving as an organizational and cognitive framework) facilitated a variety of exchanges according to individual preferences. Only this environment in all its dimensions allows for unexpected things to happen and for the freedom to make detours and mistakes!

Finally, this research group at the ZiF did more than merely teach a lesson on practising interdisciplinarity – namely, by way of inducing some interactions at some intersections of some inter-fields. In addition, it taught a lesson on how to learn to practise interdisciplinarity: there are no techniques to be learned or manuals to be compiled. Rather, interdisciplinarity is a scholarly and organizational balancing act to be learned by doing. If there is such a thing as a golden rule, then it concerns the type of organizational activities: although indispensable, they have to be as implicit and as invisible as possible. They have to be part of the group's self-organized *procedere* to produce a stimulating atmosphere, the results of which radiate via formal presentation, publication, and informal communication. That, indeed, is the icing on the cake called the interdisciplinary research group.

Notes

1 Type three is precisely what Gibbons et al. call 'transdisciplinarity' or 'mode 2': knowledge is driven by the contexts of application, organized in highly flexible and transient institutions, always on the verge of being reorganized or given up as soon as the changing context calls for it (Gibbons et al. 1994: 3–44). As opposed to this, interdisciplinarities at the ZiF are to a large degree disconnected from transcontextual demands.

2 On a methodological note, I would like to mention that while the paper is a report on past experiences and thus helpful in understanding more about *practising* interdisciplinarity, it occasionally relates to systematic analyses of cognitive, institutional-structural, and organizational aspects of inter-

disciplinarity and should be read in conjunction with those (cf. contributions to this volume).

3 It should be noted, however, that 'research' group does not denote doing research together. Rather, the groups discuss data already collected and compare theories and methods – a concept that natural scientists, in particular, deem very restrictive (cf. Immelmann 1987: 87–91).

4 Similar observations are noted by Wilhelm Voßkamp. Reporting on his research group "Funktionsgeschichte der Utopie,' he differentiates among four stages: orientation, tentative constitution, stabilization, and critical self-reflexion (cf. Voßkamp 1987: 98).

5 Ursula Hübenthal agrees that the 'uniformity' of pursuing interdisciplinary cooperation 'lies more in the *mentality* than in the *method*' (Hübenthal 1994: 74, emphasis added).

6 Sverre Sjölander describes the fate of several ZiF groups he studied in ten stages, stage 8 being 'What is happening to me?...' According to this observation, '... people will often find that they, after participation in an interdisciplinary venture, turn out to have become advocates or at least reluctant defenders of disciplines they have interacted with during the project; this in turn will strengthen or rekindle interest in further interdisciplinary work ...' (1985: 90). The last stage, then – typically enough – is entitled 'The real beginning' (1985: 90).

7 The third characteristic of interdisciplinarity at the ZiF deliberately focuses on the exercise rather than on the evaluation, because a consensus on criteria for evaluating these activities is as yet not in sight. Although originality, integratedness, (multi-)disciplinary solidity, as well as epistemological reflection will be among these criteria, it also seems likely that evaluative criteria will have to be as different as interdisciplinarities are. For instance, it is not at all conclusive that 'applicability' should be a stable criterion, as Gibbons et al. (1994) seem to suggest.

8 At this stage the role of the ZiF is very important. It provides the organizer of a research group with administrative support and advice on various issues, timing being an important one. For instance, most organizers underestimate the huge amount of time required to convene a group.

9 This, of course, is just a less-refined version of arguments dealt with by Bromme. In a nutshell, the scholar should express a (disciplinary) identity that is stable and flexible at the same time (cf. Bromme, Rambow, and Wiedmann 1998, as well as Klein 1990: 183). Similarly, Gibbons et al. point to 'a portfolio of identities and competencies [that has] to be managed' (1994: 165). Indeed, the participants of a research group must be prepared to act as one another's 'nurturing environment' (cf. Hollingsworth, this

volume) throughout the academic year – otherwise, interdisciplinarity is bound to be a failure.

10 The scholars were representatives from borders of the following disciplines: anthropology, archaeology, ecology, economics, ethnology, genetics, history, philosophy, psychology, and sociology.

11 It is important to note that lunches at the ZiF assume less central a role than they do at corresponding institutes. This is partly due to the fact that most Fellows live on campus and try to keep up with their private lives as much as possible; moreover, social events are abundant without lunches. Thus, the degree of interaction imposed on the Fellows being so high already creates the need for some freedom from togetherness, be it scholarly or social. Still, to have lunch together was accepted surprisingly often.

12 This, by the way, constrains bibliometrical analyses quite seriously. Although they can help to draw 'cognitive maps' by looking for the increase and spread of certain keywords among different fields and disciplines, these analyses need to be complemented by in-depth discourse analysis investigating the field- or discipline-specific usages of identical words and seemingly joint concepts. (On bibliometrical analysis of interdisciplinarity, cf. van Raan, this volume.)

13 This is what Bromme recasts in terms of a theory of 'common ground,' that is, a shared frame of reference. If the distinctiveness of perspectives represented by different scholars is the constitutive feature of interdisciplinarity, then the continuous reconstruction of the object of research comes as no surprise as different sets of stereotypical representations, epistemic styles, and so on are involved (cf. Bromme, this volume). Therefore, the question is how un/common is un/common enough to be stimulating instead of detrimental to multidisciplinary discourse? (On this question cf. Knorr-Cetina 1981).

14 Here it becomes apparent that it is not some magic list of personality traits that accounts for fruitful intellectual exchange within a research group but rather the institutional setting that allows for a variety of interactions to occur. Strong leadership seems to be an important element of successful work, especially within a multidisciplinary team (cf. Hollingsworth and Hollingsworth, this volume). Yet, a Center for Advanced Study hosting temporary groups does not allow for hierarchical structures to be established. Instead, it favours an egalitarian structure that permits a multiplicity of creative settings.

15 Four conferences resulted in books edited by Fellows: Weingart, Kummer, and Hof (1994); Maasen, Mendelsohn, and Weingart (1995); Velichkovsky and Rumbaugh (1996); and Segerstråle and Molnár (1997).

16 Although regarded as one of the most crucial issues to be addressed, the conference revealed only a few areas of direct comparison. Thus this exchange – wisely enough – did not result in the publication of conference proceedings.
17 Note that 'mutual understanding' is not to be understood in an emphatic way. Rather, the group had reached a level where each Fellow's remark 'rang a bell,' or, to put it in terms of cognitive psychology, gave one a strong *feeling of knowing* (e.g., Tulving and Madigan 1970) what the other was saying. Therefore it became possible to respond to remarks more easily than before. This is not to disappoint those who are searching for a common ground. Rather, it is the first step to creating it.
18 Again, it is easy to imagine that without ongoing institutional support – for example, in terms of desktop publishing – these visible results of a research group would be difficult, if not impossible, to accomplish. In addition to the conference office, a research secretary with two staff members was kept busy preparing talks and papers throughout the year. After the group left, one secretary took care of all conference proceedings as well as the book jointly written by almost all the Fellows.
19 Interestingly, the possibility of not publishing at all had not been taken into consideration – maybe not so remarkable in view of a professional system that values, among other things, an uninterrupted list of publications. Especially for younger scholars it was already considered risky to engage in this enterprise, for it was clear beforehand that the research group would not result in many publications. From the viewpoint of the institution, publications are essential in order to earn and maintain the scholarly respect and standing for such a center.
20 Dogan and Pahre's plea for this type of hybridization is radical: 'If simple juxtaposition is avoided, collaboration between scholars belonging to different disciplines can be a creative form of hybridization. In most cases, the productive collaboration involves only two authors, rarely three or more; it seems that 'two is company and three a crowd' (Dogan and Pahre 1990: 117).
21 Typically, these studies do not give a magic number but rather emphasize basic criteria that have to be met, such as the possibility of proceeding on informal terms and implicit agreements as to who is to contribute what, exert leadership, and so on. Basically, this list of criteria coincides with the sociologists' notion of 'primary groups' as opposed to secondary ones.

10

Interdisciplinary Research at the Caltech Beckman Institute

ERIC R. SCERRI

Introduction

The Beckman Institutes located at the California Institute of Technology, the University of Illinois, Stanford University, and the University of California at Irvine are a recent example of a self-consciously established project for the purpose of pursuing interdisciplinary research in the natural and biomedical sciences.[1] This is not to deny the huge body of interdisciplinary research that has occurred, perhaps incidentally, in the natural sciences, including the development of hybrid fields such as molecular biology and chemical physics. This article rather takes for granted the ubiquity of modern-day interdisciplinary research and seeks to explore the possible outcomes of institutes that proclaim inter-disciplinarity as their *raison d'être* and perhaps take active steps to attempt to foster this mode of research.[2]

As is well known there have been several studies of mission-oriented interdisciplinary projects (see Galison and Helvy 1992), such as the Manhattan project, NASA, the research conducted in a number of elementary particle accelerators, as well as the socio-anthropological studies of Latour and Woolgar on the Salk Institute (Latour and Woolgar 1979) and an Australian group looking into the Walter and Eliza Hall Institute for medical research in Melbourne (Charlesworth et al. 1989). Studies on interdisciplinary institutes devoted primarily to the natural sciences have not been as common however. In the present article I will focus primarily on just one of the four major Beckman Institutes, the one located at the California Institute of Technology, or Caltech for short.

The approach adopted here, in keeping with recent work in history and philosophy of science, will be to examine the scientific practice and context in favour of purely logical or theoretical issues. It is hoped that the present report can nevertheless provide material for those seeking to address theoretical issues, such as a classification of different forms of interdisciplinarity.

It is now widely agreed that the theoretical approach to establish the unity of the sciences within a logical positivist tradition has failed. Similarly, attempts to achieve inter-theoretic reduction among the various sciences and ultimately to reduce all the sciences to theoretical physics have also failed to bear fruit. This has led many commentators to conclude, wrongly in my view, that science is disunified not only epistemologically but also metaphysically.[3]

It would seem reasonable to suppose that the practice of interdisciplinarity and its documented rise points to an underlying methodological unity that is being tapped by researchers engaged in interdisciplinary work. Similarly, it might be thought that if science were as disunified as some have claimed, it should not be possible to practise interdisciplinary work at all. However, matters are more complicated, since the mere practice of interdisciplinarity does not necessarily rest on any unity between the sciences.

Integration incorporates the idea of unity between forms of knowledge and their respective disciplines, whereas 'interdisciplinary' simply refers to the use of more than one discipline in pursuing a particular inquiry (Klein 1990: 27).

A Tradition of Interdisciplinary and Cooperative Research at Caltech

Collaboration was more than a slogan at Caltech; its scientific leaders understood that nature does not heed human-made categories. (Servos 1990: 269)

Caltech, in Pasadena, just outside Los Angeles, is one of the most prestigious scientific institutions in the United States, if not the whole world. The very existence of an interdisciplinary institute at Caltech may at first appear as something of an enigma, given the apparent conservative institutionalism of this bastion of the scientific enterprise.[4] Furthermore, Caltech has prided itself on fostering individual brilliance and not on pursuing large-scale teamwork projects. From time to time powerful personalities in Caltech's history, such as Linus Pauling, may

well have succeeded in building themselves research 'empires,' but this
is something that seems to have been generally frowned upon.[5] However, the very institutional success of Caltech can be seen to rest on an
interdisciplinary need that arose in the 1920s when the astronomer
George Ellery Hale began looking to attract top-quality faculty to the
then little-known campus in Pasadena that was still known as Throop
Polytechnic. Hale was an astronomer specializing in observations, one
very important aspect of which consisted in performing detailed analyses of the spectra of the sun and other stars.

After moving to Caltech, Hale reasoned that, if his spectroscopic work
was going to continue to flourish, he would need a first-rate physicist
as well as a first-rate chemist, since spectroscopy combines aspects of
these sciences. The physicist turned out to be Robert Millikan and the
chemist Alfred Amos Noyes.

Historians of science generally agree that it was this triumvirate of
world-class scientists that led Caltech from an obscure manual training
college to a position of scientific pre-eminence that persists to this day.
New disciplines such as astrophysics, biochemistry, and physical chemistry began to flourish at this time, partly as a result of the use of new
instruments, partly due to the collaborative and interdisciplinary efforts
of scientists from different specialties, and partly as the result of individual efforts by scientists and foundations officers.

The next landmark event in terms of interdisciplinarity may be identified perhaps with the foundation of the Biology Division in 1928.
Caltech was able to attract Thomas Hunt Morgan, who had already
distinguished himself as a world-class geneticist and a charismatic leader
at Columbia University, where he had helped to put genetics firmly on
the biological agenda with his experiments on *Drosophila*, the common
fruit fly. Morgan's new division at Caltech was established with the
express purpose of fostering cooperation among genetics, biochemistry,
biophysics, embryology, and physiology.

The eventual establishment of the biology division in 1928 appears, at
first sight, to have been somewhat unusual in that no effort was made
to cover all the main areas in biology, attention being focused instead
on one particular promising specialty, namely genetics. But, as in many
instances before and after this date, this policy is in keeping with
Caltech's approach of emphasizing one particular area in which the
institution could make a major contribution.

Another leading figure in Caltech folklore, two-time Nobel prize-
winner Linus Pauling, who has often been referred to simply as the

greatest chemist of the twentieth century, crafted a 'new region of science' by combining physics, chemistry, biology, theory, and experiment.

George Beadle, the founder of biochemical genetics, worked at Caltech, starting with corn and moving on to fruit flies and eventually to fungi. Furthermore, both Beadle and Morgan extended their collaborative projects well beyond academe into industry and the military sphere.

Another example of Caltech's penchant for interdisciplinarity is the work of Max Delbrück, who began as a physicist, including a spell with Niels Bohr in Copenhagen, and became one of the first scientists to forge links among genetics, physics, and mathematics. In the late 1930s he founded the 'phage school' at Caltech, which under his leadership was to be the training ground for numerous future molecular biologists.[6]

More recently Caltech has continued to be at the forefront of interdisciplinary drives. For example the field of geochemistry has been pioneered at Caltech with contributions from Clair Patterson, who developed a method for measuring the age of the earth and the solar system. He was also responsible for bringing worldwide attention to the problem of lead pollution. Another more recent case is the LIGO project (laser interferometric gravitational wave observatory), which involves a team of over 100 specialists from such areas as theoretical and experimental physics, engineering, and computing.

This brief chronology is meant to underscore the strong interdisciplinary style of scientific research that has permeated Caltech almost from its inception. It was the unique combination of the interests and skills of its scientists, as well as the institutional structure and patronage relationships, that shaped the nature of research and education from the 1920s to the present and have strongly influenced what was to become the Beckman Institute. As with the foundation of Caltech itself, spectroscopy may be identified as the unifying technique that brings together workers from different disciplines at the BI. While Harry Gray, the Institute's director, personally leads the laser spectroscopy facility, there are also large laboratories dedicated to X-ray diffraction and mass spectroscopic techniques, as well as magnetic imaging techniques (MRI) machines that are the descendants of nuclear magnetic resonance spectrometers.

The fields that are being brought together at the Beckman Institute consist primarily of chemistry and biology, forging new disciplines such as bio-inorganic chemistry. Other seemingly remote fields include biological imaging, advanced computational methods, computational chemistry, biomolecular design, and the sequencing of proteins and nucleic acids. The interrelationship among these various fields is immediately appreciated when one thinks of the ubiquity of computational methods in handling large amounts of data, such as biological sequencing or performing *ab initio* calculations in chemistry, or the use of computational methods in the course of imaging work.

Beckman the Man

Before describing the findings of our research it is necessary to say something about the benefactor who has made the Caltech BI possible. Arnold O. Beckman is a scientific entrepreneur whose name has become a household word in the field of scientific instrumentation. He was born in 1900 in Cullom, Illinois. In 1919 he enrolled at the up-and-coming University of Illinois to study chemistry, eventually majoring in chemical engineering due to his interest in what Beckman himself refers to as the 'practical side.' In the course of undergraduate training Beckman gained knowledge of hydrogen electrodes, thus helping him to invent the pH meter, which was to form the basis of his industrial empire.

After gaining his MS, Beckman went to Caltech, but after a year decided to go east and take a job with Western Electric, a company that later became Bell Telephone Laboratories. But a visit by A.A. Noyes in 1926 persuaded Beckman to return to Caltech to take a PhD. In 1935 Beckman developed the world's first commercial pH meter and soon afterwards resigned from Caltech to concentrate on his business affairs. From this point onwards Beckman's company went from strength to strength and continued to be successful even through the Depression years. During the Second World War, Beckman's National Technical Laboratories developed a number of instruments and devices, including a quartz spectrophotometer that helped in the war effort by making possible the analysis of aviation fuel and artificial rubber. This instrument remained virtually unmodified from 1940 to 1964, during which time over 20,000 were sold to laboratories all over the world. A number of other notable inventions followed, including the first commercial ultra-centrifuge, used to separate chemical substances as well as measure their densities.

From a 180-square-foot shop in a Pasadena garage Beckman Instruments, as it became known in the early 1950s, grew into an international giant with interests in biomedical research, health care, process analysis and control, environmental technology, medical and industrial chemical research, communications electronics, auto and consumer production, as well as scientific instrumentation of all kinds. Arnold Beckman served as president of Beckman Instruments until 1965 and is still formally Chairman of the Board. In 1982 his company merged with the SmithKline Corporation to form the SmithKline Beckman Corporation, of which he is a director emeritus.

Beckman, unlike most wealthy people, has given away a large part of his fortune during his own lifetime and given it to basic research, contrary to most philanthropic gifts that seem to go to 'worthy social causes.' Beckman believes that he can do more good for society by promoting basic science, which has resulted in a number of major gifts to various universities. The first major gift was to his alma mater, the University of Illinois, which has allowed for the construction of the largest of the four major Beckman Institutes. The second was a gift of $50 million to Caltech to build its Beckman Institute, the subject of this study. More recently the Beckman Institute for Genetics and Molecular Medicine was built at the Stanford University campus, as was the Beckman Institute for Laser Surgery at the campus of the University of California at Irvine.

In addition, three major buildings at the Caltech campus apart from the Beckman Institute bear the name of Beckman emblazoned in large letters.[7] Such is Beckman's presence felt on campus that Caltech it is sometimes jokingly referred to as the 'Beckman Institute of Technology.'

Interdisciplinarity at Caltech

The main way in which I have examined interdisciplinarity at Caltech has been through a series of interviews with the leading researchers. In the course of these interviews I have attempted to discover something of the academic journeys that have been taken by the interviewees, with a view to building up a picture of the typical modern-day scientific interdisciplinarian. Of the fifteen interviews conducted at Caltech I have selected just four for the sake of illustration in the present short report.

Interdisciplinarity has long been a feature of work in industrial research, which is often driven by the expediencies of market forces and is not hampered by the artificial divisions that exist in university departments resulting from the need to teach the various disciplines. It is perhaps no accident that the sponsor for the Beckman Institutes was himself not an academic.[8] As I hope to document in the course of the following pages, the structure of university teaching and administration is often regarded as being detrimental to interdisciplinarity.

One of the main innovations that has occurred at the Caltech BI regarding personnel has been the establishment of positions devoted entirely to research, a feature that not surprisingly has met with considerable resistance from the members of the teaching faculty. These new positions, called Members of the Beckman Institute (MBIs), have been created to overcome such obstacles as the traditional university structure imposes. However, as will be seen, they have also created some drawbacks for the researchers themselves.

It is probably fair to say that all other factors being equal, the most interdisciplinary style of functioning at the BI would be expected from researchers holding such MBI positions. For this reason two of the selected four individual cases discussed here, Jerry Solomon and Seth Marder, are MBIs. A third researcher, Thomas Meade, is a member of the research faculty with no teaching responsibilities. Such positions are not particularly novel, either at Caltech or in universities at large. They represent something in between members of the teaching faculty, many of whom are engaged in research at the BI, and the above-mentioned MBIs, whose positions are not classed as belonging within the faculty. The final member of the quartet considered here is Scott Fraser, who holds an endowed chair at Caltech and is thus a full member of the teaching faculty. The common thread that unifies all four chosen individual researchers is their thoroughgoing commitment to interdisciplinarity. The particular positions they hold may be no more than historical accidents.

JERRY SOLOMON[9]

Jerry Solomon describes his research work as having two aspects. Firstly, he is interested in the problem of chain folding in proteins. The question is how the primary structure in the sequence of amino acids in a protein dictates the precise three-dimensional geometry that the folded chain adopts. As a recent editorial in the journal *Science* put it, 'The folding of a protein into its characteristic three dimensional shape is a biological equivalent of the big bang: The end result is evident everywhere, in every living cell, but the beginnings are shrouded in mystery.'[10]

Solomon's second project concerns the development of methods for analysing images that are generated from multidimensional data. The imaging work has involved collaboration with biologists Scott Fraser and Mel Simon, who have completely separate research programs in the Beckman Institute. Fraser has initiated revolutionary new methods of biological imaging that extend the range of microscopic techniques into the realm of real-time microscopy on such processes as biological development.

Both of these aspects of Solomon's work are highly interdisciplinary but in different ways. In the case of the chain-folding work, Solomon draws on his own combined skills as a physicist, chemist, biologist, and computer specialist. He explains that people have been working on the chain-folding problem for some thirty years and that little success has been achieved regarding the ability to predict the three-dimensional structure of a protein given just the primary structure of amino acids. However, he stresses that along the way many subproblems have been solved and that the enterprise has forced the practitioners to develop novel methods for maximizing the use of computer memory. This type of economy is necessary despite the fact that Solomon and his colleagues have access to some of the most powerful computers available anywhere in the world. He describes himself as 'a physicist now hiding out as a molecular biologist.'

Solomon was an experimental physics professor at the University of San Diego from 1972 to 1982, where he became interested in laser scattering techniques. He then took a sabbatical year at the Jet Propulsion Laboratory in Pasadena and was drawn into image analysis. He ended up by staying at JPL for the following nine years, in charge of one of the image-processing sections. He was then approached by Caltech's Lee Hood, who had heard of his image-processing talents and was interested in developing instrumentation to carry out molecular-biological manipulations such as DNA sequencing. As Solomon recalls, it was Hood who introduced him to the chain-folding problem as well. At this time Solomon also met chemist William Goddard, another present BI researcher, and the two of them began to collaborate on the chain-folding question. Solomon completed the move from JPL in 1991, becoming one of the first members of the Beckman Institute. His reasons for leaving JPL were that 'The bureaucracy has just overtaken everything and your ability to get anything done was just going exponentially to zero.'

He also recalls that he was itching to get back into doing research in physics rather than just doing image-processing work. Solomon is the epitome of the interdisciplinary scientist and speaks very enthusiastically about the role of the BI in fostering such activities. When asked how he finds the human and intellectual environment at Caltech and at the BI he responds: 'I don't think you can find a better place. I really don't. The intellectual environment both in the Beckman and on campus in general is just superb ... With almost everybody you can walk in, you talk to them, you pick up the phone and call someone and say let's talk. It's a great environment, it really is, both being a faculty member and I think being a graduate student.' On the question of how he might characterize the style of interdisciplinarity at the BI, Solomon says,

> It's hard to define an overall theme, I don't think there really is one. You know Beckman's idea was to put chemistry and biologists together and throw in some computing stuff and see what came out. I think it's really no more, no less than that. And a lot of good things have happened ... People talk incessantly about interdisciplinary studies and interdisciplinary this and that. But nobody can define an interdisciplinary operation. It's something that has to happen spontaneously, or it doesn't work.[11]

Solomon goes on to emphasize that it takes a special kind of chemistry between people for collaborations to be successful, and that this is why collaborations cannot be defined in advance. He feels that Caltech is an excellent environment for interdisciplinary ventures, since there have always been people here who are willing to cross conventional discipline lines. Enough people do this kind of thing at Caltech that individuals of this persuasion are not made to feel awkward about it, unlike in many other institutions.

My interview turned to the newly established research positions at the BI, namely the Members of the Beckman Institute positions. Solomon points out that this has been a major departure at Caltech, where there had never previously been any purely research positions for non-faculty members. The establishment of this new position allowed Harry Gray to introduce senior researchers who, like Jerry Solomon, are well beyond the postdoctoral stage. However, this innovation was met with considerable resistance from the Caltech faculty, since, unlike postdoctoral fellows, Members of the Beckman Institute have the power to initiate grant proposals, sometimes competing for the same funds that a faculty member might be seeking.[12]

Solomon likes the fact that the new positions are, as he puts it, 'a bit ill-defined,' because this gives him more leeway to operate. He likes the advantage of being able to supervise graduate students but at the same time not have any formal teaching duties whatsoever. The position carries a five-year renewable contract that guarantees personal support for the recipients, irrespective of what they may or may not achieve. Of course most holders of the position compete for grant money to extend their research activities. The situation at the BI is therefore better than at other places where research faculty are obliged to operate on a 'soft money' basis, which amounts to saying 'no grant, no position.'

One of the well-known disadvantages of doing interdisciplinary work is that of having to live dangerously on the job market. Clearly a person who, for example, works at the interface of chemistry and physics is going to suffer disadvantages when applying for positions advertised by autonomous chemistry or physics departments. Solomon points out that a lot of graduate students avoid the interdisciplinary path because of such employment risks.

> I think most of them at that stage in their life would much rather see a clear career path, that although not guaranteed, is highly likely to succeed. That's why I really wonder whether any of these formalized interdisciplinary programs can actually succeed. A lot of that has to do, I suppose, with the way people are brought up in the education system. It's always been focused even, probably from kindergarten, on the idea of compartmentalizing things ... academia is no different than any other large institution. It has incredible inertia. It's really odd but academia in some ways is almost anathema to intellectual pursuit in the sense of not being free-wheeling and open to any ideas.

SETH MARDER

Seth Marder is described by the BI director as possibly its most interdisciplinary researcher.[13] Marder holds one of the Member of the Beckman Institute positions and works in the area of non-linear optics. This field concerns the manner in which light interacts with certain materials to produce new light waves that have been altered in their frequency or their phase and other propagation characteristics. For example, light in the infrared frequency range can have its frequency doubled in order to generate light in the visible range. Non-linear optics can be used to extend the wavelength over which a laser can generate light or to effect transfer of information from one optical fibre into another one.

Marder's group focuses on an organic materials approach to non-linear optics because, as he explains, their response can be very fast and their properties can be rationally tuned. Over the past five years he and his colleagues have concentrated on developing a systematic understanding of how chemical structure relates to the various non-linear optical properties and how the various properties are related amongst themselves. This understanding has allowed the group to come up with models that other people can use to make better materials and has also allowed Marder's own group to make materials that surpass previously existing ones.

Marder describes his own work, nowadays, as sitting at the computer, talking to people on the phone, and writing papers. Other researchers in his group are mostly engaged in synthetic work, that is, making new molecules that hopefully provide better optical properties.[14] He cites Joe Perry, a spectroscopist at the Jet Propulsion Laboratory, who obtained his PhD from Caltech, as his main collaborator.

> He has a very different perspective. He's much more a physical chemist. In terms of interdisciplinary work, what has worked extraordinarily well for us is the fact that I come into it from the synthetic side and he comes into it from the spectroscopic side. We've been working together for eight and a half years. We can talk to each other and understand each other's language. As a result, we can come forth with ideas that other people who are not conversant in different languages have not and perhaps cannot develop.

Other collaborations include researchers in many diverse areas, such as computational chemistry, physics, electrical engineering, optical science, and material science, all of which need to be addressed in order to advance the field of non-linear optics.

Marder's intellectual development shows some interesting twists and turns, typical of many researchers at the Beckman Institute. He began by doing an undergraduate chemistry degree at the Massachusetts Institute of Technology, including a project on technetium compounds that can be used as pharmaceuticals. His PhD was carried out at the University of Wisconsin on mechanistic organometallic chemistry. He then travelled to Oxford to do what he thought would be a postdoctoral fellowship involving organometallic chemistry, but was advised to try something in the field of molecular sensors and materials. In the course of this work Marder was exposed, 'almost by accident' as he recalls, to non-linear optics, which was to become his forte. By examining the structure–property relationships of some of these systems he succeeded in discovering a new class of materials with very good non-linear optical properties. This work culminated in a paper that appeared in *Nature* but left Marder with the uneasy feeling that he did not really understand the physics of these systems. To grasp why such systems really worked, 'I felt personally obliged to spend enough time in the field so that I had that understanding. And the more I probed, the less I really believed that the rest of the people understood what they had done. And so in a very natural way I ended up getting into the field and developing a new way of thinking about structure–property relationships. Which I think has been widely accepted at this point.' Marder readily admits that at the beginning his proposals seemed bizarre to many people and that they were generally not interested in his work. Other people were not calculating what he wanted to know, and he was forced to take on a postdoctoral fellow and to do the theoretical work himself.

Only then, he says, did other theorists begin to take notice. Marder remembers that one of his first papers, which he still regards as one of his most important, had great difficulty in being accepted for publication. Eventually as many as eight independent groups succeeded in confirming Marder's theory. Meanwhile he continues to regard himself as an experimentalist who only does theory when he is forced to do so.[15] He considers that he has now earned enough credibility with the community that it is willing to take seriously his more far-fetched ideas.

Marder first came to Caltech and JPL, at the same time, as a National Research Council resident associate, which he explains represents a semi-independent position, something in between a postdoctoral and a faculty position. He was thinking about leaving when he was talked into staying and joining the new BI as well as retaining his JPL appointment.[16] Marder has therefore participated in the Beckman Institute right from its inception. He considers that being at Caltech has helped his research because of the strong academic environment, but that it has not helped his career. But he also believes, in retrospect, that it would have been more advantageous to have taken a faculty position on completing his stint as a postdoctoral fellow.

The subject turns to interdisciplinarity, a theme on which Marder holds outspoken views.

Everyone talks interdisciplinary research but if you look around institutions, including this one, the administrative structure is not suited for interdisciplinary research. It's suited for people to be easily pigeon-holed as a chemist or a material scientist, and if you're a chemist, an organic chemist or an inorganic chemist or a physical chemist. And when you in fact truly do interdisciplinary research, and you look for a job, if you don't fit into one of these historically based subcategories, you tend to have advocacy in many places but not a core advocacy in one group of people that in fact needs to cough up a position for you. Historically, a lot of it is due to teaching, I think.

Marder also has interesting views on the present education system and how that tends to stifle possibilities of interdisciplinarity. He points out that most people who emerge from universities with a PhD do not become professors but go into industry. However, these people have been trained in an environment that is highly focused on one person, that is, one-investigator type work. He thinks that it is harmful to impart that attitude to students, who eventually have to function in a completely different environment. Marder therefore suggests that it is not particularly beneficial from the standpoint of education to work in a narrow, unidisciplinary way.

He insists on distinguishing between interdisciplinary and collaborative research. There are people who do interdisciplinary work by themselves, but he subscribes to the notion that it's worth doing both interdisciplinary and collaborative research.

THOMAS MEADE[17]

Tom Meade took an undergraduate degree at Arizona State University, not because it was an 'exceptionally stellar institution,' as he puts it, but because it was as far away as he could get from New York where he was raised. While still an undergraduate he tried to get into a research laboratory but experienced a great deal of resistance from his college professors, since even as recently as the late seventies the notion of undergraduate research had not caught on at Arizona State. He was finally taken on by Therald Moeller, a chemistry professor, and one of the fathers of inorganic chemistry. Moeller guided Meade to pursue graduate work at Ohio State University which, as he now recalls, was hardly a hotbed of interdisciplinarity.

The buildings for biology and biochemistry were separate and were at opposite ends of the campus. The chemistry department was set up like a fort so that even subdisciplines of chemistry had walls. Organic people didn't talk to inorganic people and certainly not to physical or analytical chemists. It was a great department for their individual things but talking to each other, forget it. I wanted to be in inorganic chemistry, specifically inorganic chemistry of living systems, which starts to get multidisciplinary, but that field was just being born: bio-inorganic chemistry.

Following a rather bizarre selection procedure for deciding which graduate students would work with which professor, Meade found himself a student of a biochemist and obliged to take a Masters degree in biochemistry, which he did not particularly want to do at the time. He then went on to a PhD thesis in inorganic coordination chemistry, which is really where his roots lie. From this time Meade has developed an expertise in this branch of chemistry, which deals with metal atoms and ions surrounded by large, often organic, groups that cluster around the metal. Such coordination compounds are the key to many biological reactions, such as respiration and photosynthesis. For example, hemoglobin has an inner core that binds oxygen and releases it on demand and is a coordination complex consisting of a porphyrin ring at the centre of which there is an iron atom.

Although Meade says he did not truly understand the biological implications of this type of compound, he had become sufficiently interested in the work to contemplate doing a postdoctorate in the subject. He recalls that the career prospects for doing postdoctoral work were not so different at the time from what they are now, 'Finishing graduate students who are looking at careers are saying forget it – there is absolutely no funding in sciences. Government's drying up completely. You'll never get tenure, and if you do you'll bust your butt for six years to get it and then you might not. It isn't worth it. And I'm getting paid fifty percent less than some clown who's getting an MBA, whose degrees, I mean they're printing them – making them like a dime a dozen.'

Although he had a number of industrial offers, Meade nevertheless was determined to continue in academic work and ended by taking another unusual turn and going to medical school. He applied for a National Institutes of Health fellowship to work on MRI imaging and in particular the use of inorganic complexes as contrast agents, which allow certain features on MRI scans to be more visible. On arriving at the Harvard Medical School to take up his fellowship work, Meade realized that he did not know enough basic medical science.

When I got there it was clear to me that I was crippled in entomology, endocrinology, physiology, anatomy, I mean if I'm going to be making compounds that are going to be clinically related I've got to know the chemistry of physiological systems. So I started taking all the course works. I swore I'd never take any more course work after having being a bio-chemistry masters and a PhD in inorganic. But now I was back at it. For necessity, not for desire.

Although he was eventually promoted to assistant professor in medical school, Meade began to feel the need to work in a basic science environment once again and started to talk to Harry Gray, which soon led to his arrival at Caltech on a postdoctoral fellowship. Meade recalls that even at this stage he believed that having interdisciplinary skills would give him an edge in the job market, but he was also very aware of the fact that very few places were genuinely committed to this form of research work. 'What do most academic places want – they want themselves. They want to reproduce themselves. So when the academic appointments come up, what do they want? My research is hot, I'd like to have somebody who's related to my work. So the guys who are making the decisions, no matter what they say, they do not want interdisciplinary people.' Meade says that after a mere six hours in the building he knew that it was the right place for him. His specialty is the chemistry of contrast agents used with MRI imaging techniques, which are widely used for making three-dimensional images of the inside of biological systems. Unlike X-ray techniques, MRI is completely harmless, a fact that has contributed to its increasing application in the medical field.

Specially modified MRI instrumentation now permits image resolution of the order of microns instead of millimetres in the case of general medical usage. An important aspect of both forms of MRI imaging involves the use of chemical contrast agents that allow certain crucial features to show up more clearly on the images, and this is where Thomas Meade, one of the leaders in this field, comes into the picture.

Meade's position at the BI is one of research faculty. He explains why he preferred this to the idea of being a member of the Beckman Institute: 'Those are staff not academic positions and I wanted an academic position. Because if this didn't work out I wanted to have the academic credentials to go to. There are not that many of us in purely research positions; there are some in each division. Chemistry has none for example, because they don't believe in it. Biology has more than any other division, physics has a few, geology has a couple, it's not com-

mon.' The degree of interdisciplinarity of Meade's work can be appreciated from the following remarkable fact. Among his present seven
postdoctoral fellows, not one of them has a PhD from the same field.
The postdocs include a cell biologist, a molecular biologist, a hard-core
synthetic organic chemist, a cell biologist, a molecular biologist, an analytical chemist, and an inorganic chemist. 'We've made discoveries based
on a cross-fertilization that have changed my life.'

One of the most intriguing projects that Meade is involved in concerns the use of electron transfer reactions to analyse DNA. In fact there
is an outstanding tradition of research on electron transfer at Caltech,
including the award of the 1992 chemistry Nobel Prize to Rudy Marcus
for his mainly theoretical investigations of such processes. Harry Gray,
the director of the Beckman Institute, is the discoverer of long-range
(~ 20 Å) electron transfer in proteins.

It appears that the precise speed of electrons along a DNA chain
depends on its exact constitution in terms of the sequence of bases. This
means that any particular section of DNA that codes for a particular
genetic disease could be identified by measuring the rate of electron
transfer along the chain. It has also been found that a single strand of
DNA undergoes electron transfer at a considerably slower rate than the
corresponding double-stranded version. This feature has provided the
possibility of designing molecular probes for genetic disorders. Meade
and his collaborators hope to prepare probes that contain a single-
stranded version of the DNA sequence that codes for a particular genetic disease. When the probe comes into contact with the DNA belonging to the human subject, the single strand may pair up with the exactly
corresponding single strand from the subject. This would result in a
measurable increase in the speed of electron transfer along the double-
stranded DNA chain that is thereby formed, and hence the possibility
of detecting a potentially dangerous DNA sequence in the subject.

The eventual aim is to devise a chip that contains probes for all
known genetic diseases so that a young child, for example, could be
tested for the possibility of developing any of those genetic disorders at
a later age.

SCOTT FRASER[18]

Scott Fraser is a relatively recent newcomer to Caltech and the Beckman
Institute. Since being recruited from the University of California at Irvine
in 1991, he has been granted a personal chair, the Anna L. Rosen Profes-

sorship in Biology, and now leads the highly innovative biological imaging group in the BI.

When asked what drew him to Caltech, Fraser explains that UCI was too large a school to allow for fruitful collaborations.[19] His closest collaborator and team colleague at the BI is Russ Jacobs, who moved from Irvine to Caltech at the same time. Fraser also cites Caltech's long history of being sympathetic to people who change fields, like Norman Davidson who moved, very successfully, from chemistry to biology, and Max Delbrück, who began as a physicist and went on to become one of the founders of molecular biology. 'I knew that the culture was sympathetic with the sort of things we were interested in, which was to sort of live in a blur zone between fields.' In fact Fraser began as a physics undergraduate, moving later into biophysics. He begins to explain his work at the BI by candidly declaring, 'The philosophy of our lab is to try to steal as many technologies as we can from other disciplines and apply them to our problem.'

He regards the field of microscopy as having passed through three generations. First of all, one had optical microscopes that relied on human observers stationed at the eyepiece. Then came electron microscopes and scanning tunnelling microscopes. Not only did this result in a vast increase in resolving power, but now the recording was carried out by means of an instrument, that is, some sort of image sensor and a digital processing unit.

The third generation, of which Scott Fraser is a leading pioneer, consists in using even newer technologies, such as specially adapted nuclear magnetic resonance methods, to observe biological changes in 'real time.' For example, Fraser and his group have produced exquisite movies of the development of frogs – the first time anyone has produced a real-time representation of development in an opaque organism.[20]

The origins of the collaboration between Fraser and Jacobs and the subsequent formation of the $3.5 million Biological Imaging Center at Caltech can be traced back to meetings over a coffee machine at Irvine. In the late 1980s that is where Fraser and Jacobs, who is responsible for developing Caltech's imaging equipment, kept on bumping into each other.

During some of these coffee meetings they discussed whether MRI equipment used for diagnostic purposes in hospitals could be applied to the study of developing organisms. The technique that Fraser had been using consisted of confocal microscopy, which uses visible light but can only image living tissue to a depth of 100 microns below the surface. Fraser and Jacobs spent a total of three years discussing the possibilities of applying MRI technology to small biological structures.

An MRI machine is essentially a magnet that creates a permanent magnetic field around the subject. The presence of a permanent magnetic field causes protons in the water molecules of the organism to align in a particular fashion. An oscillating field is used to perturb the protons while they are returning to their original state, thus generating an electric potential that is then analysed and transformed into a video image.

In order to modify the standard hospital MRI machine Fraser and Jacobs had to increase the power so that the spatial resolution could be reduced from about 1 millimetre to 10 microns. They also had to decrease the time taken to obtain an image so that there would be little variation in the organism between successive images. Another problem, which was solved by Thomas Meade, was to find a method of marking cells so that they could be followed through a developing organism.

Fraser and Jacobs eventually succeeded in developing an MRI instrument whose resolving power is one million times better than the typical hospital model. A number of labs around the country are now using Fraser and Jacobs' imaging techniques, and Jacobs recently received a $5 million grant from the Human Brain Project, a consortium of government agencies, to study the developing anatomy of the brain.

The Caltech facility involves collaboration among three research teams: a group, headed by Tom Meade, that is perfecting contrast agents, as mentioned earlier; Russ Jacobs' group, which is developing the MRI technology; and a third group, led by Scott Fraser, that is applying the techniques to the biological study of embryo development.

As Fraser says: 'With three groups interacting on a daily basis, we've worked out better and better imaging protocols, made better and better chemical agents, and the embryologists in the lab have worked out better ways to apply the dyes and also much better surgical techniques for manipulating the cells.'

A recent success story to emerge from this collaborative effort has been the imaging of embryos within a pregnant mouse, a feat that was carried out without the slightest harm to the mouse or its offspring. Other experiments on the development of the brain have helped to answer the question of whether cells in a specific part of the developing brain are genetically programmed to move off in different directions to perform different functions or whether their fates are determined not by genes but by their immediate surroundings.

In the course of our interview, Fraser singled out David Laidlaw, a recent PhD from the BI who seems to be one of the major success stories in terms of interdisciplinarity. Fraser is full of praise for this young man, who has remained at the BI as a postdoctoral fellow. On talking to Laidlaw, one gets the impression of interdisciplinarity having fully arrived. When I put the question to him about the apparent lack of BI seminars, his response was: 'People who say that are just being lazy. There are plenty of meetings if you know where to look for them.'

It seems that one of the most impressive ambassadors of interdisciplinarity is not one of the principal investigators or even the much talked about Members of the Beckman Institute but one of the most recent PhDs to graduate from the BI.

Conclusions

It is difficult to draw general conclusions from interviewing a few individual researchers, but at least lines of further inquiry seem to have emerged.

Of the two MBIs featured in this article, one seems to be thoroughly contented, while the other perceives numerous drawbacks and indeed is planning to leave at the earliest opportunity. The impression gathered from Solomon is that interdisciplinarity is alive and well, whereas Marder suggests that this is not entirely the case and that a good deal more could be achieved were it not for administrative inertia. The four interviewees show evidence of having travelled very widely through the traditional academic disciplines. Solomon, for example, considers himself as much a biologist as a chemist, physicist, or computer scientist. They all appear to enjoy taking research risks and to be, as Marder puts it, 'on the steep part of the learning curve.' It is also interesting to note that some of them regard themselves as being somewhat unusual in their liking for this form of borderland research. The implicit message seems to be that interdisciplinary research does not suit everybody and that the majority of scientists will continue to work within the traditional boundaries.

All the interviewees stress that university hiring procedures work in such a way as to exclude interdisciplinarity. They are also frequently aware of the cynical side of interdisciplinary work in that everyone wants to be thought of as interdisciplinary nowadays, partly because award-granting bodies favour such projects.[21] However, in the view of our sample interviewees, very few institutions or individuals are truly committed to interdisciplinary work.

Finally, they all perceive that genuine interdisciplinarity is being practised at the Caltech BI. Those who try to characterize the style of interdisciplinarity point out that it is largely unstructured and takes the form of a loose, laissez-faire approach, which they attribute to the personal style of the director, Harry Gray.

Notes

1 Others include the Santa Fe Institute and the Scripps Institute for Biological Research. A number of large-scale interdisciplinary projects have also been funded by the National Science Foundation and the National Institutes of Health in recent years.

2 In fact, of the four Beckman Institutes, the one at Caltech appears to be the least concerned with actively promoting interdisciplinary research work. The ethos is more one of allowing things to happen of their own accord.

3 Indeed, there is a thriving subfield within the area of science studies that champions the disunity of science. See for example Galison and Stump (1996).

4 For example, the total number of women faculty members at Caltech at the time of writing stands at approximately twenty, while the number of black faculty members is just one, who happens to have lab space in the Beckman Institute. Of course there are serious limitations to equating institutionally conservative institutions with scientifically conservative ones.

5 At its height Pauling's group numbered a total of sixty researchers, while Hood's biotechnology group, which was almost all located in the Beckman Institute, numbered approximately 130, before Hood's eventual departure for Washington University in Seattle.

6 One of Delbrück's many protégés was James Watson, who throughout his assault on the structure of DNA with Francis Crick regularly kept Delbrück informed of developments by way of correspondence.

7 Other Beckman buildings at Caltech include the Beckman Auditorium, the Arnold and Mabel Beckman Institute for Behavioral Biology, and the Arnold and Mabel Beckman Laboratory of Chemical Synthesis.

8 Arnold Beckman pursued a brief academic career as a chemistry professor at Caltech, but after only a couple of years he resigned his position to concentrate on designing and manufacturing scientific instruments.

9 Interviewed 23 February 1996.

10 Quotation taken from an article on recent developments on chain folding by R.F. Service, 'Folding Proteins Caught in the Act,' *Science*, 273 (5 July 1996), 29–30.

11 Thomas Everhart, the Caltech president when these interviews were conducted, believed that it was not necessary to go to great lengths to foster interdisciplinarity at Caltech, since there has always been a strong tradition of interdisciplinarity here going back to the days of Hunt Morgan, Delbrück, Pauling, and other famous alumni.

12 Faculty members also resent the fact that they have been obliged to undergo a rigorous tenure process to ensure secure positions at Caltech, whereas MBIs have not.

13 Interviewed 16 February 1996.

14 The group includes just one full-time theoretician.

15 Of his seven current postdoctoral fellows only one is a theoretician, while the others all perform synthetic work.

16 Marder is rather unique in the BI since he still receives most of his salary from JPL while being housed entirely in the BI.

17 Interviewed 3 July 1996.

18 Interviewed 27 February 1996.

19 UC Irvine has approximately 13,000 students, making it roughly ten times the size of Caltech. The number of biology majors is typically around 5000, and the biology faculty numbers roughly 30.

20 Previous work had concentrated on transparent organisms, for obvious reasons, such as nematodes and zebra fish.

21 See the accompanying articles by Weingart and Turner, each of which deals with different aspects of what might be termed the cynical aspects of interdisciplinary research.

11

Major Discoveries and Biomedical Research Organizations: Perspectives on Interdisciplinarity, Nurturing Leadership, and Integrated Structure and Cultures[1]

ROGERS HOLLINGSWORTH AND ELLEN JANE HOLLINGSWORTH

Introduction

This paper is concerned with the structural and cultural characteristics of research organizations that influence the making of major discoveries in twentieth-century biomedical sciences, especially characteristics of research organizations that repeatedly make major discoveries across time. Although most of the empirical analysis for these findings is based on research organizations in the United States, we also make some reference to research organizations in other nations. This paper is part of a larger study involving structural and cultural characteristics of biomedical research organizations in four countries.

Why do research organizations vary in their capacities to make major discoveries in biomedical science? Science, especially in the twentieth century, has been very dynamic and has grown in unpredictable ways. Because most research organizations experience considerable inertia and change rather slowly, they have considerable difficulty in adapting to the fast pace of scientific and technological change. Too often, a research organization has been a world-class leader in an area of science, but because of organizational inertia and failure to adapt to new trends, it has lost its leading edge.

This paper argues that organizations require distinctive structural and cultural characteristics if their scientists are to make major discoveries time and time again. It is to the identification of these characteristics that this research is addressed. The questions posed in this research have their bases in the sociological literature that is concerned with how the structural and cultural characteristics of organizations influence the making of radical innovations. There is a vast and excellent literature in the history and sociology of modern science about performance in the scientific community – for example, scientific discovery, the creative process, and more generally, scientific productivity (Ben-David 1960, 1971, 1977; Merton 1961; Pelz and Andrews 1966; Zuckerman 1977; Allen 1978a, b; Olby 1979; Allison and Long 1990; Shapin 1995) – and about the organizational contexts within which science occurs (Lynch 1985, 1993; Shapin 1995). In recent years, an increasing number of studies (Latour and Woolgar 1979; Fujimura 1987; Latour 1987; Shapin 1995; Rheinberger 1997) have focused on the importance of the research lab/ department as the site of discoveries. These and other studies have emphasized the importance of tacit knowledge and have demonstrated that knowledge is highly differentiated, unequally distributed, and richly sited in local contexts (Polanyi 1966; Lynch 1985, 1993; Dasgupta and David 1993). Whereas much of the recent literature has focused on the research setting of a single organization, this paper differs in being more comparative and historical in nature. It specifies a series of research organization and laboratory and/or department-level variables and then uses brief case studies to analyse the pattern of relationships among these variables, especially as they relate to the making of major discoveries in biomedical science.

Concepts, Data, and Methods

THE CONCEPT MAJOR DISCOVERIES

Conceptually, this project defines a major discovery as a finding or process, generally preceded by numerous 'small' advances, that solved a particular problem and in turn led 'to a number of smaller advances, based on the newly discovered principle' (Ben-David 1960: 828; Merton 1961, 1973; Rosenberg 1994: 15). Historically, a major discovery might have been a radical or new idea, the development of a new methodology, a new instrument or invention, or a new set of ideas. It need not have occurred all at once; it might have extended over a substantial period of time, involving a great deal of tacit knowledge (Polanyi 1966; Latour 1987).

To implement the concept major discovery, we rely heavily on the scientific community, using criteria the scientific community has created to recognize major discoveries. Using a diverse set of strategies to operationalize our definition, we include discoveries that led either to winning or near winning of a major prize. While we rely heavily on discoveries associated with major prizes as a strategy for defining major discoveries, we are very careful not to rely on any *single* prize. These discoveries are as follows:

1 Those in biomedical science awarded the Copley Medal by the Royal Society of London since 1901.
2 Discoveries resulting in a Nobel Prize in Physiology or Medicine since the first award in 1901.
3 Those resulting in a Nobel Prize in Chemistry since 1901, if the research had high relevance to biomedical science (including discoveries in biochemistry and several other areas of chemistry).
4 and 5 Discoveries resulting in ten nominations in any three years prior to 1941 for a Nobel Prize in Physiology or Medicine, or in Chemistry (if the research had high relevance to biomedical science).

   The rationale for this inclusion is that this number of nominations indicates a broad belief in the scientific community that the research represented a major scientific breakthrough even if it did not result in Nobel Prizes.

6 and 7 Discoveries that were on the short lists prior to 1941 even if they did not result in a Nobel Prize and did not meet the criteria of ten nominations in any three years.

   Every year, the Royal Swedish Academy of Sciences and the Karolinska Institute each appointed a committee to study major discoveries and propose prize winners (in chemistry and physiology or medicine, respectively). These two committees made short lists of discoveries considered to be 'prizeworthy,' some of which received Nobel Prizes. We have access to the Nobel Archives for the Physiology or Medicine Prize at the Karolinska Institute and to the Archives at the Royal Swedish Academy of Sciences in Stockholm prior to 1946, but for reasons of confidentiality, we do not have access to these archives for the past fifty years.

To capture the variety of major scientific discoveries during this period, we also use several other criteria. We include

8 Discoveries resulting in the Arthur and Mary Lasker Prize for basic biomedical science since 1961.
9 Discoveries resulting in the Louisa Gross Horwitz Prize in basic biomedical science.

10 Discoveries resulting in the Crafoord Prize, awarded by the Royal
Swedish Academy of Sciences.

*Recognizing that not all major discoveries can result in a Nobel Prize, we have
emphatically worked at making certain that this is not a project about Nobel
Prizes.*

Once having identified a major discovery, we then have determined
when and in what research organization(s), department(s), and lab(s)
the discovery occurred.

In some instances, the research organization did not have departments. The result of this process has been to identify organizations
associated with major discoveries, and to award to them 'credit' for the
major discoveries with which they were associated. In some cases, scientists made their major discoveries by conducting research first in one
and then in another organization. All organizations in which scientists
did work directly associated with major discoveries have been credited
with the discovery.

The research takes note that all scientists who were engaged in making major discoveries were not always recognized by prize committees.
However, this is a study about major discoveries and the properties of
the research organizations where they occurred. Thus, the omission of
'unrecognized' individuals by prize committees does not significantly
bias our results. Our method of conducting in-depth studies of the
organizations, departments, and/or labs where a major discovery occurred permits us to identify those scientists who were involved but
did not receive recognition by a prize committee.

This research is not a history of scientific ideas or a study of creativity
of individual scientists, although it acknowledges that discoveries were
made by individuals and that creativity occurs in individuals. The concern of this paper is with how the context of the research laboratory
and/or department and organization influenced the making of major
discoveries. However, major discoveries did not occur at random in
organizations, labs, and departments; rather, there were regularities in
the characteristics of organizations and labs and/or departments where
they occurred.

STRUCTURAL AND CULTURAL CONCEPTS

The analysis of research organizations and labs and/or departments
revolves around seven basic concepts (see below for the concepts, and

for each concept, indicators or examples). They are the degree of

1 diversity of fields of knowledge
2 depth of knowledge within each area of diversity
3 differentiation of the organization and/or department into subunits
4 hierarchical and bureaucratic coordination (e.g., standardization of rules and procedures)
5 interdisciplinary and integrated activities
6 leadership that has the capacity for integrating scientific diversity
7 quality of the scientists in the organization and labs.

It should be noted that depending on whether the unit of analysis is the organization or the laboratory and/or department there are modest differences in the appropriate indicators (or examples) of the concepts, which are noted below.

Key Concepts: Indicators and Examples

THE ORGANIZATIONAL LEVEL

1 *Scientific diversity:* (1) The variety of biological disciplines and medical specialties and subspecialties, (2) the proportion of people in the biological sciences with research experience in different disciplines and/or paradigms.
2 *Depth:* (1) Number of scientists in each area of diversity, (2) diversity of talents in each scientific area (e.g., genetics: *Drosophila* [the common fruit fly], neurospora, maize, mice).
3 *Differentiation:* (1) The number of biomedical departments and other kinds of units, (2) delegation of recruitment to department or other subunit, (3) responsibility for extramural funding at departmental or other subunit level.
   At department level: 'research group' should be substituted for 'department.'
4 *Hierarchical and bureaucratic coordination:* (1) Standardization of rules/procedures, (2) centralized budgetary controls, (3) centralized decision-making about research programs, (4) centralized decision-making about number of personnel.
5 *Integration of multidisciplinary perspectives:* Across specialties, the (1) frequency and intensity of interaction, (2) publication of papers, (3) existence of journal clubs, (4) sharing of meals and leisure activities.

At departmental level: activities across research groups would be noted.

6 *Visionary leadership: capacity for understanding direction in which scientific research is moving and integrating scientific diversity:* (1) Strategic vision for integrating diverse areas and for providing focused research, (2) ability to secure funding for these activities, (3) ability to conduct recruitment of sufficiently diverse personnel so research groups are constantly aware of what are significant and 'doable' problems, (4) ability to provide rigorous criticism in a nurturing environment.

7 *Quality:* (1) Proportion of scientists in the nation's most prestigious academy of science, (2) research funding per scientist.

SAMPLE AND DATA

The larger study underlying this report is based on 31 research organizations in the United States: 31 research organizations where two or more major discoveries occurred, and a comparison group of 100 research organizations where one or no major discovery occurred. The research focuses on four general types of organizations (universities, medical centres, free-standing research institutes, and industrial research laboratories). For approximately two dozen of these organizations, we have completed in-depth case studies. Details about the sampling process to select organizations in which no major discoveries took place are available elsewhere (Hollingsworth and Hage 1996).

Obviously, there are many criteria by which one might evaluate the performance of research organizations: productivity, citation indices, level of funding per scientist, and, for universities, the number of graduate students trained or the quality of the graduate program or faculty. We do not suggest that research organizations where few or no major discoveries occurred are performing poorly in science. Indeed, many excellent research organizations have hardly had a major breakthrough in biomedical science. However, the underdeveloped state of knowledge about the conditions that facilitate or hinder the making of major discoveries justifies the emphasis of this research inquiry.

This paper is based on numerous kinds of data: more than 200 in-depth interviews, archival materials, oral histories, secondary published materials, and scientific papers. Constraints of space have made it possible to list only a small fraction of these materials in the References section.

METHODOLOGY

Throughout, we employ comparative and narrative methodologies in the analysis (Franzosi 1998). Since the goal of the research has been to determine how the properties of research organizations are associated with the making of major discoveries, the analysis has compared organizations where major discoveries occurred with those where no major discoveries or only one discovery took place. As an additional form of comparison, historical analysis is used. Using this method, we compare some organizations with themselves, analysing them before and after major structural and cultural changes, in order to examine how such changes related to the making of major discoveries.

Despite our emphasis on the common structural and cultural properties of organizations associated with making major discoveries time and again, it is important to recognize that there has been no single route by which research organizations have acquired these common traits. Some organizations where major discoveries occurred time and time again were major organizational innovations – that is, they were fundamentally new kinds of organizations. This was the case with the Rockefeller Institute, the Johns Hopkins Medical School, and the California Institute of Technology. Another route whereby organizations made major discoveries was through fundamental structural or strategic change within an existing type of organization. And the third route was by creating a new organization among the existing types.

Rather than being a full report of this research project, this is only a preliminary report concerned with the characteristics of organizations that influence their capacity to make major discoveries frequently. Irrespective of the route, those organizations where major discoveries occurred again and again had the following characteristics on the seven concepts in this study: They scored high on visionary leadership, scientific diversity, interdisciplinary and integrated activities, and quality; conversely, they were low on differentiation and hierarchical and bureaucratic coordination, and they were moderately low on depth.

Selected Case Studies

HIGHLY INTEGRATED, SMALL RESEARCH INSTITUTES

Two American research organizations that have had several major discoveries in biomedical science are Rockefeller Institute/University and the California Institute of Technology. Rockefeller Institute/University has been the site of more major discoveries in biomedicine in the twentieth century than any other single institution in the world, while Caltech has been in the company of a handful of other research organizations where a number of major discoveries occurred at multiple time points in the twentieth century.

The central finding in these two case studies is that major discoveries occurred repeatedly because there was a high degree of interdisciplinary and integrated activity across diverse fields of science (thus, scientists with diverse perspectives interacted with intensity and frequency) and because of leadership that gave particular attention to the creation and maintenance of a nurturing environment, though with rigorous standards of scientific excellence. These two relatively small research organizations had moderately high levels of scientific diversity and moderately low levels of depth, but had very low levels of *internal differentiation* (i.e., separate disciplinary departments) and had visionary leaders who provided strategies for integrating scientific diversity. They were also low on hierarchical coordination and bureaucratization.

Limitations of space permit us to do little more than report in a rather preliminary fashion some of the characteristics of research organizations that are associated with major breakthroughs in biomedical science. In a fuller forthcoming study there will be an extensive examination of the characteristics of numerous other research organizations – even though of very high quality – where major discoveries rarely occur.

The Rockefeller Institute

In its early years, the Rockefeller Institute acquired a culture of excellence and a structure that facilitated the making of major discoveries. With the passage of time there have been modifications in the Rockefeller organization, but even so, there has been sufficient continuity in its structure and culture of excellence to enable it to remain an organization where major discoveries have continued in biomedical science.

Unlike the Koch Institute in Berlin or the Pasteur Institute in Paris, which were founded around great scientists and their particular research, the Rockefeller was a new kind of research institute that from the beginning emphasized diversity in the biomedical sciences (Corner 1964; Dubos 1976). Not focused only on a specific area of science, the goal in the founding of the Institute was to pursue diverse areas in biomedical sciences. Whereas earlier institutes had been constructed around bacteriology, biomedical science was changing very rapidly by the time the Rockefeller Institute was established at the turn of the century. Bacteriology had become much more linked with pathology, and both fields were becoming more closely related to discoveries in organic and physical chemistry, as well as in physics. A broad conception of biomedical science became the guiding philosophy of the Institute from the beginning. The consequences of these decisions about a broad, integrated approach to science are discussed below.

In the early part of the twentieth century, there was only moderate diversity at the Rockefeller, as reflected in the variety of research laboratories and moderate depth, because there were only a few people in each lab. However, in the recruitment process, the first director, Simon Flexner, was very receptive to recruiting scientists from different cultural and scientific areas (e.g., the Frenchman Carrell, the Austrian Landsteiner, the Japanese Noguchi, the Russian Levene, and the Germans Meltzer and Loeb). This pattern of recruitment provided diverse approaches to problems and styles of thought as well as to fields of research. Almost every one of these scientists incorporated cultural and scientific diversity in his own individual cognitive make-up, which enhanced the potential to cross scientific disciplines.

Almost all of the distinguished scientists in the history of the Rockefeller Institute have internalized considerable scientific diversity, making it relatively easy for such staff to feel an affinity with others who crossed academic disciplines. From the very beginning, the Institute did not organize the production of knowledge around academic disciplines, as was increasingly the case in major universities. The Rockefeller practices were unlike those in organizations in which academic disciplines were the dominant principle for organizing and coordinating the production of knowledge, and in which there was a tendency to recruit scientists who internalized less cultural and scientific diversity. One of the distinctive qualities of the Rockefeller was its tendency to recruit individuals who had been socialized in different cultures, subsystems, disciplines, and/or working environments. And because these individuals internalized cultural and scientific diversity at the time of recruitment, they had the potential to acquire new styles of thought and scientific competence and to internalize even greater diversity. In short, the Rockefeller from the outset was a place where there was a willingness on the part of its scientists to live and work in multiple disciplinary worlds simultaneously. As Gibbons et al. (1994)

point out, achievement in science is accelerated by communication, which in turn is enhanced by scientific mobility, mobility being an important precondition for the cross-fertilization of ideas. The Rockefeller was quite unique in the early twentieth century in the degree to which it recruited from different parts of the world senior scientists who had moved among different sites of knowledge production and who had worked in multiple disciplines. This also produced a scientific hybridization that over time led to new techniques, devices, and principles (e.g., instances of scientific creativity and of sudden insights, and the opening of novel pathways to solving difficult problems).

A research institution such as the Rockefeller had several distinct advantages over most teaching institutions. Most teaching organizations attempt to present an entire field of knowledge, and they often recruit people not because of their research excellence but to cover a particular field of knowledge. A research institute has no obligation to cover an entire field of knowledge, and can be very opportunistic in terms of the fields in which research is undertaken. If it wishes, it can neglect complete fields, recruiting scientists solely on the basis of the availability of the best people who are working on problems relevant to the institute. Moreover, a research institute, unlike a teaching organization, has the flexibility to move into new areas with considerable rapidity. And because the Rockefeller was not a teaching institution, it had the luxury of being able to recruit scientists of excellence even if they were lacking in the ability to speak English (Flexner 1930).

Of course, the Institute was generously endowed by John D. Rockefeller, but a number of other institutes were also very well endowed (e.g., the Phipps Institute in Philadelphia, established by steel magnate Henry Phipps; the Memorial Institute for Infectious Diseases in Chicago, funded by Harold McCormick, a son-in-law of John D. Rockefeller; the Carnegie Institution in Washington, endowed by Andrew Carnegie). But none of these organizations acquired the distinction of the Rockefeller Institute, for while money was a necessary condition for an institute to produce distinguished science, it was not a sufficient condition.

One of the most important conditions for an organization to have major discoveries repeatedly across long periods of time is the quality of its leadership, a variable to which many organizational sociologists give scant attention. Over the years the Rockefeller has attempted to have directors/presidents who were capable of interacting in a meaningful way with its scientists and who also knew personally the leading biomedical scientists of the world. Of the eight directors/presidents since the founding of the Rockefeller Institute, six made major discoveries in biomedical science by the criteria described above, and the two who made no major discoveries (Detlev Bronk and Fred Seitz) were distinguished scientists who had been presidents of the National Academy of Sciences. Four were Nobel laureates in physiology or medicine.

The first director, Simon Flexner, left an indelible mark on the Institute. It was he who developed the expectation that the Rockefeller should be headed by an individual who had

1 a strategic vision for integrating diverse areas and providing focused research
2 the ability to provide rigorous criticism within a nurturing environment
3 the capacity to recruit sufficiently diverse personnel so research groups were constantly not only aware of significant and 'doable' problems but also able to have the flexibility to mount a successful attack on such problems
4 the legitimacy to secure funding for such activities.

Of course, not all subsequent directors/presidents have lived up to the leadership standards of Flexner, but these are the ideals by which successive leaders have been evaluated within the organization.

Flexner was aided by a Board of Scientific Directors made up of some of the leading biomedical scientists of America. The first president of the Board was William H. Welch of Johns Hopkins Medical School, considered the chief statesman in American medical research and education. The Board was responsible for appointing the scientific staff and for establishing the general policies concerning the scientific investigations to be undertaken. The Director (Flexner) was appointed by the Scientific Directors and was to be in intimate contact with the scientific staff. There was a Board of Trustees to conduct the financial responsibilities of the Institute, but the Board of Scientific Directors played an important role in recruiting some of the most outstanding scientists ever to be assembled. The distinctive role of the Board of Scientific Directors combined with the skills of the Director to facilitate such distinguished recruiting. This process lasted until 1953, when the Institute became a small university and the Board of Scientific Directors and Board of Trustees were merged into a single Board of Trustees. Since then, the Rockefeller Institute has not had a separate board of world-class scientists who have made the final decisions about personnel. The quality of recruitment, while continuing to be distinguished, has not been of the same extraordinary consistency as during the time when the Board of Scientific Directors was intimately involved in making scientific appointments.

At the Institute, permanent scientists were called Members and had indefinite appointments corresponding to appointments as professors in American universities. The next highest title was Associate Member, which carried an appointment of three years (Associate Members were eligible for reappointment), but in general after a second three-year term, Associate Members either were appointed as Members or resigned. Associates were appointed for two years; Assistants and Fellows for one. Eligible for reappointment, scientists in these ranks left the Institute after three to five years or rose to a higher rank. Like the Kaiser Wilhelm and Max Planck Institutes that later had similar policies, the Rockefeller Institute was thus providing advanced training for the élite of biomedical scientists.

The process of appointment as a senior scientist (Member) was extremely rigorous. Not all senior scientists received their initial appointments at that level. For example, in 1934, 46 percent of senior scientists had initially been appointed to the rank of Member, while 54 percent had been promoted from within. Members rarely left. Of Members, only Eugene Opie had resigned by the mid-1930s, and he returned. One former president of Rockefeller University confided to us that during much of its history, unless there was a strong belief at Rockefeller that a scientist was likely to win a Nobel Prize, the person was unlikely to have a permanent appointment.

It was not enough that the Rockefeller Institute had the above-described leadership, outstanding scientists, a moderate to high degree of diversity, and substantial funding for major discoveries to occur time and time again. Other structural/cultural characteristics were also important. If scientific diversity was to lead to scientists having rich horizontal interaction with each other, it was important that the Institute not be differentiated into academic departments or other units that would fragment the production of knowledge. The organization needed to be quite integrated, which was the case.

First, there was no institutionalization of disciplinary departments. It is true that early on the Institute was organized into the Department of the Laboratories, with a number of labs, and the Department of the Hospital. The first of its kind, essentially a laboratory for the study of human biology and pathology, the hospital was always small, with a number of its staff without MD degrees. Over time a number of its permanent staff have been members of the National Academy of Sciences. Here was the realization of the ideal of the dialectic between clinical and basic science. A case in point, Oswald Avery's discovery of the chemical substance responsible for bacterial transformations (a major turning point in the transition from medical microbiology to molecular biology) was made by a group trained in medicine and working in the Rockefeller research hospital. Their research, focused on understanding biological phenomena, influenced the practice of medicine only indirectly, but led to one of the most important biological discoveries of the twentieth century. Staff of the Department of Laboratories and the Department of the Hospital intermingled on a daily basis. Indeed, the key to much of the Rockefeller's success in making numerous major discoveries was the scientific integration of the Institute.

Diversity and depth of knowledge within a well-integrated research organization have the potential to change the way people view problems and to minimize their tendency to make mistakes and to work on trivial problems. In the final analysis, in order to make major discoveries scientists must work on significant problems that are 'doable.' And the greater the research group's diversity and depth within an integrated structure, the greater the likelihood that scientists will not stray into unproductive areas. Frequent and intense interaction among people of like minds (with low levels of diversity) tends *not* to lead to major breakthroughs.

Oswald Avery's career at the Rockefeller Institute is an interesting case in point. Appointed at age 37 to the Rockefeller, Avery at the time was a highly competent researcher who had worked across several fields but had demonstrated little creativity and very little originality as a scientist. Once in the Rockefeller context (with considerable diversity and depth), Avery's potential emerged, and by the time he published his classic paper with MacLeod and McCarty on DNA and transformation (1944), he had internalized vast areas of the fields of bacteriology, immunology, chemistry, and biochemistry. Our research on American research organizations suggests that the context in which scientists are embedded influences their performance. If scientists work in environments where there is considerable diversity and depth and have frequent and intense interaction with those having complementary interests, the probability that the quality of their work will improve increases. It is the diversity of disciplines and paradigms to which individuals are exposed in frequent and intense interactions that increases the tendency for breakthroughs.

Intellectual and social integration was maintained at the Rockefeller Institute by a variety of devices. There was high- quality food at lunch, served at tables for eight. The idea was that a single conversation could take place at such a table, but not at a larger one. Eating meals together while conversing about serious scientific matters was an important part of the Rockefeller culture and an important means of integrating the scientific diversity and depth of the Institute.

Even though there was considerable diversity at the Rockefeller, the type of diversity was very different from that which existed at the colleges of Oxford and Cambridge, where eating was also an important part of the culture. At the British colleges, diversity ranged all across the board (e.g., from archaeology to mathematics). With so much diversity, it was considered ill-mannered to talk about one's work at the high table at those colleges, as many of those present would be unable to comprehend the line of discussion. But at the Rockefeller, diversity was only within the biological sciences, and the norm was to carry on lively lunch-time discussions about biomedical and related sciences. The lunch table was the setting of a great learning experience where people had intense discussions about new approaches to biomedical problems.

Integration was also facilitated by the weekly conferences everyone was expected to attend at which scientists reported about their work. Within the Hospital Division, there were afternoon teatimes that most faculty attended. One of the most important integrating devices was the journal club, especially the Hospital Journal Club, which generally met twice a month throughout the academic year. Everyone was expected to attend and to be prepared to report on a paper outside one's research field but of general interest to everyone. No one knew in advance who would be called upon to present materials to the journal club. Why would world-class scientists agree to participate in such an activity? They did this because they knew they were at a great organization and believed that one reason it was so distinguished was that they were continuously learning from one another. This kind of regular reading outside one's own specialization and in areas of interest to others in the organization was one way of continuing to expand intellectual horizons.

When one reads the archives of the Rockefeller Institute/University, one is struck by the prominent role of Simon Flexner in establishing in the early twentieth century a culture of nurturing young scientists. Once institutionalized, this trait persisted among leaders of the Rockefeller (notably at the lab level), especially in the habits of Avery, Bronk, Blobel, and Wiesel.

Finally, the environment of New York was a great asset for the Rockefeller Institute. Before jet aircraft, most distinguished foreign scientists travelling to America arrived in New York and invariably visited the Rockefeller Institute. Certainly no other biomedical research organization in America was so favoured with foreign scientists. It was located in a magnificent part of New York City. After World War II, its neighbours were the New York Hospital, Cornell University Medical College, and the Sloan Kettering Institute for Cancer Research. The environment provided an opportunity for access to many of the latest ways of thinking about biomedical science. If a small institute could not have all the diverse ways of approaching biomedical science on its permanent staff, it nevertheless had the opportunity to have many of the world's leading scientists passing through the Institute with reports about their latest work. Rockefeller Foundation grants to young British and European scholars brought to New York the cream of the crop of young scientists for stays of varying lengths.

As a result of the structure and culture of the Rockefeller, it is still one of the world's great centres for biomedical research. Yet after the mid-1950s, it no longer excelled quite so much relative to all other biomedical research organizations as during the previous half-century. First, jet aircraft had an extraordinary effect in shifting the location of excellence in biomedical science, as the élite of the scientific community no longer believed it was necessary to be located on the east coast. Distinguished scientists were increasingly willing to live elsewhere. Moreover, as the National Institutes of Health began to fund biomedical research on a grand scale, the Rockefeller no longer had the same kind of distinctive financial advantages. Indeed, no major private institution could attain and continue scientific excellence any longer without federal funding. As a result of new modes of transportation and new sources of funding, the Rockefeller was no longer able to dominate the world of biomedical science.

The internal structure of the Rockefeller also changed, a modification that had some adverse effect on its long-term future, though not enough effect for it to lose its prominence as a centre of excellence in research. In 1953, the Institute appointed Detlev Bronk, President of Johns Hopkins

University, as its Director. As noted, under Bronk's stewardship the Board of Scientific Directors was abolished and the Board of Trustees became the sole governing authority of the organization. Also under Bronk's leadership, the Rockefeller Institute became the only purely graduate university in the United States. It was an exceptional university, as there was no formal schedule of classes, only eight courses were offered, and no courses were required. It has long had many more faculty than students, and over time the students have been unusually gifted with a very high degree of self-discipline. Because of their small numbers, students have been able to receive very rigorous training in a highly nurturing environment.

But as a result of the new role of the organization, the nature of the faculty changed. Under Bronk and his successor Seitz, a number of distinguished new faculty were appointed, and the organization (without its Board of Scientific Directors) also began to appoint some less distinguished scientists to tenured positions. One reason this occurred was the increase in diversity in the organization. With increased size, it became more difficult for the President of the University to have the same level of knowledge of the scientific qualities of each scientist. Moreover, Bronk, while a brilliant administrator with a great deal of charisma, was not in the mainstream of biomedical science when he became Director of the Rockefeller Institute. Though he had been a distinguished biophysicist, he had long been an administrator. Moreover, his successor, the distinguished physicist Fred Seitz, had been President of the National Academy of Sciences and had never been a biological scientist. Seitz simply did not know the biomedical science community with the same degree of intimacy as Rockefeller's first two directors.

More importantly for the ability of Rockefeller University to make major discoveries, its internal structure was moderately modified in response to changes in the larger funding environment. Once funding from the National Institutes of Health became accessible, various labs grew in size, turned somewhat inward, and became somewhat more autonomous. No longer did everyone have lunch together. By 1970, there were too many senior scientists, too many post doctoral fellows and students for the early-twentieth-century type of communication and integration to exist. Most labs began to have their own journal clubs, and attendance at the weekly scientific presentations dropped off dramatically. No longer was there the same degree of horizontal communication as during the first half of the century.

And yet, even if Rockefeller University today is less scientifically integrated, it is still much less differentiated internally than every other American university. The fact that there are still no departments and that a lab closes down when the head departs means that the organization has an extraordinary amount of flexibility to adapt to new knowledge. This flexibility and adaptiveness explain why Rockefeller University, despite its small size, still towers over all other research organizations in America. Today a higher proportion of its faculty are members of the National Academy of Sciences and are Howard Hughes investigators than in any other research organization in America. Moreover, its scientists receive more funding from the National Institutes of Health per scientist for biomedical research than those in any other research organization in America. And it is still an organization where a number of major discoveries occur.

The California Institute of Technology

Like the Rockefeller Institute/University, Caltech, when it was founded in the early part of the twentieth century, was a new kind of organization. Though a university, it had divisions (e.g., chemistry, engineering) but no departments, and it had a plural executive and was also to be very small. It has historically had a moderate degree of diversity and a high degree of integration. Neither organization attempted to do everything in the biological sciences. Because Caltech had no medical or agricultural school, its scope in the biological sciences was quite limited. With a somewhat narrow scope, its degree of scientific diversity was also somewhat limited, and because of its small size, it did not have great depth in many areas. In most research organizations, it is considerable diversity combined with moderate to high depth that leads to fragmentation and internal differentiation. However, Caltech, like Rockefeller, has never been differentiated into departments like large American universities.

In its early years, a triumvirate consisting of the physicist Robert A. Millikan, the chemist Arthur A. Noyes, and the astrophysicist George Ellery Hale guided Caltech to national prominence in the physical sciences and engineering. They institutionalized an organizational culture that has lasted to the present day. The Institute would do only a few things but would do them with excellence. There was to be heavy emphasis on research and advanced training, and there would be no mass education. Moderately high salaries would attract high-quality faculty, and generous fellowships would attract outstanding graduate students. There would be relatively few students, and classes would be very small. Excellence was to be the hallmark of the organization.

In a relatively short period Caltech attained a distinguished institutional reputation. By 1929 it was among the leading three physics and chemistry research centres in America. Whereas Johns Hopkins and the University of Chicago had also attained prominence in a rather short period of time as the creations of single patrons, Caltech was supported by a diverse group of local élites. And while Johns Hopkins and the University of Chicago were also relatively small organizations, each was somewhat broader in scope (Servos 1990: 264–75).

Today, Caltech is still relatively small and continues to have moderate scientific diversity and depth and a very low degree of differentiation. In the early 1990s, the Institute had 1875 students (more than 1000 of them graduate students), a faculty of approximately 270, and about 700 fellows and visiting professors. Caltech faculty and students over the years have made a substantial number of major discoveries in the biomedical sciences. Its faculty and administration have received twenty-one Nobel Prizes and thirty-one National Medals of Science.

The key to its having so many major discoveries has been Caltech's interdisciplinary culture. As recent president Thomas E. Everhart observed, people can cut across fields of inquiry more readily than in most places because of the Institute's small size. It is 'at the intersection of traditional fields of study such as physics, chemistry, and biology where major discoveries have occurred and Caltech has always been in pursuit of major discoveries' (*Los Angeles Times*, 12 January 1992: 6).

Caltech had no biology department until the late 1920s, but when the Institute decided to create one, it did so by recruiting geneticist T.H. Morgan of Columbia University, the most distinguished biologist in America. This appointment sustained Caltech's emphasis on excellence. Morgan was not only a member of the National Academy of Sciences but had also served as President of the Academy. He had excellent connections with the National Research Council and the Rockefeller Foundation, and within four years of his arriving at Caltech, his discoveries resulted in his being awarded a Nobel Prize. The award turned world attention to the Institute's new biology program. Entering the field of biology relatively late, Caltech was free of the institutional inertia facing many research organizations in the biological sciences. In a number of universities, biology was fragmented into many different disciplines (e.g., natural history, botany, zoology, eugenics).

With Morgan's arrival, Caltech developed biology with a firm foundation in genetics. In many ways this was fortuitous. No one at the time knew that by the 1950s the biological sciences would be firmly grounded in the science of molecular genetics. Building a division with strength in this area, Caltech was at the forefront of the direction in which biological research would move. While in some respects Morgan was past his prime, he was still a major leader in the biological sciences and was an excellent person to assist in building a biology program.

Morgan thought in strategic terms and wanted to develop a biology program with strong interaction with physics and chemistry. Though he did not have a strong grasp of either physics or chemistry, he played an important role in developing a culture for the Biological Division that would emphasize genetics, embryology, physiology, biophysics, and biochemistry, all in cooperation with physicists and chemists. While he lacked strength in some of these areas, he brought to Caltech a remarkable group of younger colleagues from Columbia: Alfred H. Sturtevart, Calvin B. Bridges, Jack Schultz, and Theodosius Dobzhansky. Kohler argues that Morgan's group had never been as productive and as innovative as it was in the 1930s after arriving at Caltech. The emphasis was on diversity and cooperation: 'Doors between laboratory rooms were always kept open, there were no individual offices or telephones, and work places were communal' (1994: 124).

Just as Flexner had been instrumental in institutionalizing at Rockefeller a culture of providing rigorous criticism within a nurturing environment, Morgan played an important role in institutionalizing this kind of culture in the Biology Division at Caltech. At Columbia University and at Caltech, the Morgan group engaged in a great deal of social interaction within a rigorous scientific environment. This kind of culture persisted in Caltech's Biology Division for many years.

During the 1930s the Caltech biology group attempted to connect *Drosophila* genetics with developmental and evolutionary biology (Kohler 1994: 176), a strategy that reached its apex with the work of Ed Lewis, who was awarded the 1995 Nobel Prize in medicine. The innovations and excitement came from work of the generation after Morgan and from the culture that Morgan had been instrumental in establishing. Sturtevart and Schultz in particular helped to foster a spirit of crossing fields. The group made serious efforts to integrate experimental embryology and biochemistry with genetics. The next generation working at Caltech (George Beadle, Boris Ephrussi, and Theodosius Dobzhansky) advanced new systems of development and evolutionary genetics

(Kohler 1994: 177). The culture of working across fields at Caltech facilitated the moving of maize geneticist Beadle into *Drosophila* genetics to work with Ephrussi, the Russian-born, Paris-trained experimental embryologist in genetics, and his eventual link with the biochemist Edmund Tatum.

Shortly after Morgan arrived at Caltech, Linus Pauling began to express an interest in biology and to participate in biology seminars. At a small organization like Caltech, scientists all across the campus were interested in what others were doing. And because of its culture of excellence, faculty assumed that all other faculty were outstanding people in their fields, and thus most people were anxious to learn about the work of their colleagues. Pauling was one of the leading theoretical chemists in the world. Because of his interest in molecules, he probably would have drifted into biology in any event. But by the mid-1930s, after encouragement from the Rockefeller Foundation, he began to work on the chemical bonding between the hemoglobin and oxygen materials, and later on the general problem of the structure of proteins. By the early 1950s, Pauling was producing reliable descriptions of the physical properties of giant protein molecules. Since Pauling was always interested in understanding chemical substances in terms of their protons and electrons, it is not surprising that he was the boundary crosser par excellence. One of the most important individuals in establishing the field of molecular biology, Pauling did work on the helical hypothesis that laid essential groundwork for Crick and Watson's discovery of the double helix structure (Watson 1968; Kay 1993).

It was the rich horizontal communication across fields at Caltech that was important in facilitating Pauling's discoveries in so many different areas. It is extremely doubtful, had he been at a larger American research university fragmented into many academic departments, that he would have had as much interaction with scientists in other areas and that his productivity and creativity would have been so considerable in so many different areas. To put it another way, the interdisciplinary and integrated culture of Caltech was critical to Pauling's thinking and to his achievements.

Just as scientific integration was facilitated at the Rockefeller Institute by its dining-room, similarly horizontal communication and scientific integration were promoted by Caltech's famous Athenaeum dining-room. For many years, it was the place where faculty met, learned what others were doing, and often agreed to collaborate on research projects. The Athenaeum had an ambience of comfort and prosperity. As at

Rockefeller, many of the tables seated eight people, enough for a single conversation. The incentives for the faculty to go there were multiple: the food was outstanding, it was a very comfortable place to dine, and it was a place to learn what the local faculty were doing and to meet leading scientists from all over the world who were visiting Caltech.

Despite all of Caltech's resources, divisions have from time to time fluctuated in quality. By the late 1940s, Morgan was no longer on the scene, Calvin Bridges was dead, and a number of Morgan's young associates had moved on. While Sturtevart and others were still there, the Biology Division did not have the same intellectual excitement and productivity as in the late 1930s. However, because of the interdisciplinary and cooperative culture ingrained at Caltech, the dip in the Biology Division's quality was a temporary phenomenon. Recruited to return to Caltech in 1946, George Beadle as leader of the Biology Division worked closely with Pauling to make Caltech again one of the premier centres of the world in the biological sciences. They recruited Max Delbrück, a physicist and a leader in phage genetics, and other distinguished scientists, so that Caltech soon became one of the world's premier centres in interdisciplinary biology with strength grounded in genetics but extending to physics and to various other fields of chemistry.

Delbrück did much to perpetuate the nurturing environment that Morgan and others had developed. While Delbrück was hardly surpassed by anyone in setting rigorous scientific standards, his work groups, whether at Caltech or at Cold Spring Harbor, joined hard work with play. At Caltech, his group of students, postdoctoral fellows, and colleagues frequently made trips to the desert for recreation, while at Cold Spring Harbor there was swimming and tennis, as well as other play. Everyone was on a first-name basis, but recognition was earned on the basis of excellence in science.

Over time Caltech has continued to be distinguished in the biological sciences, and one of the most important reasons for this persistent ability to make major breakthroughs has been the integration of scientific diversity. Another factor has been the foundation on which the Biology Division was originally based: strength not just in genetics but in the genetics of *Drosophila*. And finally, the Institute has exercised unusual care in the making of tenured appointments. We have thus far identified only one person who was granted a tenured appointment in the Biology Division prior to 1950 without first having spent a prolonged period of time at the Institute. They did not recruit faculty without knowing a great deal about them.

It is quite remarkable how the original strength in the genetics of *Drosophila* has continued to evolve, in substantial part because of the characteristics of the organization. The continued excellence in this research tradition has also been due to the strategic vision of Morgan of integrating genetics with other fields of knowledge. One impressive embodiment of these traditions has been Seymour Benzer. Originally trained in physics, he was inspired by Max Delbrück and moved into the fields of molecular biology and virus genetics, where he became famous for mapping the fine structure of genes. After discovering that exposure of a population of *Drosophila* to a mutagen generated an extraordinary variety of mutants affecting various aspects of behaviour, Benzer and his associates identified mutations affecting visual reception, circadian rhythm, memory, excitable membrane channels, synaptic function, as well as hereditary pathological defects analogous to such human disorders as muscle and brain degeneration. As a result of Benzer's pioneering discoveries, *Drosophila* has become a model system for molecular neurogenetics, since his work revealed that genes so involved have identifiable close counterparts in the human cell, and allow the localization of genes responsible for various human hereditary defects. This has opened the way to using knowledge obtained from fruit flies to investigate human behavioural mechanisms and their disorders (citations by prize committees for the Lasker Prize 1971, Horwitz Prize 1976, Wolf Prize 1991, Crafoord Prize 1993).

Most small institutions, as implied here, have only a limited range (e.g., scope or diversity of activity) in the biological sciences, and this is one of the key reasons why their diversity does not become so highly differentiated. It is rare that the small institution has a great deal of depth in a particular area. But in the case of Caltech, it was the considerable depth in *Drosophila* genetics since the time of Morgan, embedded in a small institution where the drosophilists could frequently and intensely interact with scientists in other areas of science, that has facilitated this field in producing so many major discoveries. One of the most significant breakthroughs was by Ed Lewis, who worked for more than thirty years in linking *Drosophila* genetics to embryology and evolution, work that eventually led to his receiving the Nobel Prize in 1995 (earlier he had won the Lasker and Wolf Prizes for this work). Lewis's work is very seminal in understanding how genes control development. Some observers herald his work as one of the most important discoveries of the twentieth century. It is significant that this work emerged at Caltech, the institution with more than half a century of experience in *Drosophila* genetics, the research organization in which from the outset of biology there had been considerable diversity and interest in using *Drosophila* genetics to pursue problems of development (Kohler 1994). The small size of Caltech facilitated the knowledge of development by a geneticist like Lewis, who learned about the chemistry of protein research of Pauling and others. In short, the structure and culture of Caltech facilitated the ability of its faculty to capitalize on its scientific diversity (interviews with Ed Lewis, 25 March 1994, 21 December 1994).

The interdisciplinary/integrated culture at Caltech is well illustrated by the interaction among basic scientists, engineers, and computer scientists on campus. Two of its very distinguished biological scientists, William J. Dreyer and his now-famous student Leroy Hood, long expounded the thesis that what drives the pace of scientific progress is not so much the quality of scientific talent but the availability of new technologies, particularly new instrumentation that permits scientists to pursue new research strategies. And because of the ease with which biologists, engineers, and computer scientists could communicate at Caltech, the development of new instrumentation for scientific advance has been particularly notable there, especially in the biological sciences.

In the early 1980s, some of the proteins of most interest to molecular biologists existed in millionths-of-a-gram quantities on the surface of cells, so that obtaining enough of a particular protein to conduct any research often required ten years and was very costly. Leroy Hood addressed the problem by constructing a machine that could work with extremely complex chemistries automatically and required only a tiny amount of protein. Hood and his co-workers developed a protein sequencer that had the ability to work with $\frac{1}{10,000\text{th}}$ of the amount of protein previously required. In one of the machine's early applications, Hood was able to determine the molecular structure of interferon. After developing the protein sequencer, Hood's transdisciplinary group went on to develop a DNA synthesizer that would create strands of DNA, a protein synthesizer for making protein in the lab, and a laser-equipped sequencer for determining the structure of DNA. The first gene synthesis required twenty assistants and almost six years to conduct, whereas Hood remarked that in 1985 his lab synthesized the same gene in less than a day. Some have compared the effect of these two sequencers and two synthesizers to the effect that cyclotrons and particle accelerators had on the field of high-energy physics, permitting physicists to penetrate the basic structure of matter. These machines, in conjunction with other technological advances of the last decade such as recombinant DNA and monoclonal antibody techniques, have allowed researchers 'to manipulate and analyze genes and proteins in a way that was utterly impossible before' (Leroy Hood, quoted in *Los Angeles Times*, 20 Oct 1985: 56; interviews with Leroy Hood, 29 July 1995, 28 August 1996).

Significantly, Hood's work was complementary to that of fellow Caltech biologists Benzer and Lewis. Like Benzer, Hood also worked in the area of neurobiology, and his research has also been quite fundamental to developmental biology, in particular to understanding how genes are regulated, how the nervous system functions, and how a fertilized egg becomes a complete organism. What was different about Hood's lab at Caltech was its size. By worldwide standards, and certainly by those at Caltech, Hood's lab during the 1980s and the early 1990s was extraordinarily large for a biology lab. The size of his operation was out of kilter with the norm of having small labs at Caltech. The friction between the norms of his lab and the norms of small labs at the Institute eventually became a contributing factor to Hood's leaving Caltech and moving to a large public university, the University of Washington in Seattle, where he has established a new Bio-Molecular Technology Department with people from genetics, medicine, engineering, and computer science. But it was Caltech that made it possible to develop the model of laboratory diversity that Hood highly values and that led to the new Seattle facility.

Some observers believe that Caltech is too small to continue making major discoveries in the biomedical sciences. Obviously, only time can tell. The suggestion of this project is that when scientific diversity is highly integrated and interdisciplinary, when there are leaders with a strategic vision, when there is a nurturing environment but with rigorous standards, and when there is the capacity to identify and recruit individuals of considerable excellence, the organization will continue to have high potential to make major discoveries.

Significantly, Caltech in the 1990s is continuing to demonstrate flexibility and adaptiveness to the fast-paced work of scientific change. In part, it is doing this by developing new structural arrangements, one interesting example being the Beckman Institute. The vision driving Caltech's Beckman Institute is that within the next several decades, chemistry, biology, and medicine will increasingly converge as fields of knowledge. The Director of the Beckman Institute, Harry Gray, Professor of Chemistry, views all of this in the tradition of Linus Pauling and the inclusive view of knowledge. Gray's view is that a science should embrace as its own the diverse disciplines to which it contributes. Gray and his colleagues argue that there is a total restructuring of the field of chemistry taking place as a result of new tools available to chemists. Others at Caltech argue, also in the tradition of Pauling, that in terms of theory, there is a narrowing of differences among the fields of biology, materials science, polymer science, and chemistry. And at Caltech, there is increasing emphasis on the necessity of making fundamental changes in the way that the next generation of scientists will be trained. According to Peter Dervan, Professor of Chemistry at Caltech, it is necessary for scientists to break out of their disciplinary boundaries and put people with different specialties next to one another so they can get inside one another's minds and learn from one another.

LARGE RESEARCH ORGANIZATIONS AND PROBLEMS OF MAKING MAJOR DISCOVERIES

As research organizations increase in diversity and depth, there is a tendency for them to experience more differentiation and less integration. These changes often lead to increases in hierarchical and bureaucratic coordination, with negative consequences for making major discoveries. Changes in biological and medical knowledge have marked consequences for the diversity and depth of research organizations, requiring specialties that reflect these new areas of research if the organization is not to become anachronistic. Thus, universities, research institutes, and medical schools added biochemistry once the field developed. Genetics, biophysics, and various medical and surgical subspecialties became attached to medical schools and other research organizations across the years, usually requiring the hiring of several or even many people so that there was enough depth in an area. New kinds of instrumentation and other technologies also require the hiring of personnel. But to add personnel in new specialties, to build diversity with the required spread of talents, and to create depth in each area implies a growth in the size of the research organization. The problem is how the organization incorporates the expansion of knowledge and growth in size. When research organizations respond to growth by differentiating into new departments and by imposing hierarchical and bureaucratic controls, these processes lead to a decline in integration and diminish the possibility of making major discoveries, even if those organizations become highly productive in the number of scientific papers produced.

Examples of research organizations that have responded to changes in biological and medical knowledge by differentiating into new departments and growing in size are found in many large American research universities (e.g., Illinois [Champaign-Urbana], California [Berkeley], Minnesota, Michigan) and many medical schools (e.g., the schools attached to UCLA, Yale, and the University of Pennsylvania). Many of these places appeared at certain moments in time to be poised to be the contexts of major discoveries, but such discoveries did not occur. It is worth stressing that after World War II, these universities and medical schools had large amounts of research funding, were highly productive, and had a number of scientists in the National Academy of Sciences. But they did not have the structural and cultural contexts suited for major discoveries or breakthroughs in the biomedical sciences.

Significantly, by the late 1970s and early 1980s, the University of California, Berkeley, recognized that the fragmented and differentiated structure of the biological sciences substantially hampered the quality of biological research, and it restructured the biological sciences, abolishing more than a dozen departments in the process. After years of attempting to restructure the biological sciences, today Berkeley finally has a much more integrated biology program and a structure that provides the potential for major discoveries to occur.

Differentiation, size, and bureaucratization are also variables that place constraints on organizational flexibility. Science is very dynamic, and if research organizations are to adapt to the changes in the world of science, they must have a structure that is highly flexible. It is flexibility in adapting to change in science that provides the potential for making major discoveries across time.

Lack of flexibility has been a problem with most of the nation's medical schools. At the time many medical schools came into existence, they were dominated by clinicians, especially in the departments of medicine and surgery. Most medical schools have been very sharply differentiated between the clinical sciences and the basic sciences. Therefore it has been difficult for the basic science departments in many medical schools to attain the autonomy and organizational environment necessary to become distinguished. Thus, although the medical schools of the universities of Michigan, Minnesota, Pennsylvania, and Wisconsin have been either very strong or quite good over time in the clinical sciences, they have produced either no or very few major discoveries in the twentieth century.

STRATEGIES FOR ADDING DIVERSITY AND DEPTH AND FOR ENHANCING SCIENTIFIC
INTEGRATION IN LARGE RESEARCH ORGANIZATIONS

Another set of findings in this research relate to different strategies for
adding diversity and depth without necessarily differentiating into more
departments, even in large research organizations. Since growth in size
leads to the differentiation of departments and hierarchical and bureaucratic coordination, and this in turn diminishes social integration and the
capacity to make major discoveries, the problem is how organizations can
respond to changes in knowledge by increasing their diversity and depth
without growing in size. We have found a number of interesting strategies that organizations pursued, several of which are briefly discussed:

1 leadership with a determination to limit growth while adding high-
   quality scientists who represent scientific diversity and new ways of
   thinking
2 maintaining a single program or department in the biological
   sciences that places heavy emphasis on interdisciplinary/integrated
   culture
3 creating a small interdisciplinary research institute within a highly
   differentiated organization

The first strategy, limiting growth while emphasizing diversity, has
been chosen by a few private research universities. Departments, seeking to increase depth and scope in their discipline, attempt to add staff
and consequently get larger, often recruiting staff more like themselves
in the process.

An interesting contrary example is Harvard, where a major function
of the President since the presidency of James Conant is to convene an
ad hoc committee of distinguished scholars to assess every tenured
appointment in the College of Arts and Sciences. These committees
have frequently contested the judgment of academic departments, veto-
ing a tenured appointment previously approved by a department. This
process, by contesting tendencies among departments to reproduce themselves, has increased diversity and has facilitated Harvard's flexibility
in adapting to the larger world of science, giving it a distinct margin of
advantage over other universities.

The second strategy is either to create an integrated program that
stresses diversity, depth, and integration or to prevent the processes of

differentiation by pursuing the same goals within a single department. Two illustrations of this strategy are the biology department at MIT and the basic sciences at the University of California at San Francisco, perhaps the two leading contemporary institutions in the biological sciences in the United States, if not the world.

Another strategy is to create a small interdisciplinary research institute or centre attached to a university or medical school, an institute that is largely autonomous and is high in diversity, depth, and integration. The University of Wisconsin followed this strategy for several decades with success with the Enzyme Institute and the McArdle Cancer Institute. Both were small institutes, which allowed for a highly focused and reflective attack on research, and permitted intense and frequent interaction among faculty from diverse backgrounds who had full-time appointments in these institutes. Significantly, after 1960, major discoveries occurred in these institutes but not in the departments of the university.

Conclusion

Organizations that have recurring major discoveries have tended to be those in which there is a high degree of interaction among scientists across diverse fields of science. Over time, biomedical knowledge has become increasingly complex (e.g., involving both more fields of knowledge and greater depth), and if research organizations are to make major discoveries, it is necessary for them to incorporate new knowledge and depth in new fields of knowledge in such a way that scientists can interact with intensity and frequency across diverse fields of knowledge. However, as research organizations add new fields of knowledge and depth, it is important that the parts of the organization be well-integrated and not highly differentiated from one another; otherwise there will not be the horizontal communication with frequent and intense interaction across diverse fields that is a prerequisite for major discoveries.

Research organizations where a number of major discoveries have occurred have had a distinctive style of leadership, that is, leaders who have had (1) a strategic vision for integrating diverse areas and for providing focused research on particular problems, (2) the ability to facilitate the obtaining of funding, (3) the ability to recruit personnel across diverse fields of knowledge so that research groups are constantly aware of what problems are significant and 'doable,' and (4) the ability to facilitate the provision of rigorous criticism of science within a nurturing environment. Nurturing here is defined as a combination of activities by leaders: rigorous and thorough review (carried out with sensitivity) of work of those in the work group; stimulation of new ideas and work arrangements, sometimes shielding researchers from outside criticism; willingness to be patient in waiting for results; and interacting socially with those in the work group.

The diversity of disciplines and depth of knowledge within a well-integrated research group or lab have the potential to change the way people view problems and to minimize their tendency to make mistakes and to work on trivial problems. In the final analysis, to make major discoveries scientists must work on significant problems that are 'doable.' And the greater the research group's diversity and depth, the greater the likelihood that scientists will not stray into unproductive areas. If scientists work in environments where there is diversity across disciplines and depth, and have frequent and intense interaction with those having complementary interests, the probability is increased that the quality of their work will improve. It is the diversity of disciplines and paradigms to which individuals are exposed with frequent and intense interaction that increases the tendency for creativity and for breakthroughs to occur. Working in an interdisciplinary environment without intense and frequent interaction among members of the work group does not tend to lead to new ways of thinking (e.g., major discoveries).

Changes in biological and medical knowledge have marked consequences for the diversity and depth of research organizations, requiring new specialities if the organization is not to become anachronistic. As knowledge expands, new disciplines and subspecialities come into existence, and there are pressures on the organization to appoint several or even many people in the new fields of knowledge so that there is sufficient depth in an area. New kinds of instrumentation and other technologies also require the hiring of personnel. But the addition of personnel in new specialities with the required spread of talents, and the addition of depth in each area, imply a growth in the size of the research organization.

Increases in scientific diversity and depth, if not properly managed, can ultimately limit the capacity of a research organization to make major discoveries. As research organizations increase in the number of disciplines and expand their depth in each one, there is a tendency for them to become more differentiated and less integrated. These changes are often accompanied by increases in hierarchical coordination and bureaucratization, with negative consequences for making major discoveries.

Over time, as research organizations have differentiated into more departments and other sub-units, recruitment and the search for additional funding have been delegated to lower levels. Academic departments are inherently socially conservative and tend to select people who reproduce their thinking. Thus differentiation has tended to limit the process of crossing academic disciplines and to hamper scientific integration, both very important for major discoveries in biomedical science.

More specifically, increases in size and the decentralization of research and personnel decisions to lower units such as departments lead to more bureaucratic rules and the use of budgetary controls. And the formalization of rules and increases in structural differentiation tend to decrease the frequency and intensity of interaction across specialities and thus social integration. In sum, this research adds to the theoretical literature the finding that increases in size lead to differentiation and to fewer major breakthroughs in biomedical science.

Notes

We are deeply indebted to Ragnar Björk, Jerald Hage, Gerald Edelman, Peter Weingart, Nico Stehr, and Julie Klein for their contributions to this paper. Julie K. Sweeney of the University of Wisconsin patiently and thoughtfully assisted with data for the project. Archivists at the Karolinska Institute, the California Institute of Technology, the Royal Swedish Academy of Sciences, and the Rockefeller Archive Center provided very valuable assistance. For their financial support, we thank the Rockefeller Foundation, the Sloan Foundation, the Andrew W. Mellon Foundation, the Swedish Council for Higher Education, and the University of Wisconsin.

1 Extensive use has been made of archival materials, interviews conducted by the authors, and oral histories of scientists. Space constraints prevent the listing thereof.

PART IV

THE PERSPECTIVE OF THE FUNDERS

It is not only the internal institutional and intellectual structure that affect the nature and the direction of knowledge production but obviously the resources allocated from external sources and sponsors also play a critical role. The exact importance of external sponsorship for knowledge production in universities, research centres and institutes varies from one historical period to another and from country to country. So do the funding mechanisms that have emerged over time, ranging basically from the German National Science Foundation (Deutsche Forschungsgemeinschaft, or DFG) as a state-funded self-administrative organization for *all* disciplines to the disciplinary Research Councils in England, with other models like the U.S. National Science Foundation und the French Centre National de la Recherche Scientifique (CNRS) lying in between. The organizational structures of the funding agencies, the philosophy of science underlying them, and their function to translate policy priorities (public or private) into funding programs undoubtedly have a decisive impact on the development of disciplines, on their relative wealth, and thus on the topography of disciplines as a whole. This is even more the case with private foundations. Although their role in economic terms is much smaller than that of the state, they usually pursue specific programs, often limited to particular areas of research and with particular objectives in mind. Funding agencies, in other words, have their own particular perspectives on the world of science, and given the dependence of science on their resources these perspectives are bound to affect the internal cognitive and organizational divisions of science – the disciplines and their interrelations. The funders are, therefore, an important part of the *environment* of research and teaching. They determine to a considerable extent whether interdisciplinarity is encouraged or stifled.

In view of this it is noteworthy that the term *interdisciplinary* is a creation that can be traced to such a funding organization. The first oral use of the concept by the psychologist Robert Woodworth (1869–1962) occurred, as far as we know, in the mid-twenties in the course of a meeting of the American Social Science Research Council (SSRC). According to the *Oxford English Dictionary* the initial written usage of the term, in the English-speaking world, also can be traced to the Social Science Research Council; that is, it may be found in an ad placed by the council in the *Journal of Educational Sociology* announcing postdoctoral fellowships. The original meaning of the term is by no means irrelevant, because one of the primary purposes of the newly founded council was 'the bringing together of men [*sic*] from different sciences, the breaking down of excessive compartmentalization' (Sills 1986: 17–18). Woodworth used the concept of interdisciplinary or coordinated work to characterize this function of the council.

The notion of interdisciplinary activities to be supported by the funding agency resonated strongly with many of the expressed intentions and hopes of the scientific community in the 1920s. As a result, programmatic and then popular ideas such as 'new fields,' 'overlapping projects,' 'borderline research,' 'interrelated research,' 'interfiliations,' 'building bridges,' or, even more generally, the project of the 'unity of science' of the Vienna circle constituted what Clifford Geertz (1986) some fifty years later described in his well-known metaphor as the 'blurring of genres.'

But even in the 1920s and 1930s, critics of these ideas quickly surfaced and complained about the obsession of the SSRC with interdisciplinary activities and expressed scepticism that the associated goals could be achieved. The University of Chicago sociologist Louis Wirth, for example, wrote in a memorandum to the Council: 'It may also be said the Council has allowed itself to some extent to become obsessed at times by catch phrases and slogans which were not sufficiently critically examined. Thus, there is some justification for saying that much of the talk in connection with council policy, especially in the early years, about cooperation and interdisciplinary research turned out to be a delusion.' The demand for cross-fertilization turned into the fear of cross-sterilization (Wirth 1937).

The role of the funding agencies continues to be as important now as it was then for promoting and encouraging interdisciplinary research. In the first contribution to this section, Edward Hackett of the U.S. National Science Foundation describes the vibrant interest of the Foundation in a variety of interdisciplinary work that is manifest in many research efforts that have been proposed and funded, such as the Human Dimensions of Global Change project.

Wilhelm Krull of the Volkswagen Foundation, the largest private German foundation, alerts us to secular trends in science funding that stress, certainly at the policy level, the growing societal importance of investments in knowledge production but are confronted with fiscal constraints that appear to disallow any real increases in science budgets.

Krull stresses the role of foundations as agents of change in higher education and research that stimulates interdisciplinary efforts in particular. The Volkswagen Foundation, which organizes its funding activities around priority areas and programs, regards interdisciplinary research as an important element of innovation and has always been supportive of it.

Obviously these two views could be complemented by others. Yet, they are exemplary of the issues at hand: The funders are an important element of the environment of interdisciplinary research, especially in the sense of mediating and translating the expectations of society on the production of knowledge. Thus, their own practice and support of interdisciplinarity is an indispensable part of the picture.

12

Interdisciplinary Research Initiatives at the U.S. National Science Foundation

EDWARD J. HACKETT

In its call to 'open the social sciences,' the Gulbenkian Commission[1] outlines the historical contingencies that led to current disciplinary differences in the systematic study of human behaviour and solicits fresh ideas to overcome the restrictive boundaries that separate the three cultures (science, social science, and humanities) (Wallerstein et al. 1996). Powerful forces for change are already at work as scholarship is transformed by rising concerns about gender, multiculturalism, historicity and context, values, and abiding problems about the nature of humanity and our ability to develop objective knowledge. In addition there are political forces, described below, that further contribute to the interdisciplinary impulse. Yet the Commission also calls for deliberate social action to extend, consolidate, and institutionalize such changes, in the form of joint appointments for faculty, cross-disciplinary training of graduate students and interdisciplinary research endeavours of limited duration (say, one to five years) (Wallerstein et al. 1996: 103–5). Among those challenged to act are professional societies, academic departments, and funding agencies, both public and private, because such agencies have the resources to initiate, support, and institutionalize the indicated changes.

This specific call for interdisciplinary social science is an instance of a broader rise in the level of interest in interdisciplinary teaching and research that affects many fields of science and scholarship. Reasons for this rise are discussed throughout the Commission report, and include intellectual opportunities, converging lines of inquiry, administrative mandates, the desire to solve practical problems or to reap economic benefits, and efforts to repeat the triumphs of molecular biology, geophysics, structural biology, biochemistry, and other successful hybrids.

In the post–Cold War era, when the intrinsic and symbolic value of disciplinary knowledge seems to have diminished, federal research-funding agencies, such as the U.S. National Science Foundation (NSF), may propose interdisciplinary research initiatives to highlight the practical value of their research investments.

Whatever the underlying causes of the current interdisciplinary drive, it is clearly in evidence within the walls of NSF. In recent years a variety of interdisciplinary activities have been proposed and funded, and more are currently in development. Drawing upon my experience with the design of interdisciplinary research and training initiatives at NSF, I will examine the possibilities and limitations of funding agencies' behaviour in such efforts. In doing so I hope to provide a glimpse into the places where the impulse to do interdisciplinary research first takes form and then takes flight, influencing the activities of researchers in many fields throughout the United States. I also respond in part to the Gulbenkian Commission's call for funding agencies to increase support for interdisciplinary research by examining the organizational dynamics set in motion when funding agencies attempt to do so.

Varieties of Interdisciplinarity at the National Science Foundation

Three main varieties of interdisciplinary activity are supported by NSF: established interdisciplinary programs, cooperative funding efforts among programs, and new interdisciplinary initiatives.

Examples of interdisciplinary programs within the social and behavioural sciences include programs in Human Cognition; Decision, Risk, and Management Science; and Science and Technology Studies. Each has a program manager, an annual budget, an approved and published program announcement (that defines the topic area and outlines the types of awards the program makes), an advisory panel that meets semi-annually to review and evaluate proposals, and a community of researchers who write and review proposals, and who depend on the program for research support. Taken together, such intellectual, organizational, and social characteristics define and institutionalize research programs: they create a distinctive problem focus, endorse a set of accepted modes of inquiry and explanation, and establish a pool of resources that are relied upon by their respective research communities. Interdisciplinary research areas may have journals, professional societies and meetings, degree programs, and departments that lend further legitimacy to their research programs within NSF. With all this institutional and organizational apparatus, it would be difficult for NSF to end an established interdisciplinary program.

A second form of interdisciplinary research activity, less strongly institutionalized, arises when two or more programs contribute support for a new project. Such interdisciplinary efforts may be as modest as a $20,000 conference or as large as a multi-year, multimillion-dollar research centre, instrument, or data-gathering effort. Cooperative funding decisions may be fluid and ad hoc, requiring as little as two program officers signing a budget form that indicates how much each will contribute to a joint project. For larger, longer-running efforts, each cooperating program will review the proposal in its own community and perhaps also seek the advice of its panel before committing funds. Compared with an established interdisciplinary program, cooperative funding has less (but still some) enduring organizational consequence, need not create or sustain as cohesive a research community, and is less likely to institutionalize new modes of inquiry and explanation.

Initiatives are a third mode of interdisciplinary activity at NSF, and the balance of this paper will examine their development, social organization, and politics. Interdisciplinary initiatives may be divided into three categories, depending on their degree of development and institutionalization. The Human Dimensions of Global Change initiative, which spans agencies of the federal government and broad fields of the physical, biological, and social sciences, is a well-established effort to understand interactions between human and natural systems. Social science research on this topic began with a $200,000 set-aside in 1988–9, peaked with a $17 million expenditure in 1994–5, and continues to this day.

Other initiatives are stillborn, or, optimistically, still aborning, such as the Human Capital Initiative. Originally conceived in 1990 as a social science initiative to fund research in six areas of national concern (productivity, literacy, aging, drug and alcohol abuse, health, and violence), this effort has had a history of rising and falling fortunes. Congress appropriated $5 million for such activities in 1994–5, but the funding level today is lower and the initiative is still searching for identity and support. A recent workshop organized by the National Academy of Sciences, and related activities within NSF, may give new form and life to the initiative.

Finally, two new NSF-wide initiatives, Integrative Graduate Education and Research Training (IGERT) and Knowledge and Distributed Intelligence in the Information Age (KDI) are well on their way to attracting intellectual interest and money. At the time of this writing, proposals for IGERT are under consideration at NSF, and the program announcement for KDI has been drafted and is in the review and revision process.

IGERT is a new graduate training initiative that will award about $20 million to support programs that integrate education *and* research, across *two or more disciplines*, to prepare scientists for careers at the *interstices* of disciplines and in non-traditional settings. In each of the emphasized ways, IGERT is intended to integrate dissimilar intellectual activities and to create new educational, research, and employment opportunities.

KDI is a research theme that will support a variety of activities on the use of new information and computer networking technology to improve learning, knowledge production, and creativity. The initiative is large and multifaceted, requesting $58 million in additional funds for fiscal year 1998 to support three distinct elements:

1 Learning and Intelligent Systems (LIS) is intended to enhance the 'human ability to learn and create' through research on human and machine-based learning and through the development of new technologies for learning and creative activity.
2 New Computational Challenges (NCC) is dedicated to supporting the 'next generation' of hardware and related software for integrating complex data across vastly different scales or levels of analysis (say, from atoms to materials and structures).
3 Knowledge Networking (KN) is designed to understand how new knowledge may be created and integrated by using computer networks to connect various sorts of users (scientists, technicians, policy-makers, citizens, students) with data resources, digital libraries, and even scientific instruments and other analytic apparatus.

The Interdisciplinary Impulse

The simplest question – where do interdisciplinary research initiatives come from? – may be the hardest to answer. Certainly there is an initial judgment that an interdisciplinary activity would yield intellectual benefits, such as students with distinctive educational backgrounds in the case of IGERT, or new knowledge and new technologies in the case of KDI. But there is also something more political and opportunistic underlying these initiatives. For example, NSF has been criticized for favouring research over teaching and, through its grants process, for influencing the preferences of university faculty and graduate students. To some degree IGERT (and other new programs) aim to redress this imbalance by explicitly encouraging activities that integrate education and research training.

Underlying KDI is the premise that the benefits of new computer technologies would increase if their development could be more firmly grounded in a systematic, research-based understanding of the needs and characteristics of the learning, creating, and collaborating processes. A speech by U.S. Vice President Al Gore to the American Association for the Advancement of Science, later excerpted as an editorial in *Science*, catalyzed the KDI initiative by proposing 'an updated metaphor that is more appropriate to the times and more muscular in its power to explain: the metaphor of *distributed intelligence*' (Gore 1996: 177, emphasis added). The Vice President's remarks suggested language for justifying a request for additional funds, though the interest and impetus for the initiative have roots that are years deep. Both IGERT and KDI reflect the understanding that, with strong downward pressure on the nation's discretionary spending, any real rise in the NSF research budget must be accompanied by a claim to meet new needs and to pursue new opportunities in striking new ways.

Initiatives of all sorts, including interdisciplinary initiatives, are very flexible in their creation, contents, and names, so they can be exquisitely responsive to the needs of the day, then disappear or take new shape. IGERT, for example, is the latest in a lineage of NSF graduate training programs. KDI borrows its name from the Vice President's speech and requests $58 million from Congress, but it is said to be the most visible and responsive outcropping of a research effort at NSF that runs some $355 million deep (Lane 1997). In each case something much like the new initiative was in fact underway at NSF, with the new name, sharper focus, and additional funds representing a significant change at the margin.

Beyond the scientific and political reasons for new interdisciplinary initiatives, there is also a serious policy purpose to be served: such initiatives establish national science priorities in a visible and measurable way without necessarily changing the existing disciplinary balance. That is, when the NSF budget is prepared for Congressional review, and when top NSF officials testify about that budget before Congress, initiatives provide good, high-profile material that resonates with the interests of members and that leads, at least in principle, to distinct, measurable outputs. In his testimony to Congress about NSF's budget request for fiscal year 1998, Director Neal Lane highlighted both IGERT and KDI, which together accounted for more than a page of his six-page testimony (Lane 1997). (Indeed, much of NSF's research budget for fiscal year 1998 is framed in terms of broad, thematic categories – KDI, Life in Earth's Environment, and Educating for the Future – that efficiently express the connection between research investments and social goals.) Rhetoric aside, the true depth and extent of the initiatives' influence will only be known if there is an assessment after a few years of experience.

Perhaps most importantly, when written as initiatives these new efforts disguise or displace priority choices between fields of science. An open request to raise support for one area of science more rapidly than another may occasion a divisive public outcry from the affected science communities. But initiatives allow a vaguer sort of priority setting between fields to occur in a more private and manageable place, with certain crucial parameters (such as the topic, budget, types of activity to be supported, and need to honour a public commitment) established in advance. Interdisciplinary initiatives also protect the core activities of disciplinary programs by providing a peripheral contact zone for exchanges with other fields and the political environment that is some distance from the intellectual core of the field.

The ideas underlying a new research initiative must also pass muster with another constituency: the external research community. Unlike disciplinary research, there is no readily identified reference community for an interdisciplinary initiative. Yet without significant consultation with outside researchers, NSF would risk strong criticism and potential failure. To succeed, a research initiative must meet a receptive public that will openly embrace the idea and freely choose to participate by preparing and reviewing proposals.

NSF creates this receptive public by sponsoring one or more workshops at which an invited group of a dozen or more scholars explore and map – and perhaps create – the new terrain encompassed by the proposed initiative. Workshop organizers and participants are chosen by program officers, who consult with one another and with outside scholars to develop a broad, representative, and expert group. The workshop serves as a sounding board for NSF's ideas, a listening post for reactions and new views from the community, a channel of communication, and a general source of legitimacy for the initiative. Workshops typically result in written reports (and, these days, electronic documents and discussions) that are used to support the initiative and to prepare its defining documents (described below).

One of the most striking features of the workshop process is the amount of reciprocal adjustment required to get all participants, from within NSF and without, talking about the same topics in a mutually comprehensible language. Precisely because the topic is interdisciplinary, emergent, and relatively loosely defined, and because broad inclusiveness is an explicit goal, workshops draw together a group with widely varied training, knowledge, and presuppositions. A workshop on one facet of KDI, for example, included scholars from departments of computer science, library and information science, science and technology studies, history, neuroscience, economics, education, geography, psychology, philosophy, astronomy, and electrical engineering. Within such groups much effort is needed to standardize vocabulary and compensate for differences in knowledge about any given topic that arises in discussion.

Perhaps most striking is the high ratio between the ideas (and paper!) generated by workshops and the amount that finds its way into the final report and, ultimately, into the program announcement. For one facet of KDI, for example, three workshops were held on different subthemes, each involving dozens of participants. At one of these workshops, which lasted two days, subgroups met separately and produced mini-reports, dutifully shared with the group. These, in turn, became many pages of raw material for a report of several pages. In the end, all the ideas, research questions, and advice generated by perhaps 100 persons meeting for two days has been distilled into three single-spaced pages of the program announcement.

That said, workshop discussion and reports have a lasting impact on the formation of an initiative. The ideas and perspectives shared during those days framed much of the ensuing discussion at NSF. And the workshops provided an argumentative resource during the drafting of the program announcement, with one NSF official telling another 'Contrary to what you might have concluded, there is a great deal of convergence and consensus in the community as to what [the initiative] should be and where NSF's new KDI program ought to be going.' This was clearly evident in the three workshops, which were participated in by over 100 leaders from all of our disciplines. The workshop reports are now on the Web and spread across a much wider audience, reaching out and energizing the diverse communities to develop and form new ideas.

I would not underestimate the influence workshops have on the development of interdisciplinary initiatives, but would emphasize that they are loosely coupled to subsequent events and that their verbal contribution is highly distilled.

Workshops also, finally, give advance notice of the initiative to the proposal-writing community, completing the circle: the community can now compete for resources from the initiative it helped shape. The importance of these community-building activities cannot be exaggerated, because the ultimate success of any initiative depends upon the participation of the scientific community.

The Politics of Interdisciplinary Initiatives

The external politics of interdisciplinary research initiatives are clear: Initiatives show that the agency's research effort is focused on achieving identifiable ends and that those ends are congruent with larger themes established by the administration. Initiatives also imply specific, observable outcomes that may be assessed to show the social benefit resulting from such expenditures. Such analyses are required by the Government Performance and Results Act of 1993, which directs every government agency first to establish strategic goals, then to assess its performance against those goals.

The internal politics of initiatives are more subtle and problematic, and those only come into view when the process of developing an initiative is examined in some detail. Initiatives of the sort discussed here (IGERT and KDI) ultimately take the form of a program announcement and a management plan. The program announcement describes for the research community the topic area of interest, the activities to be supported, the matters that proposals should address, when proposals must be received and how they will be evaluated, and offers some examples of the sorts of topics or projects the initiative is intended to support. The management plan, in contrast, is an internal NSF document that describes the handling of funds and proposals, including organizational and staffing matters, details of the review process, and even where the proposal files ('jackets') will be stored. While this may seem a tedious document to write or read, it is in fact complicated, contested, and crucial, as it presents a blueprint for the management of the initiative (that is, outreach to the community; recording, review, and disposition of proposals; and, especially, where the money will come from to support the new work and how it will get to where it will go). Since initiatives are new activities that often cut across large segments of the NSF organization, the usual organizational and institutional mechanisms – tradition, habit, culture, standard operating procedures, and the like – are not available to guide practices or may be inconsistent.

Both the program announcement and the management plan are written collaboratively and iteratively by groups of program officers and division directors (the next layer up the hierarchy). These groups draft material that is reviewed by the Senior Management Integration Group (or SMIG), whose main members are the Director of NSF, the Deputy Director, and the Assistant Directors who head each of the research directorates (Biological Sciences, Computing and Information Sciences and Engineering, Engineering, Geological Sciences, Education and Human Resources, Mathematical and Physical Sciences, and Social and Behavioral Sciences). Each assistant director must look after the interests of his or her directorate in such meetings, reconciling the initiative's scope and definition with the research interests and capacities of the constituent fields.

Those drafting the documents often find this a difficult and frustrating process, partly because the issues driving decisions at the higher levels of the organization may be inconsistent with or imperceptible to those below, and partly because communication is delayed, incomplete, and sometimes cryptic. Until one has done so, it is hard to appreciate the difficulty of imagining what sorts of projects might be proposed in an emerging, interdisciplinary research area, then crafting language to describe such imagined work and to indicate the criteria for evaluating it. Further, with tens of millions of dollars at stake, the Assistant Directors keep firm control of initiatives, demanding repeated drafts but giving somewhat vague guidance about what is desired. Finally, the amount of contingency and forward thinking involved in the initiative process confounds matters further. As the program announcements and management plans for IGERT and KDI were prepared, NSF staff were spending the last of their fiscal year 1997 budgets, following Congressional budget deliberations about fiscal year 1998 (which includes funds for both initiatives, not yet passed by Congress), and preparing the budget request for fiscal year 1999.

Establishing and using merit review procedures to evaluate proposals poses additional complications. Different parts of NSF use different review mechanisms. About a third of NSF's proposals are evaluated only by written reviews from specialists chosen to review a particular proposal. Another third are reviewed only by a panel of reviewers who collectively provide advice about a set of proposals. And a final third are evaluated using both a set of proposal-specific specialists and a panel. Other, more subtle differences also distinguish review and decision processes in different parts of NSF. Yet interdisciplinary initiatives require development of a single, consistent review process.

Panels are often the preferred mode of review for initiatives, perhaps largely because that affords program officers the greatest amount of interaction with reviewers and allows reviewers to speak freely among themselves. But panel review means that expert panelists must be identified and persuaded to serve, not an easy matter because panelists already serving on (or recently departed from) NSF panels probably should not be further burdened, and because persons who plan to submit proposals to an initiative probably should not serve on the panel reviewing proposals for that initiative. The population is also limited by conflict of interest rules that prevent mentors and their dissertation advisees from *ever* reviewing one another's proposals, and that prevent current collaborators, recent co-authors, and colleagues at the same institution from reviewing one another's work. Such rules are essential to avoid the biased judgments and the mere *appearance* of impropriety that may arise from conflicts of interest, but they have the unfortunate side-effect of sharply limiting the pool of expert advisers available for any given proposal. The established panels that advise regular research programs also develop habits, usual practices, and something akin to cultures that smooth their work, while a panel newly formed to serve an initiative lacks these advantages. Finally, program panels typically advise one (or two or three) program officers about a more-or-less established, coherent area of research, but panels serving interdisciplinary initiatives advise an ad hoc group of program officers from diverse fields of science about an equally nebulous research theme. If the initiative is large enough or broad enough, there might be two or more panels at work simultaneously, leaving it to a group of program officers to forge decisions from that varied input.

Program officers are often more comfortable with disciplinary review, characterizing it as 'more rigorous' and 'thorough.' This may be so because panels and the fields they represent develop implicit standards for choosing problems and methods, for judging results, and for evaluating the quality of journal publications, academic appointments, and graduate training. In all, it is easier to 'place' a disciplinary proposal and investigator. The uncertainty of interdisciplinary proposal review complicates, perhaps even jeopardizes, program officers' judgment.

Further complicating matters is the program officer's ambiguous position in an initiative. Since funds for the initiative are often sequestered from regular program funds, perhaps because they came as an additional allocation from Congress, or were pooled with funds from elsewhere in the Foundation (another directorate or a Foundation-wide 'opportunity fund'), or were established through a 'tax' on programs within the directorate, the program officer's calculus is changed. Instead of allocating funds from a pot of money more or less under his or her control, to support work in the field represented by her or his program, the program officer is faced with the challenge of withdrawing funds from a central pot of money, using proposals from her or his field to effect the withdrawals. This somewhat compromises the program officer's position in a panel meeting, because she or he has responsibility for running a fair and orderly meeting, but also has an interest in the success of certain proposals.

Assessment

It is difficult to know whether interdisciplinary initiatives return fair value for the money invested, and it is difficult to measure their performance against that of traditional, disciplinary activities. Partly this is a problem of yardsticks and perspective, with metrics for any sort of science performance hard to come by and with sharp differences in perspectives on the fundamental merit of any sort of interdisciplinary effort. At the highest level, NSF's investments of whatever sort will be measured against its strategic goals, which are quite general and abstract promises to improve the quality of U.S. science, technology, education, and society.

At the more concrete level of individual awards, the assessment burden is increasingly shifted to those writing the proposal. That is, program announcements for the interdisciplinary initiatives discussed here ask proposers to include in the proposal plans for assessing the project's performance. To some degree this is a form of shirking, but it has the merit of allowing new outcomes and measures to arise from the field, then to be amassed, assessed, formalized, and developed by NSF.

Conclusion

Facing stable or declining national research budgets and a political climate that demands practical, tangible justification for research spending, interdisciplinary research initiatives are likely to become an increasingly prominent feature of the science policy landscape. Interdisciplinary research certainly *seems* bold and relevant, but I know no systematic evidence that this is so. Very little is known about the workings of such initiatives, such as how research teams are formed, what are the opportunity costs of research set aside to pursue the new opportunity, and what are the processes for evaluating proposals and making funding decisions. Most importantly, virtually nothing is known about their contributions to knowledge and the quality of life.

In light of all this ignorance and uncertainty, it is difficult to embrace interdisciplinary initiatives. Yet they may be a lasting instrument of science policy, and the one area of real growth and opportunity. Our best option, then, is to proceed boldly but reflectively, giving such investments our whole-hearted support while thinking critically and systematically about their performance and consequences.

Note

1 The Gulbenkian Commission is a group of ten scholars from the social sciences, natural sciences, and humanities that was drawn together with support from the Calouste Gulbenkian Foundation to reflect on the circumstances and prospects for the social sciences.

13

Beyond the Ivory Tower: Some Observations on External Funding of Interdisciplinary Research in Universities

WILHELM KRULL

Introduction

Today, more and more governments treat investments in higher education, science, and technology as a strategic asset. The increased public policy importance of knowledge investments, however, does not necessarily correspond with increasing budgets. On the contrary, fiscal constraints have led to, at best, a steady state, and more often to budgets that in real terms have been considerably reduced. This holds especially true for Germany, which is still struggling with the grossly underestimated costs of integrating the five East German states into the Federal Republic.

Due to financial constraints that are affecting the entire publicly financed sector, more and more researchers and research policy-makers are stressing the need for a new 'public private partnership.' Although this request also aims at establishing better linkages between publicly financed research institutes and universities on the one hand, and privately run research laboratories and companies on the other, it clearly focuses on finding new sources of financial support for the hitherto publicly financed training and research work.

In Germany, as in many other European countries, citizens are used to carrying a high tax load, and therefore expect the federal, regional, or local government to cover the costs of almost all social institutions. Nevertheless, private initiatives and individual commitments as well as financial contributions from private sources have always been essential to achieving the overall objectives of the higher education and research system as well as in opening up new opportunities.

As far as funds for activities in higher education and research are concerned, more than 800 private foundations account for less than DM 1 billion per annum. Compared with the DM 2 billion that the German Research Association (Deutsche Forschungsgemeinschaft) provides for a wide variety of funding schemes, let alone the more than DM 25 billion spent by the federal and state governments to keep the universities and research institutes going, it is obviously not possible for any foundation to pursue wholesale funding policies. Even the biggest German foundation in the higher education and research area, the Volkswagen Foundation, which can spend DM 170 to 180 million per year, decided more than twenty-five years ago to focus its funding activities on specific priority areas and programs. It is mainly in view of this foundation's experiences that the following observations and annotations are made.

Interdisciplinary Research in German Universities

In almost all research systems universities have a central role to play. For the German Science Council (Wissenschaftsrat) they are the most important institutions in this respect, in particular because of their dominant position in training young researchers (Wissenschaftsrat 1989: 29). The eighty-four German universities employ more than 120,000 academics, and the catalogue of disciplines published by the German University Teachers' Association (Hochschulverband) registers more than 4000 subjects, an alarmingly high figure, or as Jürgen Mittelstrass puts it: 'eine beängstigende, für Unübersichtlichkeit im Wissenschaft und Hochschulbereich sorgende Zahl (a frightening figure that accounts for unintelligible conditions in research and higher education') (Mittelstrass 1987: 152). For him, specialization, despite all its achievements, has been taken too far, and the call for more interdisciplinary research efforts must be considered a compensatory phenomenon: 'ein Kompensationsphänomen zur Wiedergutmachung gegenüber einer Idee, die etwa für Leibniz noch das Selbstverständliche war, für uns hingegen nur noch eine Erinnerung an unentwickelte wissenschaftliche Verhältnisse oder eine Utopie ist' ('a phenomenon of compensation to restitute for an idea that for Leibniz was still the self-evident but for us is the memory of undeveloped scientific conditions or an utopia') (Mittelstrass 1987: 152).

Due to the fragmentation into thousands of disciplines, numerous institutional barriers to interdisciplinary research, and a wide variety of other obstacles for cooperating across disciplines, the universities clearly have lost in importance over the last two decades when it comes to providing the relevant knowledge base. As 'emphasis has moved away from free inquiry to problem solving and, more generally in the direction of problem-oriented research' (Gibbons et al. 1994: 71), the necessity of a realignment between the university's own values and the society's real needs has become more obvious. And yet, many universities still find it difficult to combine their disciplinary substructures with new institutional settings designed to stimulate or strengthen the interaction between researchers from different departments. Although there is by now widespread agreement on the need to overcome the tendency in many disciplines to specialize in ever narrower areas, and to bring together the best suitable persons with their specific expertises from various disciplines to tackle some of the most urgent research issues, so far only a small number of universities seem to have succeeded in providing adequate institutional responses to the challenges provided by an integrated approach to new research issues.

Several newly established research centres and institutes for advanced study, especially in East German universities (e.g., at Frankfurt/Oder, Erfurt, and Leipzig, but also in Munich, Essen, and Bremen/Oldenburg) obviously attempt to open up new opportunities for inter- and transdisciplinary research work. Right from the start, most of these new organizational structures are designed to provide these opportunities for the respective researcher or research group on a temporary basis, and membership as well as space is granted only to those researchers who are able to apply successfully for grants from other research organizations and foundations.

Foundations as Facilitators of Change: The Volkswagen Foundation

Foundations offering financial support in the area of higher education and research regard it as their duty to stimulate new developments, redress imbalances of the publicly financed funding agencies, and provide support for the most innovative, paradigmatic activities, especially when these involve the identification of important societal, technical, or environmental problems and promising contributions to their solution. In this respect foundations like to consider themselves facilitators of change.

As far as the Volkswagen Foundation is concerned, the support of science, technology, and the humanities in research and academic teaching therefore does not aim simply at meeting the costs for a specific piece of novel research or a teaching experiment. This is not to say that the Foundation does not expect projects to make significant contributions to basic scientific, technical, or cultural knowledge, but beyond the requirements of originality, competence, appropriateness of method, and so on it is usually the potential conclusions, the relevance of the expected findings to particular issues, and the prospective impact on institutional structures, policies, and such that matter when it comes to giving priority to one proposal or the other.

Since the early seventies, the Volkswagen Foundation has been concentrating its funding activities on priority areas and programs. The current programs focus on structural reforms in German universities, especially on more efficient decision-making and leadership (Efficiency by Autonomy) and on the establishment of interdisciplinary junior research groups in universities. As far as the priority areas (*Schwerpunkte*) are concerned, there are, broadly speaking, two types of priority areas: on the one hand, those offering support for basic research into specific subjects and problems, currently, for example, on the transformation of economic, political, and social systems; environmental scarcity; neuro-immunology; electron transfer; conditional mutagenesis; non-linear dynamics in production systems; and on problems and possibilities of intercultural communications; on the other hand, there have always been priority areas offering opportunities for the funding of an urgently needed infrastructure in research and university teaching and of international scientific communication, for example, for symposia and summer schools, and for research abroad. Some of the latter priority areas are especially directed to projects on and in other countries, currently especially on China, and the cooperation with researchers in Central and Eastern Europe.[1]

Out of these funding opportunities, it is mainly the program focusing on the establishment of interdisciplinary junior research groups in universities and the topical priority areas that provide a framework for highly innovative, mostly interdisciplinary research. While the former is a relatively new scheme that has just been implemented, the latter over the last two and a half decades have proven to be a useful tool for stimulating individual researchers to tackle research questions that may otherwise not have been on their agenda.

Priority areas are usually defined for a period of eight to ten years with an average annual budget of DM 5 million. Although a wide variety of different approaches to searching for new research topics and validating concepts exist, the following criteria, *inter alia*, apply to al-most all preceding evaluations of proposals for new priority areas:

Research potential and relevance
• originality and innovativeness
• expected enhancement of the knowledge base
• impact on the further development of the respective area
• incentives for inter- and transdisciplinary approaches
• career prospects for junior researchers
• opportunities for the application of results

Potential applicants and funding opportunities
• size of the respective scientific community
• relation to already existing funding mechanisms and programs of other funding agencies
• specific opportunities for the Foundation to achieve its objectives

Position in the framework of the overall funding program
• relation to other previous or existing priority areas
• impact on the Foundation's profile
• financial implications
• capacity to implement the new priority area

Opportunities and Limitations

Nowadays, in more and more universities and research institutes, the need for a reintegration of specialized research efforts is strongly felt. There seems to be widespread consensus that this can be achieved only through additional or extraordinary activities, in some cases even out-side the hitherto existing institutions. Such newly proposed institutions are designed to regain flexibility in order to provide the appropriate environment for an intensive interaction among distinguished research-ers from various institutions.

There is widespread agreement among research policy-makers that projects as well as centres for interdisciplinary research must live up to the highest standards; that is, the latter should be established as centres of excellence. However, it is not an easy task to make this happen. Unlike institutes for advanced study, such as the Wissenschaftskolleg zu Berlin, these projects and centres cannot afford to focus their atten-tion entirely on highly respected individuals. Although the quality of the researchers involved in interdisciplinary projects is crucial, the criteria of scientific excellence in a particular discipline need to be complemented by other criteria, such as the readiness and ability to develop and apply a common terminology; the openness to free communication among all members of the team; the readiness to become engaged in a permanent process of mutual learning; the acceptance of a problem-oriented, instead of a discipline- or person-oriented approach; and last, but not least, the readiness to give priority to the project's objectives instead of pursuing one's personal interests.[2]

The two personality profiles, the 'great individual' on the one hand and the 'team-oriented collaborator' on the other, are not mutually exclusive. However, if one wants to overcome the 'miseries of specialization' (Weingart 1992: 10), one has to pay attention to the capacity for teamwork of each of the researchers involved.

For a grant-making institution like the Volkswagen Foundation, it is of course difficult to assess in advance whether the proposed research team will be able to meet its objectives. Apart from taking a close look at the previous funding record of the senior researchers involved and encouraging the reviewers to rigorously apply international quality standards, there will always remain a certain degree of risk with regard to the adequacy of the project staff, the proposed methods, and the working scheme. Especially in newly developing areas it is therefore essential that the foundation and the respective research communities develop an atmosphere of mutual trust, thus encouraging those who are prepared to follow new paths beyond the academic heartland in which they hitherto acquired their reputation.

A brief description of a small number of previous and still existing priority areas may suffice to illustrate some of the issues involved in launching new activities and in facilitating their success:

- In the early 1960s, when the Volkswagen Foundation was set up, research areas like molecular biology, biophysics, and biochemistry still had difficulties in becoming regular parts of German university departments. Therefore, the foundation fairly early on decided to make this one of its priorities. Until 1975 it had already spent about DM 90 million. Through a wide variety of different approaches and funding mechanisms – ranging from scholarships designed to encourage physics and chemistry students to embark upon biological research all the way through to start up-grants for newly established research institutions – it finally succeeded in developing these research areas in such a way that they were able to sustain themselves on an internationally competitive level.

- The stimulation of interdisciplinary joint projects in the engineering sciences (from 1987 to 1995, 109 grants totalling DM 54.1 million), which often also included researchers from the biomedical and other sciences, was one of the most ambitious attempts of the Volkswagen Foundation to provide incentives for designing projects that promised to provide the most adequate, integrated response to the complex issues involved. The Foundation accepted only proposals for projects that required joint efforts of at least three institutions working in different disciplines. Due to the enormous workload involved in preparing a full proposal for such large-scale projects, the Volkswagen Foundation strongly encouraged applicants to submit as a first step only short position papers. When these – as a result of an initial review – were considered to be very promising, the researchers were asked to elaborate in a complete proposal. In most cases, this procedure took more than a year, but it was very much appreciated by the researchers as well as by the reviewers involved as a way of avoiding too much waste of effort, frustration, and disappointment.
- Another area involving engineering scientists since the 1970s has been research into complex systems, including the mathematical and theoretical foundations of the engineering sciences (1971 to 1987, 330 grants totalling DM 96.2.million), the modelling of complex systems in chemical engineering (1992 to 1996: fifty-one grants totalling DM 19.1 million), and the investigation of non-linear dynamic effects in production systems (since 1995: twelve grants totalling DM 4.4 million DM). The main objective of all of these priority areas has been and still is to stimulate research that will enhance the theoretical understanding of engineering problems and help to develop new concepts, including their validation.
- Materials research, ranging from the study of physics and chemistry of unconventional materials (1978 to 1985: 167 grants totalling DM 22.8 million) and the microcharacterization of materials (since 1985: 166 grants totalling DM 49.4 million) all the way through to modern photonics (since 1989: 151 grants totalling DM 35.1 million), has also been and still is one of the Foundation's priorities. Most of the projects involve the application of physical and chemical methods as well as engineering expertise. In recent years, an increasing trend towards cooperation with the biological sciences can be observed. It

may even open up new funding opportunities in forthcoming priority areas.

- The integration of scientific methods and techniques into archaeo-logical research was one of the foundation's priorities for more than twenty years: archaeometry (1973 to 1987: 117 grants totalling DM 46.9 million) and archaeometallurgy (1987 to 1995: 113 grants totalling DM 32.6 million). The prime objective of the priority area on archaeometry was to stimulate interdisciplinary cooperation between researchers in the humanities and the sciences, in particular with regard to developing and testing methods used in the sciences in the detection, clearing, analysis, restoration, and preservation of cultural objects. Especially during the initial stages in the 1970s, this priority area served as a very useful tool for developing a climate of mutual trust for the cooperation of researchers from very different cultural and methodological backgrounds, and in the long run, it contributed considerably to the acceptance of the use of scientific and technological methods in prehistorical and archaeological research. Thus, this first priority area paved the way for an even broader approach in archaeometallurgy that by necessity also included researchers from the engineering sciences. After having terminated these funding activities, it will now be interesting to see how sustainable these cooperative research efforts are when it comes to competing for regular funds from other agencies.
- Since 1992 the foundation has been offering support for research on problems and possibilities of intercultural communications (71 grants totalling DM 25.2 million). This priority area aims to encourage especially researchers from the humanities and the social sciences to contribute to the analysis of intercultural communications – their prerequisites, opportunities, and limitations – as well as to finding practical ways of overcoming concepts and stereotypes of 'foreign' and 'alien.' Due to the complexity of the issues involved, almost all research work in this area calls for interdisciplinary and international cooperation.

Conclusions

In Germany, as in many other countries, research investments are increasingly seen as important prerequisites for maintaining or enhancing competitiveness, economic growth, and quality of life. Due to fiscal constraints in the public domain, the federal as well as the state governments are more and more confronted with the need to make choices and to give priority to certain areas, even with regard to the hitherto undisputed provision of funds for maintaining a comprehensive infrastructure for teaching and research in publicly financed universities.

The reductions in core funding of universities coincide with a considerable differentiation among institutions involved in the production of new knowledge, that is, interdisciplinary research centres, institutes for advanced study, and applied research centres, the latter especially in emerging technologies. Most of these new institutions have been established, at best, on the periphery of existing campuses, and more often completely outside the university sector. Their ability to combine experts from different disciplines and to provide flexible responses to the changing needs of industry as well as public administrations has made them strong competitors for grants and contracts that, until a few years ago, were more or less automatically given to a university professor.

It is in the light of these changes that several universities have begun to redefine the objectives of their research activities and to reorganize their institutional infrastructure. The increasing scarcity of funds and the growing demand for more problem-oriented research makes it inevitable for the universities to develop new institutional settings that can respond effectively to the predominantly medium-term needs of interdisciplinary research. In order to be competitive, it is important for them to ensure that they can obtain the best possible team of researchers. Therefore, it is essential for universities as well as research centres to find ways to open up their internal structures and to make themselves, at least on a temporary basis, as attractive as possible for the best suitable researchers from other institutions.

The current climate of change and the readiness of many researchers to embark upon problem-oriented research projects clearly is favourable to the Volkswagen Foundation and its funding objectives. Due to more than twenty-five years of experience with external funding of interdisciplinary research activities, it considers itself well equipped to support especially those university researchers who are prepared not only to look beyond the ivory tower, but also to commit themselves to providing adequate research responses to the respective issues and to bringing about the necessary institutional changes. Due to its high quality standards, the Foundation thus indirectly may even contribute to the establishment of centres of excellence.

But there is more to it than simply making the right choices with regard to scientific excellence. In the long run, almost inevitably the following question is raised: 'Where can all the talented young people who were engaged in high-quality interdisciplinary research go after completing their project?' Often, the marked emphasis of German universities on discipline-oriented specialization prevents postdoctoral researchers, even more senior researchers who hold a 'Habilitation' (in Germany, a kind of superdoctoral thesis that entitles holders to teach at a university) from getting back into the system. As long as the involvement in interdisciplinary research is considered to be a second-best option, it is difficult for any funding organization to achieve its objectives in a university environment.

I have no clear-cut solution to this problem, but I do think that efforts must be made to look for an appropriate balance between the urgently needed commitment of researchers to interdisciplinary projects and the openness of academic institutions to consider these researchers as equally suitable candidates for professorships as their colleagues who have stayed in the mainstream of their respective field. But without external incentives and the creation of new institutional structures, it will be difficult to turn this idea from wishful thinking into good and common practice, let alone a self-fulfilling prophecy.

Notes

1 An overview in English on the current funding program of the Volkswagen Foundation is provided in the booklet 'Outlines,' which can be obtained directly from its head office in Hanover (Postfach 81 05 09, D-30505 Hannover, or e-mail: mail@volkswagen-stiftung.de).

2 For a more detailed list of criteria, based on an article by M.B. Luszki on interdisciplinary team research from 1958, see Dieter Blaschke 1986: 177f.

Concluding Comments

As we have documented, there is both in academia and in science policy a renewed interest in interdisciplinarity, its opportunities, and its institutional obstacles. This interest derives its urgency from and is fuelled by a variety of competing and even contradictory sources and commitments. There is, first of all, the persistent perception of an uninhibited trend towards ever more specialization in science driven by the search for novelty and efforts to achieve visibility. In some of its extreme forms, it is argued, this is inimical both towards the production of useful knowledge and the ideal of education and training that results in more than limited horizons of brute specialists. Among the almost taken for granted rationales, therefore, is the need that the fruits of science be much more holistic. Second, the agenda for interdisciplinarity has more recently been supported by discourses, especially in some of the humanities that are hostile to the current division of labour in academia, because the practice of disciplinary-based knowledge production fails to live up to some emancipatory social and political goals. Strong voices are heard in these movements assailing the political authority, territorial claims, and discrimination that accompany the practice and defence of disciplinary boundaries. Interdisciplinarity is seen as a cure for the enumerated symptoms and narrow special interests. These attacks and indictments by no means inhere exclusively in radical perspectives and approaches. Complaints about the breakup of intellectual coherence and transparence, the loss of a meaningful centre, and the persistent specialization in science (and the growing societal division of labour as its counterpart) also can be taken as rationales that favour the agenda of interdisciplinarity.

On the other hand, the call for interdisciplinarity as a solution to a range of cognitive as well as social, pedagogical, and organizational problems has found its detractors, not unlike those who voiced early doubts almost immediately after the U.S. Social Science Research Council first proclaimed interdisciplinarity as one of its major objectives in funding research activities. The contentions associated with what has become known as the 'science wars' are one prominent example. The very public debate about Alan Sokal's essay (1996) indicated that natural scientists had begun to take note of the work on science in such fields as radical environmentalism, feminist criticism, constructivist science studies, and literary and cultural criticism. The debate was not only motivated by concerns of the natural sciences that the damage to their public image that was feared to be incurred by these fields might result in further budgetary constraints. It also demonstrated the deep schism between the 'two cultures' of the natural sciences on the one hand and the social sciences and humanities on the other. Among many issues that surfaced in the dispute was the claim that scientific practice is not constrained in any unique sense by the world of objects it investigates but is, not unlike the humanities and the social sciences, the product of social conventions. This constructivist approach therefore denies that it is meaningful to speak about different branches of science separated by deep epistemological divisions and distant forms of practice. Those who have rejected the project of constructivism in the context of the science wars of course affirm the strength of and the need for the divisions among the sciences; at worst, the claim is made that the humanities and the social sciences finally ought to follow the successful example of the natural sciences. If nothing more, the science wars experience reveals the potential for misunderstanding and politicization between the two cultures. Only cool-hearted and open-minded observers are opting for bridge-building.

What seemed to be a high-pitched and trendy debate on the latest quirks of post-modernism actually pointed to a well-known paradox of the interdisciplinary movement, namely, that 'being interdisciplinary – breaking out of the prison houses of various specialties to the open range first of a general human knowledge and then of the employment of that knowledge in the great struggles of social and political life – is not a possible human achievement' (Fish 1994: 237). The point is familiar: the structures that organize how we know are not eliminated by interdisciplinarity, but relocated.

Among these countervailing forces, persistent commitments, opposing legitimations, and converging hopes for interdisciplinarity there is one developmental track that above all induces and pushes interdisciplinarity. There is little if any evidence that most of the arguments we have enumerated in praise of interdisciplinarity or those that can be read as assaults on the idea of interdisciplinarity have had visible or measurable effects on the *practical* project of interdisciplinarity.

Fish seems to be triumphant and disappointed at the same time that interdisciplinary programs only lead to either the emergence of a new discipline or the annexation of one discipline's territory by another. While the radical voices in favour of interdisciplinarity may imagine the world of knowledge production without any organizing structures, the more sober view sees interdisciplinarity always as a limited project in relation to a limited number of disciplines in a limited time frame. This is precisely the reason why this volume focused on the *practice of interdisciplinarity*: disciplines, or more generally, structures of cognition and knowledge production are not dispensable as such but nor are they immutable – by practice. It cannot be otherwise.

References

Allen, G.E. 1978a. 'Opposition to the Mendelian-Chromosome Theory: The Physiological and Developmental Genetics of Richard Goldschmidt.' *Journal of the History of Biology* 7: 55–87.

Allen, G.E. 1978b. *Thomas Hunt Morgan: The Man and His Science.* Princeton, NJ: Princeton University Press.

Allison, P.D., and J. Scott Long. 1990. 'Departmental Effects on Scientific Productivity.' *American Sociological Review* 55: 469–78.

Australian Bureau of Statistics (ABS). (1992–3, 1996–7). *Research and Experimental Development, All Sector Summary.* Catalogue No. 8112.0. Canberra: ABS.

Avery, O.T., MacLeod, C.M., and McCarty, M. 1944. 'Transformation of Pneumococcal Types Induced by a Desoxyribonucleid Acid Fraction Isolated from Pneumococcus Type III.' *Journal of Experimental Medicine* 79: 137–58.

Baldwin, J.M. 1902. *Development and Evolution.* New York: Macmillan.

Barthes, R. 1977. *Image, Music, Text.* Trans. Stephen Heath. New York: Hill and Wang.

Baumgartner, P., and S. Payr, eds. 1995. *Speaking Minds: Interviews with Twenty Eminent Cognitive Scientists.* Princeton, NJ: Princeton University Press.

Bazerman, C. 1995. 'Influencing and Being Influenced.' *Social Epistemology* 9, 2: 189–201.

Becher, T. 1990. 'The Counter-Culture of Specialization.' *European Journal of Education* 15,1: 333–46.

Bechtel, W. 1986. 'The Nature of Scientific Integration,' in W. Bechtel, ed., *Integrating Scientific Disciplines*, 3–52. Dordrecht, Netherlands: Martinus Nijhoof.

Beckmann, M.C. 1991. 'Tjalling C. Koopman,' in E.A. Shils, ed., *Remembering the University of Chicago*, 253–66. Chicago: University of Chicago Press.

Ben-David, J. 1960. 'Scientific Productivity and Academic Organization in Nineteenth Century Medicine.' *American Sociological Review* 25: 828–43.
- 1971. *The Scientist's Role in Society: A Comparative Study.* Englewood Cliffs, NJ: Prentice-Hall.
- 1977. *Centers of Learning: Britain, France, Germany, United States.* New York: McGraw-Hill.
Bernstein, R. 1991. *The New Constellation.* Cambridge, MA: Polity Press.
Birnbaum, N. 1986 [1969]. 'The Arbitrary Disciplines,' in D. Chubin, A.L. Porter, F.A. Rossini, T. Connolly, eds., *Interdisciplinary Analysis and Research. Theory and Practice of Problem-Focused Research and Development,* 54–66. Mt Airy: Lomond.
Black, M. 1962. *Models and Metaphors: Studies in Language and Philosophy.* Ithaca, NY: Cornell University Press.
Blanke, T., and U.K. Preuss. 1994. 'Empfehlungen zur Errichtung eines Hanse-Wissenschaftskollegs in Delmenhorst.' Memorandum.
Blaschke, D. 1986. 'Zur Beurteilung interdisziplinärer sozialwissenschaftlicher Forschung,' in R. Fisch and H.-D. Daniel, eds., *Messung und Förderung von Forschungsleistung,* 167–89. Konstanz: Universitätsverlag Konstanz.
Blewitt, A. 1992. 'Corporatisation and Change – The Reality of Commercialisation for HR Management in CSIRO.' Paper prepared for the Institute for International Research (IIR) Conference on Human Resource Management (Reposition and Realign Your HR function for Greater Organisational Effectiveness).
Bono, J.J. 1990. 'Science, Discourse, and Literature. The Role/Rule of Metaphor in Science,' in S. Peterfreund, ed., *Literature and Science. Theory and Practice,* 59–89. Boston: Northeastern University Press.
- 1995. 'Locating Narratives: Science, Metaphor, Communities and Epistemic Styles,' in P. Weingart, ed., *Grenzüberschreitungen in der Wissenschaft – Crossing Boundaries in Science,* 119–51. ZiF Interdisziplinäre Studien 1. Baden-Baden, Germany: Nomos.
Bourdieu, P. 1991. *The Political Ontology of Martin Heidegger.* Cambridge, UK: Polity Press.
Bourke, P., and L. Butler. 1993. 'Mapping Scientific Research in Universities: Departments and Fields.' Performance Indicators Project, Occasional Paper No. 1. Canberra, Australia: Australian National University, Research School of Social Sciences.
Bremische Bürgerschaft. 1995. Landtag 13. Wahlperiode, Drucksache 13/1178, Empfehlungen einer Stiftung privaten Rechts 'Hanse-Wissenschaftskolleg.' Manuscript.

Bromme, R., and R. Rambow. 1995. 'Man sieht nur, was man weiß....' *Der Architekt* 8: 451–53.

Bromme, R., R. Rambow, and J. Wiedmann. 1998. 'Typizitätsvariationen bei abstrakten Begriffen: Das Beispiel chemischer Fachbegriffe (Typicality of Abstract Concepts: The Example of a Chemical Specialist Concept).' *Sprache und Kognition* 17: 3–20.

Bromme, R., and H. Tillema. 1995. 'Fusing Experience and Theory: The Structure of Professional Knowledge,' in R. Bromme and H. Tillema, eds., *Fusing Experience and Theory*. Special issue of *Learning and Instruction* 5: 261–69.

Bundesministerium für Bildung und Forschung (BMBF). 1996. 'Technologie, interdisziplinäre Zentren für klinische Forschung in Hochschulkliniken.' Hinweise für Interessenten (Internet): http://www.dfg.de/foerder/innovation/index.html.

Burian, R.N. 1993. 'Unification and Coherence as Methodological Objectives in the Biological Sciences.' *Biology and Philosophy* 8, 3: 301–18.

Burrows, R. 1991. *Deciphering the Enterprise Culture: Entrepreneurship, Petty Capitalism and the Restructuring of Britain*. London: Routledge.

Buxton, W., and S. Turner. 1992. 'Education and Expertise: Sociology as a "Profession,"' in T.C. Halliday and M. Janowitz, eds., *Sociology and Its Publics: The Forms and Fates of Disciplinary Organization*, 272–407. Chicago: University of Chicago Press.

Calhoun, C. 1992. 'Sociology, Other Disciplines, and the Project of a General Understanding of Social Life,' in T.C. Halliday and M. Janowitz, eds., *Sociology and Its Publics: The Forms and Fates of Disciplinary Organization*, 137–95. Chicago: University of Chicago Press.

Campbell, D.T. 1959. 'Methodological Suggestions From a Comparative Psychology of Knowledge Processes.' *Inquiry* 2: 152–82.

Canada. *National Guide to College and University Programmes*. 1996. Ottawa: Human Resources Development Canada.

de Certeau, M. 1984. *The Practice of Everyday Life* (trans. Steven F. Rendall). Berkeley: University of California Press.

Charlesworth, M., L. Farrall, T. Stokes, and D. Turnbull. 1989. *Life Among the Scientists*. Melbourne: Oxford University Press.

Chubin, D. 1976. 'The Conceptualization of Scientific Specialties.' *Sociological Quarterly* 17: 448–76.

Chubin, D., A.L. Porter, F.A. Rossini, T. Connolly, eds. 1986. *Interdisciplinary Analysis and Research. Theory and Practice of Problem-Focused Research and Development*. Mt. Airy, MD: Lomond.

Clark, B. 1995. *Places of Inquiry*. Berkeley: University of California Press.

Clark, H.H. 1992. *Arenas of Language Use*. Chicago: University of Chicago Press.

– 1996. *Using Language*. Cambridge: Cambridge University Press.

Cohen, S. 1993. *Academia and the Luster of Capital*. Minneapolis: University of Minnesota Press.

Commonwealth Scientific and Industrial Research Organization (CSIRO). 1987. *Report of the Institute Model Study*. Canberra, Australia: CSIRO.

Cooperative Research Centres Program Evaluation Steering Committee. 1995. *Changing Research Culture*. Canberra, Australia: AGPS.

Corner, G.W. 1964. *A History of the Rockefeller Institute*. New York: Rockefeller University Press.

Cosmides, L., and J. Tooby. 1987. 'From Evolution to Behavior: Evolutionary Psychology as the Missing Link,' in J. Duprée, ed., *The Latest on the Best: Essays on Evolution and Optimality*, 277–306. Cambridge: MIT Press.

Crane, D., and H. Small. 1992. 'American Sociology Since the Seventies,' in T. Halliday and M. Janowitz, eds., *Sociology and Its Publics: The Forms and Fates of Disciplinary Organization*, 197–234. Chicago: University of Chicago Press.

Dahlberg, I. 1994. 'Domain Interaction.' *Advances in Knowledge Organization* 4: 60–71.

Darden, L., and N. Maull. 1977. 'Interfield Theories.' *Philosophy of Science* 44: 43–64.

Dasgupta, P., and P.A. David. 1993. 'Toward a New Economics of Science.' MERIT Research Paper 94–003. Maastricht, Netherlands: Maastricht Economic Research Institute on Innovation and Technology.

Davidse, R.J., and A.F.J. van Raan. 1997. 'Out of Particles. Impact of CERN, DESY and SLAC Research to Fields Other than Physics.' *Scientometrics* 40, 171–93.

Dawkins, R. 1982. *The Extended Phenotype*. Oxford: Freeman.

Department of Defence. 1993/94. *Corporate Plan*. Canberra, Australia.

Deutsche Forschungsgemeinschaft (DFG), Jahresbericht 1996. *Bd. 1, Aufgaben und Ergebnisse*. Bonn.

Dogan, M. 1995. 'The Moving Frontiers of the Social Sciences,' in P. Weingart, ed., *Grenzüberschreitungen in der Wissenschaft (Crossing Boundaries in Science)*, 87–105. ZiF Interdisciplinary Studies 1. Baden-Baden, Germany: Nomos.

Dogan, M., and R. Pahre. 1990. *Creative Marginality. Innovation at the Intersections of the Social Sciences*. Boulder, CO: Westview Press.

Dreyfus, H. 1995. 'Cognitivism Abandoned,' in P. Baumgartner and S. Payr, eds., *Speaking Minds*, 71–83. Princeton, NJ: Princeton University Press.

Drucker, P.F. 1993. *Post-Capitalist Society*. New York: Harper.

Du Bois-Reymond, E. 1887. *Über die wissenschaftlichen Zustände der Gegenwart,* in E. du Bois-Reymond, *Reden,* Zweite Folge, 448–64. Leipzig: Verlag von Veit & Comp.

Dubos, R.J. 1976. *The Professor, the Institute, and DNA.* New York: Rockefeller University Press.

Easton, D. 1991. 'The Division, Integration, and Transfer of Knowledge,' in D. Easton and C. Schelling, eds., *Divided Knowledge,* 7–36. Newbury Park, CA: Sage.

Eisenstadt, S.N. 1992. 'Some Observations on "Post-Modern" Society,' in N. Stehr and R.V. Ericson, eds., *The Culture and Power of Knowledge,* 51–59. Berlin: Walter de Gruyter.

Elzinga, A. 1985. 'Research, Bureaucracy, and the Drift of Epistemic Criteria,' in B. Wittrock and A. Elzinga, eds., *The University Research System,* 191–220. Lund, Sweden: Research on Higher Education Program.

Epton, S.R., R.L. Payne, and A.W. Pearson. 1984. 'The Management of Cross-Disciplinary Research.' *Rand Management* 14: 69–79.

Etzkowitz, H. 1983. 'Entrepreneurial Scientists and Entrepreneurial Universities in American Academic Science.' *Minerva* 21, 2–3: 198–233.

Etzkowitz, H., and L. Leydesdorff, eds. 1997. *Universities and the Global Knowledge Economy: A Triple Helix of University-Industry-Government Relations.* London and Washington: Pinter.

Falersweany, M.L. 1995. 'Spanning Rhetoric for a Holistic Science.' *Social Epistemology* 9, 2: 151–64.

Fischer, E.P., and C. Lipson. 1988. *Thinking about Science: Max Delbrück and the Origins of Molecular Biology.* New York: Norton.

Fish, S. 1994. 'Being Interdisciplinary Is So Very Hard To Do.' *There's No Such Thing as Free Speech,* 231–420. New York: Oxford University Press.

Fleck, L. [1935] 1979. *Genesis and Development of a Scientific Fact.* Ed. T.J. Trenn and R.K. Merton. Trans. F. Bradley and T.J. Trenn. Chicago: University of Chicago Press.

Flexner, A. 1930. *Universities: American, German, English.* Oxford: Oxford University Press.

Flood, J. 1984. 'The Advent of Strategic Management in CSIRO: A History of Change.' *Prometheus* 2, 1: 38–72.

Franzosi, R. 1998. 'Narrative Analysis – or Why (and How) Sociologists Should Be Interested in Narrative.' *Annual Review of Sociology* 24: 517–54.

Fujimura, J. 1987. 'The Molecular Biology Bandwagon in Cancer Research: Where Social Worlds Meet.' *Social Problems* 35: 261–83.

Fuller, S. 1988. *Social Epistemology.* Bloomington, IN: Indiana University Press.

– 1993. *Philosophy, Rhetoric, and the End of Knowledge*. Madison: University of Wisconsin Press.

– 1995. 'Interdisciplinary Rhetoric.' *Social Epistemology* 9, 2: 201–4.

– 1996. 'Interdisciplinarity: Fielding the Challenges.' *DIANOIA* 5, 1: 72–75.

Funtowicz, S.O., and J.R. Ravetz. 1993. 'The Emergence of Post-Normal Science,' in R. von Schomberg, ed., *Science, Politics and Morality: Scientific Uncertainty and Decision Making*, 85–123. Dordrecht, Netherlands: Kluwer.

Galison, P. 1992. Unpublished manuscript.

Galison, P., and B. Helvy, eds. 1992. *Big Science*. Stanford, CA: Stanford University Press.

Galison, P., and D.J. Stump, eds. 1996. *The Disunity of Science*. Stanford, CA: Stanford University Press.

Garrod, S.C., and G. Doherty. 1994. 'Conversation, Coordination and Convention: An Empirical Investigation of How Groups Establish Linguistic Conventions.' *Cognition* 53: 181–215.

Geertz, C. 1986. 'Blurred Genres: The Reconfiguration of Social Thought,' in H. Adams and L. Searle, eds., *Critical Theory Since 1965*. Tallahassee: Florida State University Press.

Gerson, E. 1983. 'Scientific Work and Social Worlds.' *Knowledge* 4, 3: 357–77.

Gibbons, M., C. Limoges, H. Nowotny, S. Schwartzman, P. Scott, and M. Trow. 1994. *The New Production of Knowledge*. London: Sage.

Gibbs, R. 1994. *The Poetics of Mind: Figurative Thought, Language, and Understanding*. Cambridge: Cambridge University Press.

Gigerenzer, G., and K. Hug. 1992. 'Domain-Specific Reasoning: Social Contracts, Cheating and Perspective Change.' *Cognition* 43: 127–71.

Gigerenzer, G., Z. Swijtink, T. Porter, L. Daston, J. Beatty, and L. Krüger. 1989. *The Empire of Chance: How Probability Changed Science and Everyday Life*. Cambridge: Cambridge University Press.

Gillespie, D.T.G. 1964 (Spring). 'Research Management in the Commonwealth Scientific and Industrial Research Organization.' *Public Administration*, 42: 8–72.

Goldman, H. 1995. 'Innovation and Change in the Production of Knowledge.' *Social Epistemology* 9, 3: 211–32.

Gore, A. 1996. 'The Metaphor of Distributed Intelligence.' *Science* 272: 177.

Graff, G. 1987. *Professing Literature*. Chicago: University of Chicago Press.

Green, M.L.H., S.R. Marder, M.E. Thompson, J.A. Bandy, D. Bloor, P.U. Kolinsky, and R.J. Jones. 1987. 'The Synthesis and Structure of (cis)-[1-ferrocenyl-2-(4-nitrophenyl)ethylene]: An Organometallic Compound with a Large Second-Order Optical Nonlinearity.' *Nature* 330: 362.

Gruner, S.M., S. James, P.N. Langer, and V. Vogel. 1995. 'What Future Will We Choose for Physics?' *Physics Today* (December): 25–30.

Hacking, I. 1987. 'Prussian Numbers,' in L. Krüger, L. Daston, and M. Heidelberger, eds., *The Probabilistic Revolution. Vol. I: Ideas in History*, 377–94. Cambridge: MIT Press.

Hagendijk, R. 1990. 'Structuration Theory, Constructivism, and Scientific Change,' in S. Cozzens and T. Gieryn, eds., *Theories of Science in Society*, 43–66. Bloomington: Indiana University Press.

Halliday, T. 1992. 'Introduction: Sociology's Fragile Professionalism,' in T. Halliday and M. Janowitz, eds., *Sociology and Its Publics: The Forms and Fates of Disciplinary Organization*, 3–42. Chicago: University of Chicago Press.

Halpern, M. 1990. *Binding Time*. Norwood, NJ: Ablex.

Hanson, R. 1997 (March). 'Patterns of Patronage: Why Grants Won Over Prizes.' Paper presented to New Economics of Science Conference. Notre Dame, Indiana.

Hayles, N.K. 1990. *Chaos Bound*. Ithaca, NY: Cornell University Press.

Heckhausen, H. 1972. 'Discipline and Interdisciplinarity.' *Interdisciplinarity: Problems of Teaching and Research in Universities*, 83–89. Paris: OECD.

Hesse, M. 1972. 'The Explanatory Function of Metaphor,' in Y. Bar-Hillel, ed., *Logic, Methodology, and Philosophy of Science*, 249–59. Amsterdam: Elsevier.

Hill, S., and P. Murphy. 1994. 'Quantitative Indicators of Academic Research.' Commissioned Report No. 27. National Board of Employment, Education and Training. Canberra, Australia: AGPS.

Hill, S., and T. Turpin. 1993. 'The Formation of Research Centres in the Australian University System.' *Science and Technology Policy* 6, 5: 7–13.

– (February). 'The Clashing of Academic Symbols.' *Science as Culture* 4: 327–62.

Hoch, P. 1987. 'Migration and the Generation of New Scientific Ideas.' *Minerva* 25, 2: 209–37.

– 1990. 'New UK Interdisciplinary Research Centers.' *Technology Analysis and Strategic Management* 2, 1: 39–48.

Hollingsworth, R. 1996 (September). 'Why Research Organizations Vary in Their Capacity to Make Major Discoveries in Biomedical Science: Some Observations from the United States.' Paper presented at the Royal Swedish Academy of Sciences. Stockholm.

Hollingsworth, R., and J. Hage 1996. 'Organizational Characteristics Which Facilitate Major Discoveries in the Bio-Medical Sciences.' Document presented to the Science and Technology Studies Program, National Science Foundation, USA.

Horton, W.S., and B. Keysar. 1996. 'When Do Speakers Take into Account Common Ground?' *Cognition* 59: 91–117.

Hübenthal, U. 1991. *Interdisziplinäres Denken*. Stuttgart, Germany: F. Steiner.

– 1994. 'Interdisciplinary Thought.' *Issues in Integrative Studies* 12: 55–75.

Huber, L. 1992. 'Editorial.' *European Journal of Education* 2, 3: 193–99.

Hutchins, E. 1995. *Cognition in the Wild*. Cambridge: MIT Press.

Immelmann, K. 1987. 'Interdisziplinarität zwischen Natur – und Geisteswissenschaften – Praxis und Utopie,' in J. Kocka, ed., *Interdisziplinarität. Praxis – Herausforderung – Ideologie*, 82–91. Frankfurt: Suhrkamp.

Intrilligator, M. 1985. 'Interdependence among the Behavioral Sciences.' Paper presented at World Congress of Political Science. Paris.

Isaacs, E.A., and H.H. Clark. 1987. 'References in Conversation between Experts and Novices.' *Journal of Experimental Psychology: General* 116: 26–37.

Jameson, A., T.O. Nelson, R.J. Leonesio, and L. Narens. 1993. 'The Feeling of Another Person's Knowing.' *Journal of Memory and Language* 32: 320–35.

Jantsch, E. 1972. 'Towards Interdisciplinarity and Transdisciplinarity in Education and Innovation,' in CERI, *Interdiscipinarity: Problems of Teaching and Research in Universities*, 97–120. Paris: OECD.

– 1980. 'Interdisciplinarity.' *Prospects* 10, 3: 304–12.

Johnson-Laird, P. 1982. 'Mutual Ignorance: Comments on Clark and Carlson's Paper,' in N.V. Smith, ed., *Mutual Knowledge*, 40–45. New York: Academic Press.

Kargon, R. H. 1978. 'Temple to Science: Cooperative Research and the Birth of the California Institute of Technology.' *Historical Studies in the Physical Sciences* 8: 3–32.

Kash, D.E., and Rycroft, R.W. 1994. 'Technology Policy: Fitting Concept with Reality.' *Technological Forecasting and Social Change* 47: 35–48.

Kastner, M., and G. Sprenger. 1993. *ZiF: 1968–1993. Daten aus 25 Jahren Forschung*. Bielefeld, Germany: Universität Bielefeld.

Kay, L.E. 1993. *The Molecular Vision of Life: Caltech, the Rockefeller Foundation and the Rise of the New Biology*. New York: Oxford University Press.

Keat, R. 1991. 'Consumer Sovereignty and the Integrity of Practices,' in R. Keat and N. Abercrombie, eds., *Enterprise Culture*, 216–30. London: Routledge.

Kedrov, B. 1974. 'Concerning the Synthesis of the Sciences.' *International Classification* 1, 1: 3–11.

Keil, F.C. 1989. *Concepts, Kinds, and Cognitive Development*. Cambridge: MIT Press.

Kenneth, W. 1995. *Sex, Ecology, Spirituality: The Spirit of Evolution*. Boston: Shambhala Press.

Kingsbury, D. 1968. 'Manipulating the Amount of Information Obtained from a Person Giving Directions.' Unpublished doctoral thesis. Harvard University, Cambridge.

Kingsbury, S.J. 1987. 'Cognitive Differences between Clinical Psychologists and Psychiatrists.' *American Psychologist* 42: 152–56.

Klein Thompson, J. [1983] 1986. 'The Dialectic and Rhetoric of Disciplinarity and Interdisciplinarity,' in D. Chubin, A.L. Porter, F.A. Rossini, and T. Connolly, eds., *Interdisciplinary Analysis and Research. Theory and Practice of Problem-Focused Research and Development*. Mt Airy, MD: Lomond.

– 1990. *Interdisciplinarity: History, Theory and Practice*. Detroit: Wayne State University Press.

– 1996. *Crossing Boundaries: Knowledge, Disciplinarities, and Interdisciplinarities*. Charlottesville: University Press of Virginia.

Kline, S.J. 1995. *Conceptual Foundations for Multidisciplinary Thinking*. Stanford, CA: Stanford University Press.

Knorr-Cetina, K.D. 1981. *The Manufacture of Knowledge: An Essay on the Constructivist and Contextual Nature of Science*. New York: Pergamon Press.

Kocka, J., ed. 1987. *Interdisziplinarität: Praxis – Herausforderung – Ideologie*. Frankfurt: Suhrkamp.

Kohler, R.E. 1994. *The Lords of the Fly*. Chicago: University of Chicago Press.

Krauss, R.M., and S.R. Fussell. 1990. 'Mutual Knowledge and Communicative Effectiveness,' in J. Galegher, R. Kraut, and C. Egido, eds., *Intellectual Teamwork: Social and Technological Foundations of Cooperative Work*, 111–46. Hillsdale, NJ: Lawrence Erlbaum Associates.

– 1991. 'Perspective-Taking in Communication: Representations of Others. Knowledge in Reference.' *Social Cognition* 9: 2–24.

Kuhn, T.S. 1962. *The Structure of Scientific Revolutions*. Chicago: University of Chicago Press.

– 1977. *The Essential Tension*. Chicago: Chicago University Press.

Küppers, G., P. Lundgreen, and P. Weingart. 1978. *Umweltforschung – Die gesteuerte Wissenschaft?* Frankfurt: Suhrkamp.

de Lacey, P., and G. Moens. 1990. *The Decline of the University*. Tahmoor, Australia: Law Press.

Lakoff, G. 1987. *Woman, Fire, and Dangerous Things: What Categories Reveal about the Nature of Thought*. Chicago: University of Chicago Press.

Landau, M.H. Proshansky, and W. Ittelson. 1961. 'The Interdisciplinary Approach and the Concept of Behavioral Sciences,' in N. Washburne, ed., *Decisions, Values, and Groups*, 7–25. New York: Pergamon.

Landsberg, J. 1989 (June). 'The Management of Scientific Research.' *Prometheus* 7, 1: 75–91.

Lane, N. 1997. Testimony on NSF's Fiscal Year 1998 Budget Request, 6 February 1997.

Lassman, P., and I. Velody, eds. 1989. *Max Weber's 'Science as a Vocation.'* London: Unwin Hyman.

Latour, B. 1987. *Science in Action: How to Follow Scientists and Engineers through Society.* Cambridge: Harvard University Press.

Latour, B., and S. Woolgar. 1979. *Laboratory Life: The Construction of Scientific Facts.* Princeton, NJ: Princeton University Press.

Law, J. 1973. 'The Development of Specialties in Science: The Case of X-Ray Protein Crystallography.' *Science Studies* 3: 275–303.

Ledermann, N.G. 1992. '"Students' and Teachers" Conceptions of the Nature of Science: A Review of the Research.' *Journal of Research on Science Teaching* 29: 331–59.

Lepenies, W. 1978. 'Toward an Interdisciplinary History of Science.' *International Journal of Sociology* 8, 1–2: 45–69.

Levin, L., and I. Lind, eds. 1985. *Interdisciplinarity Revisited.* OECD/CERI. Swedish National Board of Universities and Colleges, Linköping University.

Los Angeles Times, 20 October 1985, 12 January 1992.

Lovell, B. 1990. *Astronomer by Chance.* New York: Basic Books.

Lowy, I. 1992. 'The Strength of Loose Concepts.' *History of Science* 30, 4, no. 90: 371–96.

Lübbe, H. 1987. 'Helmut Schelsky und die Interdisziplinarität. Zur Philosophie gegenwärtiger Wissenschaftskultur,' in J. Kocka, ed., *Interdisziplinarität. Praxis – Herausforderung – Ideologie,* 17–33. Frankfurt: Suhrkamp.

Luszki, M.B. 1958. *Interdisciplinary Team Research: Methods and Problems.* New York: New York University Press.

Lynch, M. 1985. *Art and Artifact in Laboratory Science: A Study of Shop Work and Shop Talk in a Research Laboratory.* London: Routledge and Kegan Paul.

– 1993. *Scientific Practice and Ordinary Action: Ethnomethodological and Social Studies of Science.* Cambridge: Cambridge University Press.

Maasen, S. 1994. 'Who Is Afraid of Metaphors?' in S. Maasen, E. Mendelsohn, and P. Weingart, eds., *Biology as Society, Society as Biology: Metaphors. Yearbook Sociology of the Sciences,* Vol. 18, 11–36. Dordrecht, Netherlands: Kluwer.

Maasen, S., E. Mendelsohn, and P. Weingart, eds. 1995. *Biology as Society, Society as Biology: Metaphors. Yearbook Sociology of the Sciences,* Vol. 18. Dordrecht, Netherlands: Kluwer.

Malt, B. 1994. 'Water Is Not H_2O.' *Cognitive Psychology* 27: 41–70.

Markova, I., C. Graumann, and K. Foppa, eds. 1995. *Mutualities in Dialogue: Intrapersonal and Interpersonal Processes.* Cambridge: Cambridge University Press.

Mathiesen, W.C. 1990. 'The Problem-Solving Community: A Valuable Alternative to Disciplinary Communities?' *Knowledge* 2, 4: 410–27.

Mayr, E. 1963. *Animal Species and Evolution.* Cambridge: Harvard University Press.

McGauran, P. 1996. *Science and Technology Budget Statement 1996–97.* Canberra, Australia: AGPS.

Merton, R.K. 1961. 'Singletons and Multiples in Scientific Discovery.' *Proceedings of the American Philosophical Society* 55: 470–86.

– 1968. 'The Matthew Effect in Science.' *Science* 159: 56–63.

– 1973 [1963]. 'The Ambivalence of Scientists,' in N. Storer, ed., *The Sociology of Science,* 383–412. Chicago: University of Chicago Press.

– 1973. *The Sociology of Science: Theoretical and Empirical Investigations.* Chicago: University of Chicago Press.

Messer-Davidson, E., D.K. Shumway, and D.J Sylvan, eds. 1993. *Knowledges: Historical and Critical Studies in Disciplinarity.* Charlottesville, VA: University Press of Virginia.

Miller, G.A., E. Galanter, and K.H. Pribram. 1960. *Plans and the Structure of Behavior.* New York: Holt.

Mischel, W. 1990. 'Personality Dispositions Revisted and Revisted: A View After Three Decades,' in L.A. Pervin, ed., *Handbook of Personality: Theory and Research,* 111–34. New York: Guilford Press.

Mithen, S. 1996. *The Prehistory of the Mind, The Cognitive Origins of Art, Religion and Science.* London: Thames and Hudson.

Mittelstrass, J. 1987. 'Die Stunde der Interdisziplinarität,' in J. Kocka, ed., *Interdisziplinarität: Praxis – Herausforderung – Ideologie,* 152–59. Frankfurt: Suhrkamp.

Muller, J., and N. Taylor. 1995. 'Schooling and Everyday Life: Knowledges Sacred and Profane.' *Social Epistemology* 9, 3: 257–6.

Murphy, G.L. 1996. 'On Metaphoric Representation.' *Cognition* 60: 173–204.

National Research Council. 1986. *Scientific Interfaces and Technological Applications.* Washington, DC: National Academy Press.

Neurath, O. 1938. 'Unified Science as Encyclopedic Integration,' in O. Neurath et al., eds., *International Encyclopedia of Unified Science,* Vol. 1, No. 1, 1–27. Chicago: University of Chicago Press.

New Alliances and Partnerships in American Science and Engineering. 1986. Washington, DC: National Academic Press.

Norem, J.K. 1989. 'Cognitive Strategies as Personality: Effectiveness, Specificity, Flexibility, and Change,' in D.M. Buss and N. Cantor, eds., *Personality Psychology: Recent Trends and Emerging Directions,* 45–60. Berlin: Springer.

Noyons, E.C.M., R.J.W. Tijssen, A.J. Nederhof, and A.F.J. van Raan. 1996. 'Bibliometric Mapping of Agricultural Research. Report to the Netherlands Council for Agricultural Research (NRLO).' The Hague. Working paper, available on http://sahara. fsw. leidenuniv.nl/ed/nrlo/nrlo00.html.

Noyons, E.C.M., and A.F.J. van Raan. 1998. 'Monitoring Scientific Developments from a Dynamic Perspective: Self-Organized Structuring to Map Neural Network Research.' *Journal of the American Society for Information Science* (JASIS) 49, 1: 68–81.

OECD/CERI. 1972. *Interdisciplinarity: Problems of Teaching and Research in Universities.* Paris: OECD.

Ohio State University (OSU) Task Force for Interdisciplinary Research and Graduate Education. *Report on Recommendations for Fostering Interdisciplinary Research and Graduate Education.* Columbus, OH: OSU. 1991 (April 19).

Olby, R. 1979. *The Path to the Double Helix.* Seattle: University of Washington Press.

Pahre, R. 1995. 'Positivist Discourse and Social Scientific Communities.' *Social Epistemology* 9, 3: 233–55.

Palmer, C. 1996. 'Practices and Conditions of Boundary Crossing Research Work.' PhD dissertation. University of Illinois at Urbana-Champaign.

Palmer, S. 1995. 'Gestalt Psychology Redux,' in P. Baumgartner and S. Payr, eds., *Speaking Minds,* 157–76. Princeton, NJ: Princeton University Press.

– 1999. *Vision Science: Photons to Phenomenology.* Cambridge: MIT Press.

Parthey, H. 1996. 'Kriterien und Indikatoren interdisziplinären Arbeitens,' in P.W. Balsiger, R. Defila, and A. Di Guilio, eds., *Ökologie und Interdisziplinarität – eine Beziehung mit Zukunft? Wissenschaftsforschung zur Verbesserung der fachübergreifenden Zusammenarbeit,* 99–112. Basel, Switzerland: Birkhäuser.

Paulson, W. 1991. 'Literature, Complexity, Interdisciplinarity,' in N.K. Hayles, ed., *Chaos and Order,* 37–53. Chicago: University of Chicago Press.

Paxson, T. 1996. 'Modes of Interaction between Disciplines.' *Journal of General Education* 45, 2: 79–94.

Pearson, A.W., R.L. Payne, and H.P. Gunz. 1979. 'Communication, Coordination, and Leadership in Interdisciplinary Research,' in R.T. Barth and R. Steck, eds., *Interdisciplinary Research Groups,* 112–27. Vancouver, BC: International Group on Interdisciplinary Programs.

Pelz, D.C., and Andrews, F.M. 1966. *Scientists in Organizations: Productive Climates for Research and Development.* New York: John Wiley.

Physics in Perspective. 1971. Washington, DC: National Academy of Sciences.

Pinch, T. 1990. 'The Culture of Scientists and Disciplinary Rhetoric.' *European Journal of Education* 5, 3: 295–304.

Polanyi, M. 1966. *The Tacit Dimension.* London: Routledge and Kegan Paul.

Porter, A.L., and D.E. Chubin. 1985. 'An Indicator of Cross-Disciplinary Research.' *Scientometrics* 8: 161–76.

Putnam, H. 1975. 'The Meaning of "Meaning,"' in H. Putnam, ed., *Philosophical Papers: Volume 2. Mind, Language and Reality*, 215–71. Cambridge: Cambridge University Press.

Renfrew, C. 1983. *Towards an Archaeology of the Mind*. Cambridge: Cambridge University Press.

– 1993. 'Cognitive Archaeology: Some Thoughts on the Archaeology of Thought.' *Cambridge Archaeological Journal* 3, 2: 248–50.

Rheinberger, H.-J. 1995. 'Remarks on Epistemic Practices,' in P. Weingart, ed., *Grenzüberschreitungen in der Wissenschaft (Crossing Boundaries in Science)*, 168–82. ZiF-Interdisciplinary Studies 1. Baden-Baden: Nomos.

– 1997. *Toward a History of Epistemic Things: Synthesizing Proteins in the Test Tube*. Stanford, CA: Stanford University Press.

Rosenberg, N. 1994. *Exploring the Black Box: Technology, Economics, and History*. New York: Cambridge University Press.

Ross, L., D. Greene, and P. House. 1977. 'The False Consensus Phenomenon: An Attributional Bias in Self-Perception and Social Perception Processes.' *Journal of Experimental Social Psychology* 13: 279–301.

Russell, S.J., and P. Norvig. 1995. *Artificial Intelligence: A Modern Approach*. Englewood Cliffs, NJ: Prentice-Hall.

Sakaiya, T. 1991. *The Knowledge-Value Revolution*. New York: Kodansha.

Salter, L., and A. Hearn, eds. 1996. *Outside the Lines: Issues in Interdisciplinary Research*. Montreal: McGill-Queen's University Press.

Schaffner, K.F. 1993. 'Theory Structure, Reduction, and Disciplinary Integration in Biology.' *Biology and Philosophy* 8, 3: 319–47.

Schelsky, H. 1971. *Einsamkeit und Freiheit*. Gütersloh: Bertelsmann Universitätsverlag.

Schneider, H.J. 1988. 'Interdisziplinarität: Floskel oder Notwendigkeit?' *UNIVERSITAS* 12–15.

Schober, M.F. 1993. 'Spatial Perspective-Taking in Conversation.' *Cognition* 47: 1–24.

Schön, D.A. 1963. *The Displacement of Concepts*. London: Tavistock.

Schurz, R. 1995. 'Ist Interdisziplinarität möglich?' *UNIVERSITAS* 11: 1080–89.

Searle, J. 1995. 'Ontology Is the Question,' in P. Baumgartner and S. Payr, eds., *Speaking Minds*, 203–13. Princeton, NJ: Princeton University Press.

Segerstråle, U., and P. Molnár, eds. 1997. *Nonverbal Communication: Where Nature Meets Culture*. Mahwah, NJ: Lawrence Erlbaum Associates.

Service, R.F. 1996 (5 July). 'Folding Proteins Caught in the Act.' 273: 29–30.

Servos, J.W. 1990. *Physical Chemistry from Oswald to Pauling: The Making of Science in America*. Princeton, NJ: Princeton University Press.

Shapin, S. 1995. 'Here and Everywhere: Sociology of Scientific Knowledge.' *Annual Review of Sociology* 21: 289–321.

Sigma Xi. 1988. *Removing the Boundaries*. New Haven, CT: Sigma Xi.

Sills, D.L. 1986. 'A Note on the Origin of Interdisciplinarity.' 17–18.

Sjölander, S. 1985. 'Long-Term and Short-Term Interdisciplinary Work: Difficulties, Pitfalls and Built-In Failures,' in L. Levin and I. Lind, eds., *Interdisciplinarity Revisited*, 85–92. Stockholm: Liber Förlag.

Snow, C.P. 1964. *The Two Cultures: And a Second Look*. New York: New American Library.

Social Epistemology. 1995 (19, 2). Special issue on Boundary Rhetorics and the Work of Interdisciplinarity.

Sokal, A. 1996. 'Transgressing the Boundaries: Towards a Transformative Hermeneutics of Quantum Gravity.' *Social Text* 14: 217–52.

Sperber, D. 1985. 'Anthropology and Psychology: Towards an Epidemiology of Representations.' *Man* 20: 73–89.

Sperber, D., and D. Wilson. 1986. *Relevance: Communication and Cognition*. Cambridge: Harvard University Press.

Sproull, R., and H. Hall. 1987. *Multidisciplinary Research and Education Programs in Universities*. Washington, DC: National Academy Press.

Squires, G. 1992. 'Interdisciplinarity in Higher Education in the United Kingdom.' *European Journal of Education* 27, 3: 201–9.

Star, S.L., and J.R. Griesmer. 1988. 'Institutional Ecology, "Translations," and Boundary Objects.' *Social Studies of Science* 19: 387–420.

Stehr, N. 1994. *Arbeit, Eigentum und Wissen: Zur Theorie von Wissensgesellschaften*. Frankfurt: Suhrkamp.

Stehr, N., and R. Ericson. 1992. 'The Culture and Power of Knowledge in Modern Society,' in N. Stehr and R. Ericson, eds., *The Culture and Power of Knowledge: Inquiries into Contemporary Societies*, 3–29. Berlin: Walter de Gruyter.

Stocker, J. 1992. 'Australia's Economy – A Stool Missing a Leg?' Speech to the National Press Club (March 11). Canberra, Australia.

Stocking, G.W., Jr., and D.E. Leary. 1986. 'History of Social Scientific Inquiry.' *Items* 40: 53–57.

Straker, S. 1970. 'Kepler's Optics: A Study in the Development of Seventeenth-Century Natural Philosophy.' PhD dissertation. Indiana University. Ann Arbor, MI.

Tijssen, R.J.W., and A.F.J. van Raan. 1994. 'Mapping Changes in Science and Technology: Bibliometric Co-occurrence Analysis of the RandD Literature.' *Evaluation Review* 18: 98–115.

Toulmin, S. 1972. *Human Understanding. Volume I: General Introduction and Part I*. Oxford: Clarendon Press.

– 1990. *Cosmopolis: The Hidden Agenda of Modernity.* New York: Free Press.

Tulving, E., and S.A. Madigan. 1970. 'Memory and Verbal Learning.' *Annual Review of Psychology* 21: 434–37.

Turing, A.M. 1950 'Computing Machinery and Intelligence.' *Mind. A Quarterly Review of Psychology and Philosophy* 59: 433–60.

– 1991. 'The World of the Academic Quantifiers: The Columbia University Family and Its Connections,' in M. Bulmer, K. Bales, and K. Kish Sklar, eds., *The Social Survey in Historical Perspective: 1880–1940,* 269–90. Cambridge: Cambridge University Press.

– 1996a. 'The Pittsburgh Survey and the Survey Movement: An Episode in the History of Expertise,' in M.W. Greenwald and M. Anderson, eds. *Pittsburgh Surveyed: Social Science and Social Reform in the Early Twentieth Century,* 35–49. Pittsburgh: University of Pittsburgh Press.

– 1996b. 'Review of *Patronage, Practice, and the Culture of American Science: Alexander Dallas Bache and the U.S. Coast Survey* by Hugh Richard Slotten.' *Minerva* 34: 393–401.

Turner, S. 1990. 'Forms of Patronage,' in S. Cozzens and T.F. Gieryn, eds., *Theories of Science in Society,* 185–211. Bloomington: Indiana University Press.

Turner, S., and R. Factor. 1984. *Max Weber and the Dispute over Reason and Value: A Study in Philosophy, Ethics, and Politics.* London: Routledge and Kegan Paul.

Turner, S., and J. Turner. 1990. *The Impossible Science: An Institutional Analysis of American Sociology.* Beverly Hills: Sage.

Turpin, T. 1997. 'CRCs and Transdisciplinary Research: What Are the Implications for Science?' *Prometheus* 15, 2: 253–65.

Turpin, T., D. Aylward, S. Garrett-Jones, and R. Johnston. 1996b. 'Knowledge-Based Cooperation: University-Industry Linkages in Australia, Evaluations and Investigations Program.' Department of Employment, Education, Training and Youth Affairs, No. 96/17. Canberra, Australia: AGPS.

Turpin, T., and A. Deville. 1994 (April). 'Research Cultures and Organisational Change: Case Studies within the CSIRO.' Draft Report to the CSIRO, Centre for Research Policy.

– 1995. 'Occupational Roles and Expectations of Research Scientists and Research Managers in Scientific Research Institutions.' *R&D Management* 25, 2 (April): 141–57.

Turpin, T. and S. Garrett-Jones. 1997. 'Innovation Knowledge Networks in Australia and China,' in H. Etzkowitz and L. Leydesdorff, eds., *Universities and the Global Knowledge Economy: A Triple Helix of University-Industry-Government Relations,* 21–32. London and Washington: Pinter.

Turpin, T., S. Garrett-Jones, and N. Rankin. 1996. 'Bricoleurs and Boundary Riders: Managing Basic Research and Innovation Knowledge Networks.' *R&D Management* 26, 3 (July): 267–82.

Turpin, T., S. Garrett-Jones, N. Rankin, and D. Aylward. 1996a (March). 'Using Basic Research – Part 2: Socio-Economic Connections to Academic Research in Australia.' Commissioned Report No. 45, National Board of Employment, Education and Training. Canberra, Australia: AGPS.

Turpin, T., and S. Hill. 1995 (January). 'The New Cultures and Organisation of Science.' Paper presented at Conference for Centers for Interdisciplinary Research. Bielefeld, Germany.

Turpin, T., N. Sullivan, and A. Deville. 1993. 'Crossing Innovation Boundaries: The Formation and Maintenance of Research Links between Industry and Universities in Australia.' Commissioned Report No. 26, National Board of Employment, Education and Training. Canberra, Australia: AGPS.

Van der Steen, W.J. 1993. 'Towards Disciplinary Disintegration in Biology.' *Biology and Philosophy* 8, 3: 259–75.

van Raan, A.F.J. 1990. 'Fractal Dimension of Co-Citations.' *Nature* 347: 626.

– 1996. 'Advanced Bibliometric Methods as Quantitative Core of Peer Review Based Evaluation and Foresight Exercises.' *Scientometrics* 36: 397–420.

van Raan, A.F.J., and T.N. van Leeuwen. 1999. 'Assessment of the Scientific Basis of Multidisciplinary, Applied Research: Application of Bibliometric Methods in Nutrition and Food Research.' To be published, preprint version available on http://sahara.fsw.leideruniv.nl

Velichkovsky, B., and D.M. Rumbaugh, eds. 1996. *Communicating Meaning: The Evolution and Development of Language*. Mahwah, NJ: Lawrence Erlbaum Associates.

von Stutterheim, C., and W. Klein. 1989. 'Text Structure and Referential Movement,' in R. Dietrich and C.F. Graumann, eds., *Language Processing in Social Context*, 39–76. Amsterdam: North-Holland.

Voßkamp, W. 1987. 'Interdisziplinarität in den Geisteswissenschaften (am Beispiel einer Forschungsgruppe zur Funktionsgeschichte der Utopie),' in J. Kocka, ed., *Interdisziplinarität. Praxis – Herausforderung – Ideologie*, 92-105. Frankfurt: Suhrkamp.

Wallerstein, I., et al. 1996. *Open the Social Sciences: Report of the Gulbenkian Commission on the Restructuring of the Social Sciences*. Stanford, CA: Stanford University Press.

Ward, T.S., S. Smith, and J. Vaid, eds. 1997. *Creative Thought: An Investigation of Conceptual Structures and Processes*. Washington, DC: APA.

Wasser, H. 1990. 'Changes in the European University: From Traditional to Entrepreneurial.' *Higher Education Quarterly* 44: 111–22.

Watson, J.D. 1968. *The Double Helix*. New York: Athenaeum.

Weingart, P. 1987. 'Interdisziplinarität als List der Institution,' in: J. Kocka, ed., *Interdisziplinarität: Praxis – Herausforderung – Ideologie*, 159–68. Frankfurt: Suhrkamp.

- 1989a. 'In Search of Compatibility between Biological and Sociocultural Evolution: Exposé.' Manuscript. Bielefeld, Germany.
- 1989b. 'Biological Foundations of Human Culture. Proposal for a Research Group at the Center for Interdisciplinary Research (ZiF) in 1991/92.' Manuscript. Bielefeld, Germany.
- 1992. 'Interdisziplinarität zwischen falschen Hoffnurgen und bescheidenen Erwartungen.' *DAS MAGAZIN Wissenschaftszentrum Nordrhein – Westfalen* 2: 10.
- 1995a. 'Interdisciplinarity.' Paper presented at Conference for Centers for Interdisciplinary Research. Bielefeld, Germany.
- 1995b. 'Die Einheit der Wissenschaft – Mythos und Wunder,' in P. Weingart, ed., *Grenzüberschreitungen in der Wissenschaft (Crossing Boundaries in Science)*, 11–30. ZiF Interdisziplinäre Studien 1. Baden-Baden, Germany: Nomos.
Weingart, P., ed. 1995c. *Grenzüberschreitungen in der Wissenschaft (Crossing Boundaries in Science)*. ZiF Interdisziplinäre Studien 1. Baden Baden, Germany: Nomos.
Weingart, P., H. Kummer, and H. Hof, eds. 1994. *Verhaltensgrundlagen des Rechts – zum Beispiel Vertrauen*. Baden-Baden, Germany: Nomos.
Weingart, P., P.J. Richerson, S.D. Mitchell, and S. Maasen. 1997. *Human by Nature – Between Biology and the Social Sciences*. Mahwah, NJ: Lawrence Erlbaum Associates.
Weingart, P., R. Sehringer, and M. Winterhager. 1990. 'Which Reality Do We Measure?' *Scientometrics* 19, 5–6: 481–93.
Whitley, R. 1984. 'The Rise and Decline of University Disciplines in the Sciences,' in R. Jurkovich and J.H.P. Paelinck, eds., *Problems in Interdisciplinary Studies* 2, 10–25. Aldershot, UK: Gower.
Wilenski, R. 1995. 'Why Play the Philosophy Game?' in P. Baumgartner and S. Payr, eds., *Speaking Minds*, 265–82. Princeton, NJ: Princeton University Press.
Wing, P. 1993. *This Gown for Hire: A History of the Australian Tertiary Institutions Commercial Companies Association*. Canberra, Australia: Anutech.
Winter, M. 1996. 'Specialization, Territoriality, and Jurisdiction in Librarianship.' *Library Trends* 45, 2: 343–63.
Wirth, L. 1937. *Report on the History, Activities and Policies of the Social Science Research Council*. Prepared for the Committee on Review of Council Policy. New York: SSRC.
Wissenschaftsrat. 1988. *Empfehlungen des Wissenschaftsrates zu den Perspektiven der Hochschulen in den neunziger Jahren*. Cologne: Wissenschaftsrat.
Woolgar, S., and D. Pawluch. 1984. 'Ontological Gerrymandering.' *Social Problems* 32, 3: 214–17.
Ziman, J. 1996. 'Postacademic Science: Constructing Knowledge with Networks and Norms.' *Science Studies* 9, 1: 67–80.

Zuckerman, H. 1977. *Scientific Elite: Nobel Laureates in the United States.* New York: Free Press.
Zadeh, L. 1995. 'The Albatross of Classical Logic,' in P. Baumgartner and S. Payr, eds., *Speaking Minds*, 301–11. Princeton, NJ: Princeton University Press.

Contributors

Rainer Bromme: Main research fields are applied cognitive psychology and research on teaching and learning. PhD in Psychology 1979. Until 1992 senior researcher at the Interdisciplinary Research Institute on Mathematics Education (IDM) at the University of Bielefeld, Germany; at present professor of psychology, University of Münster, Germany.

Marc De Mey: Professor of cognitive science at the University of Ghent (Belgium), Fulbright scholar at the Center for Cognitive Studies at Harvard University; Peter Paul Rubens professor at the University of California at Berkeley; author of *The Cognitive Paradigm. An Integrated Understanding of Scientific Development* (University of Chicago Press, 2nd ed., 1992).

Sam Garrett-Jones: Senior Fellow at the Centre for Research Policy, University of Wollongong, Australia. Joined the university with more than ten years' experience in senior policy development positions with Australian government science and technology advisory agencies. PhD from the Australian National University's Research School of Pacific and Asian Studies. Publications include papers, reports, and book chapters on university–industry cooperation in research and training in Australia and on measuring the development of science and technology in several East Asian countries.

Edward J. Hackett: Professor of Sociology at Arizona State University. Recent work concerns the social organization and dynamics of research groups in science and engineering, peer review, and misconduct in science. In 1996–8 directed the Science and Technology Studies Program at the U.S. National Science Foundation.

Ellen Jane Hollingsworth: Director of Research at the Mental Health Research Center of the University of Wisconsin (Madison). Has written and edited several books on social policy and social services, and on services to people with severe mental illness.

Rogers Hollingsworth: Professor of Sociology and History and Chairperson of the Program in Comparative History at the University of Wisconsin. Awarded honorary degrees by the University of Uppsala (Sweden) and Emory University, author or editor of numerous books and articles on comparative political economy. Research on the study of creativity and innovation. Recent publications: *Comparing Capitalism: The Embeddedness of Institutions* (with Robert Boyer, Cambridge University Press, 1997), *Governing Capitalist Economies* (with Philippe Schmitter and Wolfgang Streeck, Oxford University Press, 1994). He is immediate Past President of the Society for the Advancement of Socio-Economics.

Julie Thompson Klein: Professor of Humanities in the Interdisciplinary Studies Program at Wayne State University (Michigan). Author of *Interdisciplinarity: History, Theory, and Practice* (Wayne State University Press, 1990), and *Crossing Boundaries: Knowledge, Disciplinarities, and Interdisciplinarities* (University Press of Virginia, 1996), editor of *Interdisciplinary Studies Today* (1994, with William Doty). Represented the United States at OECD- and UNESCO-sponsored meetings on interdisciplinary issues. Visiting Foreign Professor of English in Japan, Fulbright Lecturer and Academic Specialist in Nepal, and Distinguished Foundation Visitor at the University of Auckland in New Zealand.

Wilhelm Krull: Secretary General of the Volkswagen Foundation (Hanover, Germany) since 1996. DAAD-Lector University of Oxford (1980–4); Scientific Administrator at the Wissenschaftsrat's headquarters in Cologne (1985–7); Head of Research Policy Unit at the Wissenschaftsrat's headquarters (1987–93); Head of Section I at the Max Planck Society's headquarters in Munich (1993–5). Member of various national and international committees, such as the OECD's Group on Scientific and University Research, and various panels for the evaluation of European Community research and development programs.

Rhodri Windsor Liscombe: Doctorate from the University of London in the history of art and architecture. A major contributor to the catalogue of the *Council of Europe Exhibition. The Age of Neoclassicism* (1972). Publications include *William Wilkins* (Cambridge University Press, 1980), *Altogether America: Robert Mills, Architect and Engineer* (Oxford University Press, 1994) and *The New Spirit: Modern Architecture in Vancouver 1938–63.* Elected Fellow of the Society of Antiquaries of London in 1987, and Vice-President of the Society for the Study of Architecture in Canada in 1996. Professor in the Department of Fine Arts, and Chair of the Individual Interdisciplinary Studies Graduate Program at the University of British Columbia.

Sabine Maasen: Research Coordinator at the Max Planck Institute for Psychological Research in Munich. Research assistant 1988–90, worked at the Center for Interdisciplinary Research 1990–4, received her doctorate in sociology from the University of Bielefeld 1996. Articles and books in the sociology of science and knowledge, including *Vom Beichtstuhl zur therapeutischen Praxis* (Bielefeld: Kleine, Verlag 1988), *Die sogenannten Geisteswissenschaften* (with P. Weingart et al., Frankfurt: Suhrkamp, 1991), *Biology as Society, Society as Biology: Metaphors* (with E. Mendelsohn and P. Weingart, Kluwer, 1994), and *Die Genealogie der Unmoral. Therapeutisierung sexueller Selbste* (Frankfurt: Suhrkamp, 1998).

Eric R. Scerri: PhD in History and Philosophy of Science at King's College, London University, postdoctoral research at the California Institute of Technology on Interdisciplinarity at the Beckman Institutes. Assistant Professor of chemistry at Bradley University in Illinois; Visiting Professor of Chemistry at Purdue University, and editor-in-chief of *Foundations of Chemistry* (http://www.wkap.nl/journals/foch). Various publications in philosophy of science journals, including *Synthese, Erkenntnis, British Journal for Philosophy of Science,* and *International Studies in Philosophy of Science* and in chemical education journals.

Nico Stehr: Fellow of Green College, University of British Columbia, and Senior Research Associate in the Sustainable Research Development Institute of UBC. Fellow of the Royal Society of Canada and editor of the *Canadian Journal of Sociology.* Publications: *Society and Knowledge* (with Volker Meja, Transaction Bodis, 1984), *Knowledge and Politics* (Routledge, with Volker Meja, 1990), *The Knowledge Society* (Reidel, with Gernot Böhme, 1986), *Practical Knowledge* (Sage, 1992), *Knowledge Societies: Labour, Property and Knowledge* (Sage, 1994), and *The Culture and*

Power of Knowledge: Inquiries into Contemporary Societies (with Richard V. Ericson, W. de Gruyter, 1992).

Stephen Turner: Graduate Research Professor of Philosophy at the University of South Florida. Publishes on the history and prehistory of disciplines, especially in relation to funding. Publications include *The Impossible Science: An Institutional History of American Sociology* (with Jonathan Turner, 1990) and articles on early American geology, the Social Survey Movement, and the role of Rockefeller funding in the professionalization of American sociology.

Tim Turpin: Director of the Centre for Research Policy, University of Wollongong, Australia. PhD in Sociology from La Trobe University; teaching sociology, anthropology, and management. Academic interests cover the general areas of cultural theory, institutional change, and the communication of knowledge and culture. Field work on research cultures at universities, research institutions, and enterprises in Australia and elsewhere. Recent publications have been concerned with cultural change and organizational boundaries.

Anthony F.J. van Raan: Professor of Quantitative Studies of Science at the University of Leiden, The Netherlands. Director of the Leiden Centre for Science and Technology Studies since 1985. Studied mathematics, physics, and astronomy at the University of Utrecht. Postdoctoral fellow, University of Bielefeld, Germany, 1973–7. Senior lecturer and research fellow in Leiden, 1977, professor, 1991. Visiting scientist in universities and research institutes in the United States, United Kingdom, and France. In 1985, switched fields from physics to science studies. Has published (as author and co-author) about thirty articles in physics and about 100 in science and technology studies. In 1995, together with American sociologist Robert K. Merton, won the Derek de Solla Price Award, the highest international award in the field of quantitative studies of science.

Peter Weingart: Chair of sociology of science at the University of Bielefeld (Germany) since 1973. Director of the Center for Interdisciplinary Research (ZiF) 1989–94, Fellow of the Wissenschaftskolleg 1983–4, 1997. Member of the Berlin-Brandenburg Academy, heads the Institute for Science and Technology Studies (IWT) at Bielefeld. Numerous books and articles in the sociology of science and science policy.